DEALING WITH SEXUAL ABUSE

A Young Australian's Insights

by Hannah Baker

With illustrations by
Sarah Millicent Elliott

Copyright 2015 Hannah Baker
Published by Wallace Press

Front cover artwork by Hannah at age nine.
Back cover artwork and pictures inside book copyright of and kindly
donated for use by Sarah Millicent Elliott. (Please support Sarah's
generosity by checking out her website http://www.elliottmydear.com/)
Cover and text design: Ben Galpin Graphic Design
Book formatting: UpLoad Publishing Pty Ltd

First published in 2015

National Library of Australia Cataloguing-in-Publication entry
Creator: Baker, Hannah, 1988- author.
Title: Dealing with sexual abuse :
                  a young Australian's insights /Hannah Baker.

ISBN: 9780994315809 (paperback)

Subjects: Baker, Hannah, 1988-
                  Sexually abused children--Australia--Biography.
                  Sexual abuse victims--Australia--Biography.
                  Sexual abuse victims' writings.

Dewey Number: 362.76092

NOTE FROM THE AUTHOR

Half proceeds towards helping Australian children and young people

At Hannah's request, half of the proceeds from book sales will be split between the following two Australian organisations that directly support children and young people who have experienced abuse:

Kids Helpline
Australia's only free, private and confidential telephone and online counselling service specifically for young people aged 5–25. Kids Helpline provided ongoing support to Hannah for nine years as she grappled with the abuse and its impacts on her life: http://www.kidshelp.com.au

George Jones Child Advocacy Centre
Located in Perth, Western Australia and opened in 2011, the centre supports children, young people and families who have been affected by abuse. Counselling, medical services and police are all located in one child-friendly building to make it as easy as possible for those who have been abused. Centre staff have been very supportive of Hannah's efforts with her books: http://www. parkerville.org.au/Child-Advocacy-Centre

Please see the back of the book for more information about these services.

Stay updated: Website: www.dealingwithsexualabuse.com.au

Thank you to Adam Guerin at Oz Web Shop for kindly sponsoring and managing this website free of charge.

Facebook page: Search "Dealing With Sexual Abuse: a young Australian's insights"

Thank you Jayneen and Mark Sanders who have generously volunteered their time to assist with production of this book. Jayneen has her own books to protect kids from abuse, check out her website: somesecrets.info/

BOOKS BY THE SAME AUTHOR

Hannah's Diaries: a young Australian's experience of *dealing with abuse*

This book is appropriate for all teenagers and young people who have or have not been abused, and who are strong readers. Hannah has shared her real-life teenage diaries to help other young people understand what it is like to be abused by someone you care about. She then explains what it was like when she reported the abuse to police and went through the legal process. She explains what abuse is, and gives ideas on what to do if you have a friend who is being abused. She also provides clear advice for any young people who are currently being abused, and explains that it is possible to get help and deal with what has happened.

The book contains several beautiful illustrations which were kindly donated for use by Sarah Millicent Elliott.

Hannah's Hope: How I dealt with abuse

This book is aimed at kids age 10+ or teenagers who are not strong readers. It is best suited to those who have been abused and are being supported by a trained professional or understanding carer. The book aims to help readers who have been abused to know that they are not alone, that it is okay to have whatever feelings they have, and that things will get better. It also provides important information about where kids and young people who are still being abused can go to receive help. The book contains cartoon pictures and is equally appealing for boys and girls.

CONTENTS

INTRODUCTION

In this book, I have shared my personal story, starting with my teenage diaries, to give you rare insights into the experience of child abuse and its devastating impacts.

The abuse I endured only stopped when I moved out of home in 2006, the year I turned 18. Up to this point I had been let down by several adults in my life. I received inadequate education about sexual abuse at school so was unable to find the words to tell anyone about it until I was in my mid-teens. By this time, my faith in adults had been all but shattered. The particular teacher who I tried to confide in about the abuse took years to report it, and by the time she did, I was 16 years of age and had decided that the only person I could trust was myself. I slipped through the cracks of the child protection system, who closed my file with the words "no further action" without even meeting me. The child protection report was written with such little care for detail that at one point the case worker had even gotten my name wrong and called me 'Natalie'. I cried when I read it a few years later and wondered why nobody had even pretended to care about me.

Thankfully, I did not give up. It was through developing an anonymous relationship with a **Kids Helpline** counsellor that I started to build up the confidence to keep trying to get help. I started telling adults little bits of information to test the waters, gradually telling them a bit more, until I knew if they were 'safe' or not. With these adults, I yo-yo'd back and forth with my trust for them, and sometimes denied that the things I had told them were true. Eventually when I was 17, I found a sexual assault counsellor who listened to me and helped me to move out of home. If it hadn't been for this counsellor and Kids Helpline, it is hard to say whether I would have been able to keep going.

At the age of 18, a few months after leaving home, I built up the courage to go to the police, so that my father could never hurt me again. In reading this book, you will see just how tough the legal system is for victims of crime, particularly when you have already been so badly violated as a child. Sadly, there are no real winners in this system. At an age where I should have been out having fun and enjoying new freedom, I spent six years navigating through court appearances, a trial, several appeals, and then parole hearings. Getting 'justice' in the legal system was of very cold comfort for me. There were many conflicting feelings of grief, denial, loss and guilt that came with the prospect of my dad being sent to jail. When the guilty verdict came through, I wasn't celebrating. I was bawling my eyes out.

At the time of publishing this book, I am 26 years old and in the "rebuilding" phase of my life. I still have many issues that make it difficult for me to be the person I want to be. Some of these issues can be disabling at times, despite not being obvious to people who don't know me well. I go through patches of dissociating and having flashbacks, have ongoing sleep difficulties that only respond to medication, and also experience suicidal periods. I am scared of not having the future I dream of – which has always been to have kids and a family of my own. The enormous trust issues I have developed sometimes make me feel terrified that I have no future to look forward to.

I'm going to be honest with you in saying that I wish I did not feel compelled to write this book. I firstly wish that I had never been abused. Sadly, I was. Secondly, I wish that the service response in my situation had been effective, respectful and comprehensive. Sadly, it wasn't. And more than anything, I wish that the abuse had not impacted on my life in such a soul-destroying way. Unfortunately, I cannot change what happened to me, but it is of some small consolation that I can help people to understand the difficult situation that I and countless other Australian children have faced.

I hope my book will make you aware of the importance of educating kids about abuse so that they have the words to tell an adult what is happening to them. I hope I will make you aware of the importance of listening to and helping children, instead of assuming that they are 'coping well despite what is happening at home' and can be left in an abusive situation. Please do not underestimate how heartbreaking it is to read a callously written child protection report about yourself, and to know that nobody at school or the child protection department bothered to intervene. You might not realise how crucial a role you play in helping a young person in a bad situation and in giving them hope for the future. When no one listens, many of these kids will consider killing themselves, because they already feel so worthless anyway. When you do listen, you teach them that it is possible to have a different life.

Since first publishing my story as an e-book in May 2014, I have been amazed by the response from around Australia and beyond. It has been downloaded thousands of times. Government agencies and support organisations around the country have been extremely interested in what I have to say. My story was even featured in a well respected newspaper, The Weekend Australian.

On one level, it has been hugely satisfying to see that my story has sparked so much interest. On another level, all I can see is irony. Now that I am an adult and have the skills to speak up, suddenly I have the attention I needed as a child. Suddenly, my words and actions are seen as 'powerful' and 'inspiring'. The painting I did at age nine screaming out for help, which received no attention when I needed it to, has now been featured in a national newspaper.

Even though I have a lot of attention now, I have not forgotten that less than 10 years ago, some services and government departments couldn't close my file fast enough. I think I was much more powerful and inspiring when I was turning up at school day after day, doing my best to be a nice person despite the endless abuse I was enduring. Doing my best to protect everybody but myself.

Too often in the public sphere, discussions are held and decisions made about the protection of children without truly hearing the voice of kids and young people themselves. I believe my story shows that on many levels, as a society, we are still getting it wrong so often here in Australia. There is huge potential for improvement, and I truly hope that readers of this book will feel passionate enough to push for change. I know you might find my story blunt and confronting, but the reality is that there are so many more stories that are similar to mine that you will never hear. Kids who have been abused are an extremely vulnerable population, and I daresay that most young people who have endured it, and the often damaging system responses, simply do not have the energy or skills to go and give feedback about what changes are needed. More to the point, they probably don't expect anyone to care about what they have to say.

This book is dedicated to every child who has endured awful abuse by people they thought they could trust. To every child whose child protection file has been closed with "no further action" without any investigation. To every young person who has turned to suicide out of despair at the damaging abuse they have endured. To every child who was not listened to by an adult they needed to help them. To every child who has felt completely alone, worthless and like there is not a single person they could turn to. To every child who has been tossed around in the 'support systems' following a disclosure of abuse. To any child or young person who has endured the humiliating criminal justice system.

This book is dedicated to every child and young person who deserved so much better.

Please note: If you are supporting a young person who would benefit from a shorter, more child/teen friendly version of this book, please visit www.dealingwithsexualabuse.com.au for more details about:

Hannah's Diaries: a young Australian's experience of dealing with abuse which is suitable for teenagers and young people who are strong readers, or

Hannah's Hope: How I dealt with abuse which is suitable for kids age 10+ or teens who are not strong readers.

DEALING WITH SEXUAL ABUSE: A Young Australian's Insights

PART ONE:
MY DIARIES (2002–2007)

Painting by
Sarah Millicent Elliott

All alone!
Whether you like it or not
Alone will be something
You'll be quite a lot

(Dr Seuss, in *Oh the Places You'll Go*)

INTRODUCTION

The picture on the front cover was painted by me in school art class when I was in Grade 4. By this time, I had been abused at home for several years. I knew that I badly wanted someone to help me, but was so ashamed that I kept it to myself.

At the age of 13, I started writing the diaries that you will see on the following pages. Writing was the only time I could be honest, and my diaries were kept very private. Nobody even knew of their existence until I was 18, when I let my Aunty Susie look at them. I truly believe that my diaries helped stop me from killing myself. I was so terrified that if I died, someone would find the diaries and think I was crazy and disgusting. More importantly though, writing gradually helped me to make sense of the situation I was in, urge myself to keep going, and build up the confidence to seek help.

You might notice in my diaries that I took a while to really 'take in' the abuse and its realities. When I was living at home I was so disconnected and numb, just coping and getting through the day. It was only when I moved out that I could really start to understand what had happened, and could see that it was going to keep impacting on me for many years to come. I started to realise that moving out and escaping the abuse was only the beginning of my recovery, not the end of it. That is when the crippling depression set in.

2002

4th March 2002

I've kept diaries before but they've always been so stupid and pointless. All I ever did was write facts, like 'today I went to the shops and bought a blue skirt', or 'tomorrow I am going to Kristy's house for a sleepover, it will be fun'. It's not that I wasn't a good writer – I have always loved writing since I started school. It's just that I didn't know how to say what I really felt, well I guess I didn't understand myself (I still don't!).

Nobody knows how alone I feel, all the time. They don't realise that the bouncy happy girl they see is totally fake, just putting it on. Well I guess people don't think I am normal because I am really hyperactive at times. But nobody knows how crazy and sad I am because I never tell anyone how I feel. I sometimes think I don't have feelings at all. And when I do, the last thing I do is let anyone know how I'm feeling. It's easier to just joke around and try to make people laugh!

I don't have any true friends because none of them know me at all. I am so desperate to talk to someone that I am starting a stupid diary!

7th March 2002

I'm quite excited about having a real diary, where I can write how I really feel. I was thinking about it a lot at school today, all during 'silent reading'. Instead of reading I was thinking of all the things I would like to write, that I'd never be able to say to anyone. Can you imagine having a real friend who you can tell anything? I can't.

I had so much in my head today but now that I'm sitting down to write, I don't know what to say! Maybe I should just write some of the 'getting to know you' stuff today.

Okay. I'm called Hannah. I'm the youngest in the family. I am 13 but will be 14 in July. My birth stone is Ruby. I have the world's best dog, his name is Max. We got him last year and I love him so, so much.

I'm in Year 9. Everyone says Year 9 is the worst year because all the girls fight, but my group has been pretty good. My sister Bec is three years older than me. She's in Year 12 and thinks she's soooo important. I think she's annoying and needs to get over herself. My dad works in the city, and Mum works in sales at the moment. My sister doesn't have a job. I do! I do a paper round. Mum was a bit surprised when I went and organised it, they had an ad in the paper. I am a very independent person. I am saving money, I don't spend much of it at all. It's annoying when there aren't that many pamphlets in the round, because you still have to go the same number of houses, but you get paid less! The best I ever got paid was $29. The least you get is about $14. It is not very much fun on the really, really hot days but other than that I quite like being outdoors anyway. I am thinking I might spend some of the money on buying a bike so that then I can do more deliveries.

I don't get along that well with Mum, I suppose to her I've always been the 'difficult child', and my sister is the goody two shoes. Bec is very focussed on school and doing well (she's an 'extreme nerd'!) and lately I've been cruising through doing hardly any work. Dad is usually pretty nice to me, he doesn't say much. He's like me, he doesn't really have emotions and you can never really tell what he is thinking, at all. Bec and Mum won't shut up sometimes, they just go on and on when they're together, and I feel like I don't belong. Sometimes I can't stand to be around Dad but that's just me being stupid and I get over it. He favours me over Bec. He can be quite critical of her especially when he's talking alone with me. He makes fun of her a lot to me and says I am pretty. He says nice things to me most of the time. I think that is because I am quiet and he likes me. And Bec is just so annoying.

I am obsessed with running, I run everyday even though my knees and hips are getting screwed up (and I'm only 13!). It's what keeps me going. I train twice a week with Wes Taylor on the oval near my house in summer and on the sand tracks in winter, and by myself most other days. Wes is amazing – he trains us for free because he loves running so much, and is retired himself now. There are about 8 of us at the moment. He makes us run really hard. The hardest days are when we run at 4pm in summer when it's still about 35-40 degrees, and also the first few weeks in April on the sandtracks when it's still quite warm and there hasn't been enough rain, so it is hell running on that dry sand!

I can run until I am dizzy and about to throw up, in fact, I like feeling that sick because then I know I have tried my hardest. Normally I try to stick with Ellie until I can't anymore, because she is faster than me. I am pretty good at getting into a rhythm and blocking out the pain. But lately I've been taking an iron tonic because I have so little energy the rest of the time. I don't know how I have any energy to run, because I don't get enough sleep at all. I haven't for years though, so I'm pretty used to it.

26th March 2002

I haven't written for a while because I didn't know what to write anymore. I still feel like such a loser for keeping a diary, I don't think any of my friends do, but I haven't told them about mine. If I had a 'real friend' I could tell them about my diary. But I don't have anyone I could call a real friend. My friends would probably be really offended if they saw what I just wrote. I hang out mainly with Cassie, Nat, Zoe, Jasmine, Lisa, Jade and the boys – Dirk, Paul, Jason and Tyler. I spend the most time with Cassie and Nat – we're never serious and joke around all the time. Zoe is more serious and works harder than the rest of us but she's really nice. Jasmine, I don't really like, because she's the biggest flirt EVER (e.g. with Tyler) and I think she's the kind of person who'd drop all her friends for a guy. And then she'd come crawling back if things didn't work out. Also, I've always felt like she looks down on me and Nat, and seems to compete with us for Cassie. It's annoying! Cassie doesn't seem to realise though, it's so stupid. Or maybe she does realise and just enjoys being the popular one – I'm not sure.

Jade and Lisa, well they don't really hang out with our group but I go and hang out with them some lunchtimes. Actually, I've been spending more and more lunchtimes with just Lisa lately, which seems to be annoying Nat. Oh well. I also take the bus with Jade and Lisa every day, and have been really good friends with Jade since Year 4.

The boys are really nice, Paul and Jason are probably the easiest to get along with, followed by Dirk, followed by Tyler who I think is an idiot because he is so up himself. Actually, my favourite is definitely Paul – after Callum Rogers (who I secretly really like) he is my 2nd favourite boy in the whole year.

3rd April 2002

Today I am so tired and I wish I could write more, but I don't know. I don't know what to write. And also, if anybody ever found this diary I'd be dead! I have to be careful to not write too much about myself, because if someone finds it they'll realise how crazy I am and I'll get in so much trouble.

16th May 2002

Fight with my sister... I think she's a baby and needs a reality check. Mum always stands up for her! I always try to help out with the cooking for no thanks, and then when I don't it's all my fault. But Bec never has to because she's so important having exams and all... I even got in trouble for hitting a tennis ball against the garage wall on the weekend because it was too annoying for her when she was studying. What a princess! What else am I supposed to do when it's pouring with rain?

29th June 2002

The crazy part of me wants to write something and I will just this once, but it is all lies, and it isn't about ME okay?

It started when she was very small, just little things at first but she can't remember exactly how old she was. He used to touch her and made her take her clothes off. It felt so wrong and every muscle in her body would go tense. When she was 7 or 8 is when it first got really bad. He hurt her, hurt her, hurt her so many times but I don't believe it, I think she's crazy.

5th July 2002

It was the last day of term and we got our reports today. Mine could have been better – a lot of C's, including for maths, science and English! Last year I got an A for every single essay in English, so that's a pretty big drop. I guess I haven't been paying enough attention to the books we're meant to read, and all me and Nat do is sit up the back and talk. Nat sucks at English! I don't know how anybody could find Shakespeare interesting. I hate all the different words. Nat has been sent outside for talking a few times, it's funny because no matter what it always seems to be her who gets sent outside – even when we have a relief teacher! I must look innocent or something!

My parents didn't seem too thrilled about my report but they were nicer about it than I'd expected. Probably because I'd warned them that it wasn't going to be as good as it could have been. They know I've been slack this semester. I'd rather focus on running for now anyway – it's one of the few things that keeps me sane these days.

(Undated – July 2002)

I am trying to scrub away the dirt, scrub, scrub keep on scrubbing and maybe one day I will be clean. Or will I be dirty forever? I scrub until I have no skin left – I am raw and bleeding but I am still so dirty. I have dirt in my blood. I try to keep scrubbing but the sponge is so full of dirt that I can't hold it anymore. It's too big and heavy with dirt.

There's no use, the dirt won't go. I am a dirty, disgusting girl.

19th July 2002

I am nearly 14, can you believe it?

20th July 2002

I'm 14 now. I don't feel any older, but it feels weird to think that I am 14. I feel like I only just turned 13. Time flies even when you're not having fun!

It wasn't the most exciting day. Cassie had a party on Tuesday for her birthday, so I didn't bother to do anything because our birthdays are so close anyway. But I made a cake for my birthday to bring to Cassie's party. They all laughed at it soooo much because it was bright pink, and kind of ugly...

So yes as birthday's go, it wasn't that exciting. Aunty Barb dropped round in the morning, but she stayed for ages! Mum got on the phone to someone from work, just after Aunty Barb came, and said 'I'll be back in a minute'...

So poor Barb (and me!) sat and waited and waited for at least an hour. In my head I was thinking "wow this had better be a really important phone call Mum..." I was still in my pyjamas and had to sit making awkward conversation the whole time. Like she would ask "sooo, how's school going?" and I'd say, "yehhhh, good..."... Long awkward silence then she asks, "You getting much homework these days?" and I said "aaahh, yeh, same as usual, yeh..."

BLAH, BLAH, BLAH!

Even Max (the dog) doing a massive fart didn't get rid of her...

8th August 2002

Not much happening lately, just same as usual. School, athletics, etc, etc. State athletics championships are coming up soon so I've been training pretty hard. Nat says she never trains but I bet she does. I hate when she beats me at cross country because that's my thing, and she is way better than me at the field events like high jump. I can't do high jump, I'm too short!

I've been getting as little sleep as ever but that's life. Whenever I'm really tired, I just take Panadol to get rid of the headaches, and even though it makes me feel a bit numb sometimes, it helps me to get through. Weird, because some people reckon that Panadol makes you drowsy, but it actually helps to wake me up. Last year I had barely slept before school sports day so took a Panadol just before the 800m.

I've also started taking stuff from the medicine box to help me sleep better at night, but they haven't helped me at all. The only thing that works on me is night-time cough medicines (Benadryl and Dimetapp are best), but I've found that the more often I take them, the more I have to take for it to work. And it doesn't stop me from waking up. Still, at least it helps me to fall asleep instead of lying there for hours.

(Undated between 8th August 2002 and 17th August 2002)

I must stay quiet, I must stay quiet, I must stay quiet. I need somebody to hear me but I must stay quiet.

Good girl, Daddy will be proud.

17th August 2002

I came 6th at states in cross country, which is okay, but not a medal. It was a very hilly course which was good for me because I always catch the tall girls on the hills – they're easier if you're short.

Anyway, it looks like I am going to have to train a lot harder if I want a medal next year. Even though sixth isn't that far from medal positions, the top 4 girls were way ahead of the rest of us. So I have to get into the top pack next year, if I want any chance – right up with Amber Jackson and Emily Wickham.

29th August 2002

Nighttimes have been bad lately. I have tried so, so hard to not write much about that stuff in here, but I might have to soon because it's always in my head. I can't keep it to myself much longer.

But I don't have the energy to write about it now.

31st August 2002

Okay I feel dumb writing this, and I don't know what to write. But I'm going to try anyway, and since you're just a diary, you can't laugh at me.

Well. Where do I start? Well, ever since I was about seven, I have been having the craziest nightmares. At first it was like a giant, like in the BFG. It didn't make any sense to me. He would lie on top of me and hurt me but it got so confused and jumbled in my head, and I would just black out.

I know it's not a giant, it's a person, and he's been hurting me all these years, and says that is what happens when someone loves you.

Once when I tried to tell him to stop he said that I like it, that I make him do it. It's my fault for letting him think that but I don't want to upset him. I guess it's not such a big deal but it seems to be ruining my life. I can't stop thinking about it but could never tell anyone because they would say I was crazy or gross. But I don't think I can handle it much more. Mum just seems to care about what other people think of our family. I don't think she cares about me at all, she's fake and I HATE HER, HATE HER, HATE HER.

2nd September 2002

I feel so guilty reading over my last diary entry. I can't believe I wrote that stuff. I'm going to have to hide this diary really well now.

27th December 2002

I tried to stop writing in this because I didn't want to think about the bad stuff anymore. You know how sometimes you think, "Well the only problem here is me for being so negative all the time, so if I just focus on positive things, my life will be fine". I just wanted to forget it all and pretend it's not real. But even if I act like that to other people, I think I am lying to myself and it's not working as well as it used to.

I'm glad Christmas is over. I hate it sooo much. Just the whole pretending to be a normal family thing – it's painful! I went for a long run at the park even though it was stinking hot. Then in the afternoon we went to Aunty Susie and Uncle Roy's, which was really fake too. Roy gets along great with Dad, and Susie hates me, probably because I'm so boring at family stuff and don't talk to any of the adults. I can't be bothered, I have nothing to say to them. Bec always sits at the 'adults' table because she thinks she's so grown up or whatever. Jeff (my cousin) does the same sometimes too, even though he's only 13. I couldn't care less whether I'm acting grown up or not. Katie and Jack never try to, so I stick with them. The adults table is boring anyway.

2003

2nd February 2003

Another school year begins tomorrow, and I've decided that this year I'm going to do well. Hopefully putting it in writing will help motivate me – especially because if you do badly in Year 10, you can only do the dummy subjects in Year 11 and 12.

Last year I was so lazy and it made me feel even worse about myself, because of the grades I was getting. Even though I act like I don't care, I hate doing badly and I want to get mostly A's this year.

23rd February 2003

I've drifted further from my friends than ever before in these past few months. I used to love the time I spent with them but now I just want to be on my own more and more, because I can't relate to them. Sometimes I have been wandering off 'to go to the canteen', just to give myself a break from it all. It takes so much energy to chat when you are struggling to stay with it. I've been going to the library before school some days to do some extra work and also to avoid talking to people. It's hard to make conversation. My friends don't understand me at all, and I can no longer pretend that my life is as easy as theirs. The things that are important to them are just background distractions to me. Every day is a struggle, even just getting out of bed in the morning is almost too much for me these days. I'm starting to realise that I can't go on like this forever. I can't last much longer.

24th March 2003

Because of the bad stuff, I feel like I am nothing. I feel wrecked, drained. I just want to get over it and forget it, but I can't. When I was younger, it didn't affect me as much because I didn't understand it, so I seemed to just block it out. I thought I must be having crazy nightmares, that it wasn't real. I NEVER let myself think about WHO it was. I only started to comprehend it all in the last few years and ever since, life has been so hard.

I feel like I am so fake, like I am always pretending everything is okay when it's not. It's not okay. I am not okay. Do you understand?

Will it ever get better?

Will I ever get over this?

I'm so desperate for someone to understand me but there's not a single person in the whole world who could. I feel so horrible and disgusting, so used, so stupid! It's like I exist, but not really, I just do what other people want me to do.

I am so lonely and nobody realises. It's like I'm trapped inside my mind because of this horrible secret. It's taken over, but I can't get rid of it. I want to be normal but I never will be. I've lost my body, and I've lost my mind.

4th April 2003

I can't remember how old I am in the memory but I feel little. He called me to him, sat me down in front of him and gave me a hug. He says he'll protect me.

He's resting his hand on my leg. Nothing wrong with that, is there? I am lucky that he cares about me.

He's running his hand up my leg – does he even realise he's doing it? I don't think so. Anyway, it doesn't really matter. I can ignore it.

His hands keep moving up my leg and he stares at me. His other hand is on my face. Has it been there all along? I'm starting to drift off anyway.

'What music do you want to listen to?' – that's all I can hear. I think it's me saying it, in my head.

Suddenly I am lying down now. How did that happen? I don't know. He's pulling my pants down but it's not really him. It's a new person, I just don't know who.

'What music do you want to listen to?'

I don't know, any music.

5th April 2003

I keep having memories, they won't go away.

I'm lying in bed. He's holding my face in his hard hands. I am pretending to be asleep.

He runs his hands through my hair. But then he starts touching me and I try not to breathe. He's breathing all over me now and I start screaming inside my head, a terrible scream – I've never heard anything like it in real life. It feels like I am using every bit of energy I have in my body, every single muscle, to scream. I want it to stop, I promised myself that next time I'd scream out loud but no sound is coming out. I'm paralysed.

So I go to the beach, leaving my body behind to face this battle on its own.

(Undated, sometime in April 2003)

MY BEACH

I am going to write all this down so that I remember it even better.

My beach looks like this:

Sparkly aqua water

Soft, white sand

Sunny skies

Nobody there/only nice people

Barely any waves

I can go there whenever I want and there is always good music too.

5th May 2003

This might sound stupid but I've been thinking a lot about what it might be like for me to die now. I haven't been happy for so long. I don't have anybody that I can talk to, I don't have any friends because they don't know me at all. I can't stop thinking about all the bad stuff that happens – it's not going away!

All I can think of is overdosing on sleeping pills, at least then it would look like an accident. But I'd have to take heaps, because last year when I tried taking sleeping pills they never seemed to help much.

9th May 2003

You hurt me so much, you took so much. I have nothing left now. You stripped me of more than just my clothes. You took it all and keep coming back for more. And now I want to die.

15th May 2003

I really feel like I need to talk to someone because my mind is falling apart and I can barely cope. But I don't know who to talk to. I keep trying to talk to my phys ed teacher, Mrs Stanley, but she's not listening! I have known her for two years. I see her pretty much every day because she's also in charge of the athletics and cross country teams. I see her more than any other adult really, and always find reasons to go and talk to her. Whenever I drop hints she brushes over them, it's as if she feels awkward and doesn't want to get involved. It's as if listening is too much effort.

She's the first person I've really tried to reach out to and she isn't at all interested in helping me. But for some reason I keep trying, in the hope that one day she might care. I need her to care, well I need somebody to listen to me, otherwise nothing will ever change. More than anything, I just need somebody to give me a hug and tell me that everything is going to be okay. Even better, they can adopt me, like how Miss Honey adopted Matilda in the movie, and I can just forget about my family forever.

I wish there was somebody I could call, who could save me when bad stuff's about to happen. But I never have anybody, no one ever saves me. I always have to face everything alone because everyone is too caught up in their own lives to care. It's a selfish world.

16th August 2003

Today was states again (cross country) and it seems like my hard work paid off — I finally got a medal. I psyched myself up so much that I just HAD to get a medal. I haven't come better than 5th all season but I wasn't going to let that stop me.

I should feel happy, I'm trying to feel excited, but I don't really. My family didn't seem to realise how big a deal it was to me. And then Dad was saying that the girl who won in the age group below me got a faster time than me. That I'll never be a good runner unless everyone else breaks their legs, that I'm wasting my time trying.

I'd hoped he would be proud of me but obviously not. I really hate it when he criticises me, it makes me feel even worse about myself.

Painting by
Sarah Millicent Elliott

So now I'm so grumpy! Getting a medal at states has been my goal for over 3 years. It's kept me going. But who am I fooling? Medals won't make me happy. They won't get me anywhere in life. No matter what I achieve, deep down I know that it's all fake. Underneath I am still that horrible, disgusting, crazy girl.

Author's note: I stuck the medal into my diary with sticky tape, along with the caption: "A medal's not going to make you a nice person, fool"

4th September 2003

Today in English period in the library, I was reading a book called 'Letters to Judy' by Judy Blume. It's a book with all the letters Judy had received from young people about a whole range of things. Like bedwetting, drugs, bullying. It was really interesting.

My heart stopped a beat when I read a letter from a girl named Tracey. Her older brother had been doing to her what my dad's doing to me, but luckily for her he moved away when she was 11. I've never read about this sort of thing and I could feel my cheeks burning. Then on the next page Judy had written about sexual abuse and the pain it causes. She gave a definition of sexual abuse, and what's been happening to me fits perfectly. If I'm being totally honest with myself, I've known that it was abuse for a couple of years now, but I've always managed to convince myself that it can't be abuse because he's my dad.

I can't stop thinking, thinking, thinking about all of this. I keep re-reading that part of the book. I'm going to go to the school library first thing tomorrow to see if I can find any other books about this sort of thing. I don't want to look on the internet in case someone in my family figures out what I've been searching.

5th September 2003

The library had quite a few books about abuse. When I found them I felt guilty, as if nobody should see me looking at them because if they saw me they might figure out it's happening to me. Why else would I be interested in those books? I really wanted to get one of them out but I didn't because I didn't want any of the librarians to ask questions. They probably wouldn't have but still, there's always a chance. I can't even use the photocopier because only teachers can use them. You can never be too careful, and I can't afford for anybody to get suspicious.

12th September 2003

Last night, I really wanted to stop it from happening, but he got so mad at me that now I have a bruise on my face. Now I realise just how stupid I was. I can't stop it.

16th September 2003

I've had a big bruise on my face for the last few days, I can't even remember which night I got it to be honest, I barely remember getting it. Doesn't matter anyway. Zoe's noticed the bruise, she asked what happened, I can't remember what I told her. Jade's noticed it too, but that's because I sit next to her in half my classes – we're in so many of the same classes, even the same form.

Even Ms Cippolina's been asking me if I'm okay lately, because she's noticed how tired I am. I don't know why she notices (I sit up the very back of the room), but she does. I hope she hasn't figured it out but I don't think she has – she probably just thinks I'm strange or stay up too late watching TV or something. I've never talked to her at all so she doesn't know anything about me.

(Undated sometime between September and November 2003)

The hands of love have come to get me. They grab my face and hair, a kiss on the lips and 'I love you, don't you love me too?' I can't bring myself to say anything – no sound leaves my mouth. I nod, I have lost the battle now, my body is yours. You snatch the invitation and there's nothing I can do. All I can do is close my eyes and go to the beach, and forget about the unwelcome guest who is gatecrashing my body.

19th November 2003

Today for sport we went to the pool down the road to do water aerobics. It was the only time in the whole year that we're doing it but guess who chucked a sickie? Yep, me... I have some big bruises at the moment and I don't want anyone to see them. The big one is near my ribs.

I think Mrs Stanley has noticed by now that I always do everything I can to get out of swimming (all first term) – I 'forgot' my bathers at every possible opportunity. The worst she can do is give me a detention but she hasn't. She doesn't come down as hard on me as she does on other people – it's like she knows that I can't help it. If I did get a detention, chances are I'd be doing it with Lisa because she never brings her bathers either. Her excuse was worse than mine: 'my boardies don't fit anymore'. Haha! Mrs Stanley said "just wear bather bottoms then", and Lisa acted like this hadn't occurred to her. She's a funny one.

25th November 2003

I got a card from my old running coach Wes in the mail today. He wants to know why I stopped training, poor guy, he trained me for free and put lots of effort into me, I get a medal at states then suddenly just disappeared. It's because I felt so bad about myself and couldn't be bothered with running anymore.

(I stuck the card into my diary, here is what it said):

Dear Hannah,

It is not the same not seeing you at training, you were always so considerate and spoiled us with your baking. I have enquired through Lena and she said she thought you might be with another club now.

Hannah, even if this is the case that doesn't mean you cannot train with me, I hope you know that I coach anybody no matter what club they compete for.

So Hannah, if you liked training with me I would love to have you back.

Sincerely,

Wes.

13th December 2003

There's big news at school right now and I'm sick to death of hearing about it — it was the first story on the news last night and on the front of today's paper. On top of that, every kid in the school has been issued with a special newsletter warning us about stranger danger etc (I didn't even show it to my parents).

What happened is, yesterday morning a Year 8 girl from my school got assaulted behind the school — and by assaulted I mean she just got pushed to the ground. She got away because the guy heard other people coming, so yeh, apart from getting pushed to the ground, nothing happened. As far as I know, he didn't even touch her.

So, WHAT'S THE BIG DEAL?

People think it's terrible because she's so young (13). Thirteen isn't young when you think how young I was when I had way worse stuff happening to me. She only got pushed to the ground, and she got away. She didn't get raped, she didn't even get touched. And it only happened once, not over and over again. It was just some random stranger, not someone who is supposed to love and care about her. And it happened in a random place, not in her own home, where you're supposed to feel safe. She was able to run to the front office and tell people straight away. The police got called immediately and her parents rushed into the school to check she was okay.

Do you think I would ever get that much support if I said anything???? Absolutely not! Nobody wants to know what's happening to me because there's no easy solution! When someone is attacked by a stranger it's easy to react — everyone just says "What a monster! Put him behind bars!" But when you think about it, there's people doing way worse stuff to their own children, but nobody wants to know because it's too disgusting to understand or believe. People would rather think that people who do these sorts of things are monsters from another planet — outsiders. It's not true though. They are upstanding citizens, 'good blokes'. They only act differently behind closed doors.

2004

20th January 2004

I had a serious talking to with myself and have decided not to let this year go to waste like last year. I spent so much time dwelling on the bad stuff and feeling sorry for myself instead of working for a better future.

Here's my new plan.

It's quite exciting but I have to be so, so hard on myself. It will require lots of discipline. I need to get extremely good marks in my leaving exams next year, so that I can try and get a scholarship for uni – an interstate scholarship. That way, I would get out of the state (out of this house for good) in a way that wouldn't make either of my parents angry or scared that I would tell – instead, it would give them something to boast about! They would feel as if it was a result of their great parenting! Imagine it though! It's nice having a goal like that to work towards, and I will have to study my arse off so that I can make it happen. If I nail Year 11, there's no stopping me in Year 12.

2nd February 2004

Another school year has begun… but this one's going to be different. I'm gonna kick arse at school and get me a scholarship out of this crazy house!

14th May 2004

First semester exams are coming up so I shouldn't be thinking/writing about anything bad, but I'm really struggling. I don't think many people have any real concept of what it's like to live with someone who is abusing you. It is hard to keep going sometimes.

Painting by
Sarah Millicent Elliott

16th June 2004

My first semester exams were all good, straight A's just as I'd hoped. I have been working so hard to do well! I've really stuck to my plan to do well and work for a scholarship.

But you know what? Despite doing so well, I'm fooling myself if I think I'm not struggling. That hit me today during history class, when I could barely keep my head off the desk – that's how tired I've been. I don't know how I can keep pushing myself like this for another year and a half of school.

I've been thinking more and more lately about going to talk to someone at school – a counsellor or something. We have a school psych and a chaplain but I've never met either of them. I think I'll try the chaplain because it's not serious enough for me to need a psychologist – I'm not that screwed up and it's not that bad. I just need to talk to someone about how I can't sleep. I wouldn't tell them anything else straight away or else they'd definitely think I was crazy.

Before I try the chaplain, I'll need to check if you have to be religious to talk to her. I don't think you do.

17th June 2004

I went to see the Chaplain today. I arranged the appointment with her before school, and I was so, so nervous. All day I couldn't stop thinking about it. I got to school very early because I didn't want my friends knowing that I was going to talk to her. But then Cassie spotted me before I had a chance to go. So, just before the bell went I ducked into the student services building, and nobody saw me that time.

My appointment was in Period 6 – straight after lunch. It was so, so nerve-wracking. The first thing she said to me was: "this is something I have to tell everyone. Before you start talking to me, I have to warn you that although this is confidential, there are some things that I have to report."

I must have looked very shocked or very disappointed, I'm not sure which. She tried to reassure me: "Only really serious stuff, like if you're at risk of being harmed by yourself or somebody else. Not the kind of things that most people talk to me about, like problems with friends, relationship problems, school problems. Any of that kind of stuff is all confidential".

I just stared at the wall. She kept trying to reassure me, until finally she said: "Look, I didn't mean to scare you, I just always try to be upfront with students. I only ever report really serious stuff. Like if you'd been raped or something. I mean really serious stuff.

I tried to stay calm and asked her "what if it was a while ago?' Then she stared at me as if she was thinking "wow okay, looks like this is more serious than I thought..."

I started shaking and I couldn't stop. Even my chin was twitching like how it does when you're about to cry but trying not to.

Thank god I kept my lips firmly sealed, and she didn't force anything out of me. She just guessed that whatever was bothering me was pretty serious, and that I didn't want her to tell anyone about it. She respected that. Then she suggested that I try calling an anonymous helpline, like Kids Helpline or Lifeline if I don't feel able to talk to her just yet. I'm thinking about it.

19th June 2004

You know what? I've already taken the Chaplain's advice and called Kids Helpline. I've called them before doing prank calls with my neighbour when I was younger.

Today it was weird and so hard to talk to someone I didn't know and couldn't see but in a way that felt safer — it's not as if the counsellor had any idea who I was. I tried my very hardest to tell the counsellor what my real problems were but it was hard to tell him much — especially because it was a guy. I only hinted that things in my family aren't that great, but didn't feel able to give details. His name was Frederick — I thought he was kidding at first, I've only ever heard that name in the Sound of Music!

If I call again, I'm going to ask to talk to a female because it might be a bit easier. I'd like to try again sometime because even though I wasn't able to say much today, I kept wishing that I could say more. Imagine if I actually DID tell someone all the stuff I want to, and they wouldn't tell anyone because it's confidential and they have no idea who I am anyway! It would be a huge weight lifted from me, and maybe it would stop it from drumming around in my head all the time.

16th August 2004

Another diary. I didn't think I'd stick at it for this long but I guess it's helped me a lot. I'm going to keep leaving some pages blank so I can go back and stick photos etc there.

I should be happy about starting another diary but the news is pretty depressing today. I should have written about it last week but I've felt too horrible and depressed and haven't been in the right frame of mind to write about it.

Last week, my neighbour Ben committed suicide. He jumped off a mobile phone tower near the sand track. Even though I haven't been close to him in the last couple of years since he quit athletics, it's affected me and so many people, so much. I can't even begin to imagine how his family and really close friends are feeling, if I'm as upset as I am.

The person who actually found out was Dad, because he saw the police car outside their house. When Mum told me, I sat numbly for a few minutes after she left, then it suddenly hit me and I almost threw up. Just the sudden 'oh my god this is real' feeling. People my age are not supposed to die! Mum went over to try and help Anne (Ben's mum) but I stayed at home.

Then, after a couple of days I felt angry at him, because why should HE do that? What made his problems worse than mine? I don't even know what his problems were or if he had any major ones but something must have been pretty wrong if he did that. I felt so mad at him for taking the easy way out while I'm still facing my stupid life – why can't I just take the easy way out too? I suppose I felt mad because seeing how big the impact of suicide is has been a real eye-opener. It has such a ripple effect. Such a huge chunk of the community has been affected by this, and I really doubt Ben would have predicted that.

I always thought that if I killed myself, only close family and a few friends and maybe even a teacher or two would be upset enough to go to the funeral. But Ben's death has made me realise how many people cared about him, and I wish he'd known that. His funeral (which was this morning) was packed – some people didn't even get seats. I never in my whole life would have predicted that one death could have such an impact. It made me feel guilty for thinking about killing myself last year, if I'd have hurt people anywhere near as much as they've been hurt by this.

Now I'm just sad, because I can see his death for what it really is – a terrible waste of a talented, kind and funny boy's life. 16 does seem a young age to die. I so badly wish that I'd been closer to him in the last couple of years. Maybe we could have helped each other. But we drifted apart since we went to different high schools, and especially since he quit athletics.

17th August 2004

Aaron Peters has been really struggling with Ben's death (they played soccer together). He went to see the school psych about it and told her that I knew Ben pretty well, so now, under our year coordinator Mrs Sampson's insistence, I have to go and see the psych (Ms Lynch) too! I think Jake has to as well. I suppose I could get out of it if I really wanted to, but I secretly do want to go. I've never seen a psychologist before and this will be my chance to suss her out. You never know, she may be able to help me a bit with the bad stuff. All during Ben's funeral the people who spoke were saying stuff about how we should talk to people if we have problems, that there is never a problem too big to share. So maybe, if things go well with the psych, I'll consider telling her about my problems.

18th August 2004

The school psych... Big let down, I have to say! To put it bluntly, she was terrible! My initial thought when I saw her was 'lady, you need a mirror, and possibly a hairbrush!' I'm not even kidding. It all went downhill from there. She was trying to get me to be angry about Ben's death and said something about how she wished she could smash his head in because he'd hurt everybody so much... Bit insensitive?!? Especially considering that she didn't even know him! She was trying to get a response out of me but that's not the way to go about it...

Then I said I could kind of understand what Ben had done because when I was younger, I'd wished I could be dead sometimes. I was trying so hard to tell her stuff, I really wanted to tell someone... Then I said I have trouble getting to sleep and have nightmares, because of something bad that happened when I was about 8. She said:

"Well you may be exaggerating in your nightmares, it's not necessarily what happened. For example, I worked with a girl once who was in a car crash. She always had nightmares about the car getting hit by a truck, when in fact it was just a car that hit them."

That's helpful... So you're jumping to conclusions and telling me I'm exaggerating when you don't even know what the problem is?? Uhhh, thanks! Then she started drawing a diagram of the sleep cycles and telling me to get a regular sleep routine, etc etc. All the really obvious answers. Oh, and try taking magnesium tablets too. What the hell? I felt like she was skirting around what I was trying to say. I was trying to tell her something really important but I didn't know how. And instead of trying to help me to do this, she just gave me the easy answers. I left her office feeling frustrated with myself and disillusioned with her!

I only want to talk to somebody who actually cares, who will really listen to me. Ms Lynch is definitely not that person.

8th September 2004

Today I did one of the hardest things I've ever done and I feel really ... strange! I can't really describe it.

For some reason, this morning I decided that enough was enough, and that it was time to talk to somebody, despite my disastrous time with the school psych. So, I told Mum I felt sick and asked for the day off school (she said yes because I haven't missed a single day of school all year). I felt a bit bad because it's Nat's birthday and I wanted to see her, but I really couldn't hold up for any longer.

I waited for Mum to go out, then I tried Kids Helpline again. I asked for a female but none were free. I called back half an hour later and still no females were free so I grabbed the phonebook and looked at the emergency numbers listed on the inside cover, to see if there was anyone else I could talk to. I was desperate by this point.

I found an emergency number for a sexual assault crisis line. Like Kids Helpline it's a 1800 number which means it's free. Which means it won't show up on the phone bill, which MEANS that nobody at home will know I called!

I'm really glad I called that number because I got put through to a counsellor, who I ended up telling a lot more than I ever thought I could tell anyone. I told her a lot about the abuse, but when she asked if it was still happening I said no. I told her that it stopped a few years ago because I didn't want her to tell anyone, and also because she would think I'm so stupid for letting it still happen when I'm 16 years old. I wouldn't tell her who had abused me either, because that's the worst bit of the whole thing. I didn't want her to know. I'm so embarrassed! And also, imagine what would happen if she traced the call and talked to my dad or the police or something? That is such a scary thought and at least being vague keeps me a little bit safer if she does tell anyone. But I didn't say my name – I told her it's Jenna. I've got to stay one step ahead or else I will be in so much trouble.

The counsellor was good though, she didn't push me to tell her stuff that I didn't want to, but encouraged me to tell her the things I was ready to say. She suggested that I make an appointment to come in and see a counsellor, but I said I'd think about it first. It's near the city, so I could get there by bus, but I'm not sure that it'd be a good idea. At least talking on the phone she had no idea who I was. But if I go in to see somebody, they'll know who I am and I won't be anonymous anymore. And I have a bad feeling about that – I reckon they'd tell someone.

21st September 2004

I bit the bullet and called the sexual assault helpline again yesterday. Talking to that counsellor on Nat's birthday left me wanting to talk again. It's like I've opened a can of worms once I started talking about this stuff, and I've wanted to keep on talking, to get rid of it. It made me feel so much better when I first talked, knowing that someone knew some of my secrets, even if she had no idea who I was. I also felt less crazy after talking to her because she kept saying that my reactions to everything are totally normal. I don't know if she is just saying that to make me feel better but still, it was nice to hear and she sounded genuine.

I'd decided that I wasn't going to tell the people there my real name, but when the person arranging my appointment asked, I automatically told her, like a reflex! So they know my real name, including surname, which means I have to be very careful not to say too much now. I made sure to tell her that I wasn't being abused anymore, and that the person who did it didn't live with me anymore. But I refused to tell her who did it.

We arranged an appointment for the next school holidays so that I won't be missing any school (otherwise Mum and Dad might found out). The counsellor is called Tanya but I've never spoken to her before so I am already scared, scared, scared! But at the same time it's given me a bit of hope, that I will be able to get rid of the terrible thoughts and craziness in my mind.

1st October 2004

I called Tanya today because I wanted to get an idea of what she's like before I come in. Basically, I was trying to figure out if she's nice or not. She didn't seem that nice. At first she seemed to be wondering why on earth I was calling her when I could just wait for the appointment, but then she seemed to get it – that I just wanted to get a bit familiar with her so that it's not as scary next week. I felt really disappointed after talking to her. I don't know what I'd expected – the nicest person in the world maybe? Well I at least wanted someone who seemed nice and caring, and I didn't get that impression during our brief call!

8th October 2004

I was too hard on Tanya after that first phone call, she actually is nice. She's younger than I expected, and she's got dreadlocks. She's probably in her late 20's or early 30's, and she seemed to have a sense of humour which was good.

I was so scared when I first walked in. It's like a little cottage, near the hospital where I was born. I was so nervous on the bus. When I pressed the button to get off, my hands were shaking. Then when I actually got to the cottage I felt like a little kid, all on my own. I went and sat down in the waiting room trying to engross myself in a magazine and feeling so, so small. Wishing that I had someone by my side, supporting me and telling me that I was doing the right thing. But you can't have everything and I'm old enough to do these things on my own anyway.

I couldn't trust anyone enough to tell them where I was going, not even my best friends. Firstly because they would think I was the most disgusting person ever, and secondly in case they told people.

I pretended to Mum that I was meeting friends in the city, and she believed me. Meanwhile there I was figuring out the bus routes – got there early and all. You can't say I am not independent.

Tanya came out and guided me to her office and she could tell how scared I was. But it wasn't quite as scary as the time I went to the chaplain back in June because that was the first time I'd ever tried to talk to anyone about this stuff.

I had to be so careful to make sure she didn't get concerned enough to tell anyone anything I said, and I asked her a million and one questions about confidentiality. I can't imagine how everyone would react if this got out – my family would kill me! I told her that it stopped a couple of years ago, that I don't live with the person who abused me anymore (I refused to say who it was). I also made sure she realised that he's not a bad person, that he does lots of nice things too apart from the abuse. He's just a human being who has flaws just like everyone else.

15th October 2004

I had another appointment with Tanya but decided that I'm not going to go back anytime soon. There's no point because I can't really tell her anything, unless I want it to get reported to police or social workers. And it's too hard to tell her bits and pieces without telling her the whole story. Also, I won't be able to go now until the end of the year, because school goes back next week.

She was talking about how I'd been 'groomed' for the abuse since I was little, which makes me think that she thinks I am stupid. I couldn't really have been so stupid, could I have? I don't know what to think.

18th October 2004

I've been having so many bad dreams lately. All this stuff just won't go away now that I've started talking about it. I knew counselling was a bad idea! I am never going back. I feel so guilty for telling. I've had this one dream over and over again, where I get burnt alive for telling, because I'm such a horrible person. It's weird though, because when I wake up I feel so hot and as if my skin really is on fire. It's like I am burning up with guilt.

I don't understand myself at all.

19th October 2004

Ever since I started talking about this stuff, it's like I have to keep talking until I get rid of some of the baggage. But it's too risky going to see Tanya. So I've decided that from now on I am only allowed to talk about this stuff to people who don't know who I am – anonymously.

24th October 2004

Today I called Kids Helpline to try talking about how I've been feeling, because I've been so confused lately. I talked to a counsellor called Lindy and she was so, so nice. She has a similar sense of humour to me so I found it really easy to get along with her and talk to her. I didn't tell her much, but she was understanding. I told her bits and pieces, but not as much as I'd wanted to. That's always my problem – there's so much stuff inside me that I need to get rid of, need to tell someone, but can't bring myself to say.

Lindy gave me her future shift times so I can call her back and talk again. I'm definitely going to. For some reason I really clicked with her and was able to trust her from the word go. a part of that might be because she has no idea who I am – she doesn't even live in the same state as me! So I feel as if it's safer to open up to her than someone who knows me.

30th October 2004

I called Lindy again and told her about the abuse. Only after asking her a million questions about if she has to report stuff, and she said she only has to if someone is currently being abused. So I told her that I'm not.

BUT I did tell her that it was Dad. She's the first person who I've ever told that, the first person to ever know that he is the person who has sexually abused me. I pretended that I don't live with him anymore, so that she wouldn't tell anyone. I don't want her to tell the police! I would get in SO much trouble with my family.

When I told her it was Dad, I felt myself burn up with guilt all over again. That horrible feeling that I am betraying him, my own dad, the guy who taught me how to ride my bike without training wheels, who used to play board games with me all the time. (Who has molested me and raped me for almost my entire life). I don't know why, but it really hits you when you say these things out loud. It's as though it makes it sink in a bit more, even though I've been living with it every day for so many years. Lindy was very understanding but every time she mentioned my dad (or even said the word dad) I could feel that burning again – as though I shouldn't have said something like that out loud.

I really don't know how I feel right now. a bit sick because of the guilty feeling, a bit relieved to have someone finally know it's Dad who's done this stuff to me, and extremely exhausted, from being so confused.

Painting by
Sarah Millicent Elliott

15th November 2004

I helped out with the measuring and timing at athletics last week. I like going along and helping because I like being a role model for the younger kids. Some of them are so cute! I mainly helped with the under 8 girls such as Kelsey, Sharna and Amber. They're all 7 years old and so tiny.

It's hard to believe that I was that young when the really bad stuff started happening to me. If anybody ever tried to do that kind of stuff to these kids I would want to kill them. They're so tiny, innocent and defenceless. It's weird, when you're a kid you don't realise how little you are, until you look back. Was I really like them? Gap-toothed, doing clapping songs and laughing hysterically if someone pokes their tongue out? I suppose I was. Kelsey reminds me of myself the most at that age – she is very, very shy just like I was. I hope to God that nobody ever takes advantage of her quietness. Maybe if I hadn't been such a quiet kid, this would have ended way earlier. But I was a 'good girl' and kept my mouth shut.

26th November 2004

School's out for the year, we just had exams. It's awesome being in year 11 and finishing before the younger grades!

9th December 2004

I had another strange dream last night, about Ben. I can't really remember what happened but when I woke up I lay there for ages feeling shocked that Ben is dead. I don't know why but it just suddenly sunk in how shocking it is that he killed himself. It's not like I was that close to him in the last couple of years, but it's so hard to believe that he would do that. And that he's now dead. No coming back. I can't even begin to imagine what it must be like for his family, and how hard it must be to wake up to such a harsh reality each day. I really have no idea what it's like. It is nearly 4 months since his death.

On a lighter note, I got my school report today. Straight A's, right on track.

11th December 2004

I've been thinking about the abuse a lot lately. I get to a point where I think that everything will be okay and that I can ignore it and pretend it's not happening, but I can't always. It's unbelievable how draining it is sometimes. But I don't feel like I clicked with Tanya very well, so I wish I was able to talk to someone else. I guess I can't afford to be picky and I should just be grateful for what I've got. I prefer talking to Lindy on the phone but it's difficult because her shift times have changed – they're nearly all in the early morning now and school hours. I really hope our school's old chaplain is back next year because I definitely won't go and talk to the new one (it's a guy). And the school psych – I wouldn't go near her. She's a freak! But I don't think there's a big chance that the old chaplain will come back. If she does, I'll go see her when I have a free period. I need to talk to someone, and seeing the chaplain is a lot easier than trying to see Tanya, because I can't miss school to go to Tanya without having to explain.

16th December 2004

I've been doing more research into university scholarships interstate. The easiest possible one I think I could get is in Tasmania – they have quite a few interstate scholarships, and pretty low entry scores so maybe not as competitive. When you look at scholarships for University of Melbourne – you need to get like 99.95 as your TER. Realistically I can't get that score, I don't do physics or those subjects you need.

A scholarship would mean that I am away from home! In another state! I really want to get one of those scholarships. Even if you do need to get 99.95 in the exams, I'll give it a shot. I doubt there are many people who want it as much as me. Who NEED it as much as me!

19th December 2004

I'm still dreaming and scheming about going to uni in Tasmania. I hope that I can stay motivated to work really hard, and maybe it can happen. But as my maths teacher would say, there might be "a snowball's chance in hell."

24th December 2004

Yesterday I looked on the University of Tasmania website to find out more about their scholarships. It turns out they only offer six of the national scholarships (you get about $10,000 per year for accommodation etc). Six??? I thought it would be close to 20. Damnit, that would be so hard to win. I want that scholarship so, so much and I'm already forming plans in my head about how I can organise my time next year. I should get up early every morning and do some study before school, and after school as well. I need to work so, so hard to create a wonderful new life for myself.

27th December 2004

One thing I am learning lately is that I am a very independent person compared to some of my friends, and well and truly capable of looking after myself. I have my parents to thank for that to a large degree, for driving me so insane that I haven't wanted much to do with them for a long time. That's why I don't get along with Mum. I should talk to her about it so we can work together to get along better. That would make life easier for everyone. Deep down I now realise that I do want to get along with her, and that I do love her. I think she knows that.

30th December 2004

I'm trying to figure out how to get this scholarship.

RULES FOR MY STUDY TIMETABLE:

1. I need to make summaries for each subject

2. I need to do lots better in biology – that was my weakest subject last year.

3. I should remind myself all the time why I am working so hard. I am going to stick a picture of Tasmania in front of my desk or in my school diary.

4. I shouldn't get distracted by the bad things that happen. It can be sorted out later, it's not too hard to forget it for a while.

I'm going to have to keep in mind how little time I have left at school so that I knuckle down. I have to stay motivated and keep my Tasmanian dream alive. Otherwise I'll be stuck living in this boring hellish house instead of living happily and independently in Tasmania. I've never been there before but I'm sure I'd like it. I'd like anywhere! It's SO worth studying for.

Later that day:

Just then on the radio they played one of the songs they played at Ben's funeral. I still can't believe that he's dead, and the way in which he died. It's such a huge shame – he could have done whatever he wanted to do. He was a very social person and had lots of friends, and it's a real shame that he wasn't able to open up to any of them. Could he have called anybody? He had his mobile phone with him when he died, so why didn't he use it? Maybe he just wasn't able to verbalise his feelings – I can understand that. The first time I tried talking to a Kids Helpline counsellor they thought it was a prank call because I wasn't able to talk and I kept laughing nervously. But I have kept trying and trying, and it gets easier each time. I wish Ben had been able to do the same. I wonder if he ever seriously considered calling for help, because I distinctly remember a Friday evening in Year 8 where we did prank calls to Kids Helpline. The sad thing is that we both probably had problems that needed help, but couldn't bring ourselves to be serious. I am so sad that Ben is gone.

There are so many unanswered questions but either way it's too late now. He's dead now and his family is suffering so much. They really don't deserve this, no one does, not even MY parents. I really love Anne (his mum) and have done since I was little. She is so warm and caring, so I don't know why Ben didn't feel able to approach her. Or his dad! I guess Ben wasn't thinking straight at the time but again, nobody knows.

Wow, that's enough depressing stuff for now.

2005

1st January 2005

My mind keeps slipping towards the abuse today but I keep reminding myself that I can't afford to think about it this year. I can get it sorted out after my final exams, make it stop and get all the counselling I want, but now is not the right time. It will just drain me like it did last year and I'll spend all my time thinking about it. It's a waste of time, and energy. I remember how many evenings I spent with my head on the desk last year, just thinking about it. And on those nights, I got no homework done. I remember days spent sitting in class with my head on the desk, too tired to even listen. How did I get straight A's by doing that? I have no idea. But I have to remember to NOT MAKE LIFE HARDER FOR MYSELF! There's a time and a place for everything, and this is definitely not the right time. The old Chaplain probably won't be back this year which is probably a blessing in disguise, because then I won't be tempted to talk to her. The only other person at school that I might ever trust is Mrs Stanley but I don't see her as much as I used to. I keep telling myself that I can't let myself talk to her but I know deep down that I should. But I can't give in, I need to stay in control of myself and keep my stupid mouth shut! I have to stay strong, I can't give up now. I've come this far and the end is in sight, if I'm willing to work hard enough.

31st January 2005

Back to school... we're big Year 12's now, as we keep being reminded, and we have to be great role models for the younger students blah blah blah. And we have to study hard for exams etc etc. DUH! We already knew that.

We have a new principal who is sooo nice! I'm so glad he came because he's a million times better than our old principal. It was so hot today (like 40 degrees) and we had to sit outside for a start-of-year assembly, and he came out and talked to us and was very nice. In contrast, at LAST year's first assembly, Ms Strachan addressed us over the P.A. from the comfort of her air-conditioned office, while we fried outside in the heat! We all hated her for it.

My teachers for this year seem okay. I have Mrs Bartlett who is really short and a bit strange! My English teacher is Mrs Fisher, I've never had her before but people who've had her say she's nice. I've got Mr Cheung for biology again, which is great because if I didn't have him I probably wouldn't do very well – he's very patient at helping anyone who needs it, without making you feel dumb.

I've still got Frau Strauss for German, and the same people in my class as last year. It's the best class ever, we're all great friends.

And my maths teacher Mr Jones, well he seriously looks like the character 'Mole' from a show I watched when I was little called 'Animals of the Farthing Wood'. He also dresses to the maths teacher theme by wearing checked shirts that look like graph paper. But all round he seems like a nice guy which is lucky because he's also my homeroom teacher.

15th February 2005

I keep thinking about the abuse and wondering whether I should change my mind and go and see Tanya again. There's more than 7 weeks until the holidays, can I last that long? I could always call Lindy but there's never a convenient time. Mostly she works during school hours and she doesn't do her weekend shift anymore. It really sucks! That's when I used to be able to catch her.

I wish I had clicked more with Tanya. I clicked a lot better with the counsellor I talked to when I was arranging the appointment.

I'm my own worst enemy. Why do I make life so hard for myself? I just don't understand why I let something crazy like this dominate my thoughts. Seven weeks is too long. If only I liked the school psychologist. I need need need help NOW.

17th February 2005

Hannah. You are fine. Stop feeling sorry for yourself. Stop thinking crazy thoughts, you can't let your insane side beat you. That's all it is – insanity. Your life is not hard, you've got pretty much everything you could ever want. Be happy for once instead of being so miserable all the time. You don't want people to know what you're really like, do you? Didn't think so. So put on your happy smile and GET ON WITH YOUR LIFE.

8th March 2005

I called Tanya on Friday because I couldn't handle things anymore. I needed to talk to someone and she seemed to be the best option for now. The old chaplain never came back, and there's no way I would go talk to the new guy, and as for the school psych – noooo thanks! The soonest I can go to Tanya is in 3 weeks because we have a pupil free day from school. I can't go on a school day without my parents finding out so I'll just have to wait. It is not too far away and I've been booked in for 11am.

30th March 2005

I went and saw Tanya yesterday, I think she could tell that I was quite exhausted. I kept asking her questions about what she has to report because I want to tell her more. But I don't know if it's safe for me to do that.

I'm not sure how useful it was to see Tanya because I'm not able to say much, even when I want to. The only person I've been able to tell much is Lindy at Kids Helpline – she knows that it was my dad (I told her he's moved out so she doesn't know it's still happening). I've been able to tell her quite a bit about what's happened and how I feel, and I get along with her really well. She's so nice. I wish she lived in the same city as me so I could go to see her face to face. But maybe that would be too weird – maybe it's easier talking to her because I don't know her at all.

17th May 2005

I've been finding it really hard to concentrate in the last few days which is really bad because I have exams starting next Monday! It's gotten very bad because there was a storm yesterday and storms don't have very good memories for me. But I have to try and forget about that right now because I need to study. I need to be harder on myself instead of being my own worst enemy, and always thinking of the bad stuff.

23rd May 2005

Today has been a crazy day. CRAZY. Where do I start? As I said – crazy.

Well I suppose it started off last night really. You know who came into my room and did you know what. I tried to roll into the wall to stop it but that never works. He just grabbed my arm anyway. I don't remember much after that, I just slip away most times. I could feel the bruise on my arm this morning when I got in the shower. You can see the finger marks.

Anyway, off I went to sit my 9am English exam, feeling pretty sleep deprived but that's nothing new. Usually I'm good at English, because I love writing. But I couldn't get in the right headspace today. I could hardly remember the texts we'd studied, and could only think about my disgusting arm, I could feel it every time I moved.

I can't remember what the essay question was, but I ended up writing about family secrets and abuse and how it wrecks families. Even the world's biggest fool would have been able to figure out that I was writing about my family – I was so obvious. When I was writing it I felt sick in my stomach because I knew that if I write something like that I'll get caught and the cops will get called and this nightmare will get 100 times worse. But stupidly, I didn't seem to care at the time.

Okay, so I didn't care AT THE TIME. But as soon as I walked out of the exam room, actually as soon as they said "Pens down", I knew I had made a huge mistake. I felt so sick and scared. I was really freaking out and when I got home (nobody was there) I was starting to feel hysterical. I decided to try calling Tanya to see what the rules are about teachers reporting stuff. I needed her to reassure me that it was okay, that nothing bad was going to happen. But when I called her she wasn't there – she's been sick since last week apparently.

I spent quite a few minutes being angry at Tanya for not being there when I needed her (I know, mature). Then I decided to give Kids Helpline a try. Lindy wasn't there, but I wasn't surprised because she doesn't usually work afternoons. It's been so long since I have managed to catch her. So I decided to chat to another counsellor, the one who answered my call was called Leah. I knew that anyone who worked there would probably be able to give me the information I needed – they talk to kids everyday so know the rules about what gets reported. Leah was really nice and I asked her my questions about what teachers have to report. Except, she didn't let me off the hook that easily. She kept asking me questions ("So what did you write? Is it true? Who abused you?"). The worst bit is, by this point I was so exhausted and sick of keeping my secret that I answered every single question honestly. I let my guard down – I let myself down.

I didn't tell her outright that it's Dad who did these things to me but she asked me if it's an immediate family member and I said yes. Then she asked if they are male or female and I said male. Then she asked who else is in my family, besides me, and after I'd answered her she said:

"So if your dad is the only male in your family, are you trying to tell me that he is the one who abused you?"

Me: Yes

L: "Is he still abusing you?"

Me: Yes
(did I really just say that?)

I even ended up telling her about how I sometimes get bruises when I make him mad by not doing what he wants. It's scary to think how much I told her.

Suddenly I realised how big the repercussions of what I'd told her could be if she told anyone else, and started freaking out and back tracking in a major way. I asked her about a million times whether she had to report it to anybody and she said she wasn't going to at this point, and to call her back on Thursday (her next shift time). By then I'd been talking to her for two hours, and was totally exhausted, and lay in a heap after I hung up the phone.

Dad came home about an hour later and I was still lying on the couch. I felt as guilty as all hell to think that I'd been saying these things about him and our family. I really need to tell someone and I need it to stop. But at the same time I don't want to tell because I know that he will be so hurt if I do. I will be betraying him and despite the bad stuff, he is a good Dad the rest of the time.

If I hurt him like that I'll make him so angry, and there's no point in that. Better to keep quiet than to get burnt alive. I've had that dream a few times – I don't know where it came from, but it started after the first time I saw Tanya, when I would wake up in a hot sweat burning with guilt. First my hair would crackle and fall out, then my skin would melt. My eyeballs would burn away so they would just be empty sockets. And I wouldn't be able to scream because my mouth would have burned away, my teeth turned to ash. People would find nothing but a burnt skeleton and they would think I'd set myself on fire, that it was my fault. And they'd just think I was stupid for doing that and wouldn't care, and wouldn't be upset or anything.

I really need to move out, hopefully for uni. But if I let my exams slip like today's English exam, there's absolutely no hope that I'll get an interstate scholarship. Anywhere is fine, just not here! It's time to knuckle down. Come on.

26th May 2005

Oh my god. OHHH MYYYY GODDDD. You're only a piece of paper but there's no one else I can trust in this crazy world.

After Ben, I thought suicide was a bad idea. Now I can see its merits, loud and clear!

I'm not overreacting. I called Leah from Kids Helpline back today, feeling good that I'd been able to trust her because she said she wouldn't tell anybody about this stuff. And what's the first thing she says when I call her up?

"We're going to have to tell someone about this. I need you to work with me so that we can get you some help".

WHAT a BITCH! I hate her, I HATE HER, and I made that pretty clear. I swore at her, told her that she was a liar, that I hated her — and I meant every word of what I said. I HATE HER! I can't believe I trusted a phone line counsellor, HOW COULD I BE SO DUMB?

I tried to convince her that none of what I'd said is true, that I made it all up, that it was only a bad dream I'd had. But she wasn't that stupid and didn't buy into it. She ended up having to hang up on me because I was getting so angry, and she told me to call her back when I'd calmed down. She gave me her future shift times because she knew that wasn't going to be anytime today. I was fuming. I can't believe how stupid I was to call her in the first place. I don't know what's going to happen. I don't know what to do, I really have no idea — and I don't have anybody to talk to about it all. I feel so powerless and alone right now. But that's nothing new.

27th May 2005

This has been the most dramatic week of my life and I'm so confused. I think I'm falling apart.

Today was our interschool cross country and we had to wear the school athletics singlets. Not really the best outfit for someone with a massive bruise at the top of their arm but luckily for me the teachers from my school (Mrs Stanley and Mrs Jeffs) and the other students sat in a place on the opposite side of the track. So when I ran past them they saw my 'normal' arm, not the bruised one.

After the race I went over to where the people from my school were sitting to grab my bag, and a year 8 boy — oh god. To say he put his foot in it is a huge understatement.

"WHOA, WHAT'D YOU DO TO YOUR ARM??"

By this point, everyone within earshot is staring at me. Including Mrs Stanley, who happened to be standing less than a metre away.

"Oh I just banged it," I said, trying to shut him up. But he kept going:

"Musta banged it pretty hard!"

At this point, Mrs Stanley walked over to me to see what all the fuss is about. She walked around to see the arm that the Year 8 kid was going on about. She held onto my arm, stared at it, and looked like she felt sick. This bruise has come up really badly, it's dark purple and covering the whole top of my arm. She didn't say anything, and I stared into space. Then she changed the subject: "Have you seen Kerri? Mrs Jeffs was looking for her."

I feigned interest in her question but my mind was racing at a million miles an hour. Why didn't she say anything about my arm? What was she thinking? Was she mad at me? She seemed mad.

Silence was so scary, I would have preferred she shout at me.

Now in my mind, it's been confirmed that she knows what's going on. I think she's suspected it or known about it since at least Year 10 but I've always thought, oh, maybe she doesn't really know. I know that I don't want this to get reported but I feel even more hurt that Mrs Stanley, who I've clung to as a mother figure in the last few years, really doesn't care about me. How can you see bruises that massive and not care? Not even say "is everything alright at home?"

Especially in light of some of the very hinty conversations I've had with her about abuse. She would be a fool not to have figured it out by now.

I know it sounds dumb and I'm the world's biggest hypocrite, but I feel absolutely worthless right now. One of the few adults that I've looked to for support and I've wanted to help me so badly, who I've trusted enough to drop a million clues to, doesn't give a damn about me. She'd rather forget about it because I'm just a pesky student and she's only paid to care from 9am–3:30pm. So no point in bothering to get caught up in kids' problems. It's just a job after all.

It's pretty painful when you look at it that way. I don't have any adult in my life who I know will always be there for me, who genuinely cares about me. That is definitely the worst part of all this. I feel like I could get through anything if I had someone by my side. Isn't that what mums are supposed to do?

It's all too scary to face alone.

3rd June 2005

Nothing's happened with Kids Helpline, because I never called Leah back.
If they were going to trace the call they would surely have done it by now, right?
So I think the danger has passed. Lesson learned. I'm going to wait a couple
more weeks then try calling Lindy again, using my fake name.

8th June 2005

We got our exam results back today and I didn't do very well – which didn't
surprise me. In history and English I got 20% below what I usually get!
Oops. I cringed when I read the essay I wrote on family secrets. It was so
random and totally unrelated to the essay question and the texts we studied.
It was so obvious that I was writing about me but whoever marked it didn't seem
to care. Or maybe they just didn't even read it properly! In one bit I'd even written
"as someone who has been abused..." and somehow related that to the big guy
(corporations) vs. little guy (Michael Moore) theme in 'Bowling for Columbine'.
At one point the teacher had even written "An honest response". Yup, pretty
honest alright. No wonder I got so nervous afterwards. Thankfully, as I have
already realised, teachers don't care enough to take notice of these things.

13th June 2005

I have had such a big day and as usual I don't know how to feel.

It started off early this morning. Before school I went to training like I do on lots
of Monday mornings (sometimes with Jade). Mrs Stanley was there as usual,
as well as a bunch of Year 10 girls. Everything was normal until the Year 10 girls
all left early to go to something, leaving just me and Mrs Stanley.
Almost immediately, the conversation started to shift.

"It's amazing what kids can cope with, isn't it?" she said.

Bit out of the blue, really.

I didn't know how I was supposed to answer that so I just nodded.

Then she started talking about how some of the kids in her Year 10 class are
absolutely feral. I didn't know what she was trying to get at so I got defensive
and said:

"Maybe they've got problems. You shouldn't just blame them, they might have real problems."

"Oh I know some of them have problems, but that's no reason for them to hurt other people," she replied.

I really didn't know where this was heading. So was she mad at me for having problems, was that it?

Then she asked me:

"So do you think kids like these, who have big problems, can be helped?"

I said something about listening to them, talking to them.

Mrs Stanley: "Hannah, do you think there's something going on in your life that you need to talk to somebody about?"

Oh my god. She actually cared. I didn't know what to say so I just nodded. It looked like this was my chance to talk to her but before I did, I asked her if she has to report stuff.

"Yes I do.' She hesitated. "I've already had to report you to Ms Lynch".

WHAAAAAAAAT!

I reacted pretty badly. I was almost in a trance, all I could say was "No, no, no." I was so shocked. And I was so, so scared. She said that I have to go and talk to the school psych.

I asked her "What's going to happen to me?" but she didn't seem to know. This was the first time in her 25 or so years of teaching that she's ever had to report anything. She said she'd been thinking about it lots over the weekend after the cross country, and had to do something. She said some things I'd said and done over the five years she's known me hadn't been quite right, and that she'd always had "an inkling that something was amiss". She said she remembers how timid and scared I seemed to be of adults way back in Year 8 at athletics training. Weird huh? It's surprising what people notice.

Oh god. So she does care. Even though having it reported is so scary and I have no idea what's going to happen, at least I know that Mrs Stanley does care about me. I am so, so glad and I wish she could adopt me. Her kids are all grown up now anyway. I wish she was my mum. No matter what happens, at least she cares. That's what I keep reminding myself.

I made an appointment to see the school psych tomorrow before recess. I think I'm still a bit too shocked to know how to feel about it all. I tried to subtly run the idea past Mum this afternoon but she didn't exactly respond well. You see, I got my exam marks back and they're pretty bad by my standards – 20% below what I'd usually get in every subject except one. I suggested that the school psych might be good to talk to so I could figure out what went wrong, but Mum was just saying "Go to your teachers, they can tell you where you lost marks".

Mum. Has it ever occurred to you that there may be an underlying problem? Oh that's right, you'd rather not know.

14th June 2005

After speaking to the school psych, I'm feeling a mixture of disappointment and relief. This morning I was a bundle of nerves because I was sure that the school psych had told someone else by now, that this would all get out of control and before long the police would be knocking on our door.

Not the case.

Cassie was the only person I told that I was going to see the psych. I was hanging out with her before school and I was freaking out completely, and told her an 'edited' version of what's happening... something like "Mrs Stanley saw a bruise on my arm and reported it to the school psych. They think it was my dad who did it, but I actually hit it on a doorframe. But I'm really scared they're going to tell my parents."

It didn't even occur to Cassie that the bruise wasn't from banging it on a door frame – and since it's gone now she couldn't see it for herself. I must be the world's worst friend if I can lie to my friends like that. But I already knew that – fake, fake, fake.

So anyway, I went to the psych. She was as big an idiot as I remember her being – it was hate at first sight!

Every time I see her, my first thoughts are:

1. Brush your hair

2. Get a mirror

3. Don't wear foundation unless you're going to put it on ALL of your face, not just randomly splash it around. Otherwise, you look like you've got a splotchy rash.

Mean, yes, but they were my initial thoughts.

She didn't have anything particularly useful to say, and it was obvious that she didn't really know the facts. Firstly, she said that she'd received the report from Mrs Smith, when it really came from Mrs Stanley. It became clear to me quickly that she didn't really care, that's how she came across at least. I felt as if she was talking down to me, and I've felt that way ever since I met her last year. I pretty quickly decided that she was the last person I wanted to help me, so told her that nothing is wrong, that I am fine. She asked me if it's true that I have problems with my dad and I tried to reassure her that it's just me being a teenage brat having disagreements with my parents like everyone else does.

It was pretty obvious that she didn't believe me that everything's fine, but there's nothing she can do since I didn't tell her anything. I asked her if she had to tell anyone else about it and she said she wouldn't, unless I'd told her that I was being hurt by someone. Well, she didn't use the word 'hurt', she preferred to try and impress me with the word 'maltreated'. Seriously, what the hell! Who says that? Who do you think you are, lady? You're here to help us and try to relate to us, not to try to impress us with your politically correct jargon!

Note to psych: Get over yourself. And brush your hair – seriously!

8th July 2005

Ooh this week has been tiring. I've been doing work experience at a childcare centre. Hyperactive kids from 8am–5pm all week! But it's been good because it keeps my mind busy. I was supposed to be seeing Tanya next Friday morning but decided to cancel, because there's no point in going. I need to focus on the 2nd half of Grade 12, and there's nothing she can do to help me. It's been months since I've seen her, and I couldn't tell her much at all. I need to just focus on school for now. I have to do well. I need to stop getting so distracted.

30th August 2005

Today I ended up being sent to the school psych again....... Ugh. Mrs Sampson wanted me and the other people who knew Cody (yet another guy I went to primary school with who has just committed suicide) to go. I didn't really mind going, I wasn't close to Cody though. I don't know when the last time I even talked to him was, even though he lived on the street next to mine! I used to see his dad and brother more, because his dad helped at the footy at the same time as I would be going running. His brother called me the 'running machine' once!

I think I'm more upset because it was a reminder of Ben's extremely similar death – it was pretty much a copycat suicide. I feel so sorry for the guys they hung out with, I don't know how they can deal with such a double-blow. They must be devastated. And his family. And Ben's family, my god. They must definitely be feeling the awful déjà vu of the situation.

As usual the psych wasn't very helpful. She's not good at talking about anything that's relevant, she just goes off on her own tangent, without reading my bored body language. I want to talk to her and I've given her plenty of chances, but there's no way I could ever feel comfortable enough to talk to her. She even answered the phone while I was in her office (it was her husband) and had an argument with him about something pathetic – about who was making dinner or something ridiculous like that.

If people called when I was in one of the appointments with Tanya, she didn't answer (let alone have an argument) because she had more respect than that. It's really disheartening to have someone answer the phone! Even though I didn't really click with Tanya, I honestly do think that she's good at her job and very professional too.

I don't think you can be good unless you genuinely respect the people you work with. Just because the school psych deals with kids doesn't make her a better person than us. She should treat us as equals instead of acting all superior. It doesn't make her look good, it makes her look like an idiot who is in the wrong profession!

5th October 2005

He's so genuinely nice to me sometimes that I really can't imagine how he ever hurts me so much. It's so confusing because it makes me start questioning whether anything really is happening, or if I'm just imagining it all. And I feel so guilty because I think all these horrible things about him sometimes, and I talked to Tanya earlier this year, and still talk to Lindy sometimes, when I know that I shouldn't. I even sent Lindy a letter with all the details of stuff that happened when I was younger! I was in a trance when I wrote it and didn't let myself think too much before posting it. It's like it wasn't me who wrote it and posted it. But now, I feel like doing that is like betraying him.

At the same time, I'm scared that he's never loved me at all, that he just pretended to so that he could use me. That's the scariest thought of all for me, because at least if I can believe that he does it because he loves me and can't help it, then I can make some sense of it all. But if he's never loved me, if he just does it because he loves himself and is greedy, then what am I?

Very stupid, that's what.

He used to always say how special I was when he was about to hurt me. Back when I was little and gullible and believed everything he said. He would put his hands on my face and tell me he loved me. And then he would rape me. I would just hear myself screaming inside my head but I was never able to make any noise.

But I always hoped I was good enough for him, I wanted to make him happy because he loved me. I can't believe I fell for it, that I ever thought I was special. I was such a dumb, dumb kid. These days I try to be good for him so he doesn't hit me.

Yes, I suppose I am in a pretty bad mood tonight, because it's stormy. This kind of weather always brings back some memories.

Author's note: Kids Helpline held on to that letter, and handed it over to the police a few years later as part of the investigation. I had signed it with my fake name – it took a few years before I trusted Kids Helpline enough to tell them my real name. The fact that I was anonymous is what made me feel safe enough to tell them so much.

I didn't see this letter until 2011 after the court case. I found it quite upsetting to read. Here is what it said:

To Lindy,

I wrote you a letter ages ago but never sent it. It's pretty outdated now so I decided to write a new letter. It will probably be pretty confusing to read because I'm a confusing (crazy) person and my mind is all over the place. Oh well!

Today is the first day of the school holidays, but I probably won't have a lot of privacy to call you. Even if I do, I won't be able to talk about really personal things if I'm on a public phone.

I'm really glad that I was able to have a good chat with you a few weeks ago, because I haven't talked to anyone about that stuff for ages. It's so hard pretending to be happy all the time and it makes me feel so bad about myself because I seem so fake and superficial. It's so frustrating that I can't confide in anyone that I know, I've come close a few times with a few different people, but I always chicken out. I'm scared that they'll think less of me or not care or something.

I'm trying to make myself go and see Tanya (face to face) again sometime. She'll probably just talk to me about the grooming process again. It's just such a huge thing for me to get my head around, it is so hurtful. Even little, everyday things that happened make me wonder if they were a part of some grand plan. Like if he brushed my hair, or gave me a hug, or held my hand. Or gave me a piggy back – was that because it was fun for me, or because he liked the feeling of me wrapping my legs and arms around him? There are so many questions, and I will never know the answers to them.

I do remember being touched – molested – from a very young age. The first memory I have is somewhere between age 3 and 5, I was lying on my bed and it was daytime. All I remember is that I didn't have any clothes on and he touched me, but I have no idea how long this went on for or how the situation started. Maybe we'd been playing a game or something, but I have no idea. It's strange that I can't remember much, because I have a lot of memories of us playing games that became sexual. I told you about 'playing doctor'. It was so much fun at first. One time he wrapped my arm up in a sling! He let me stick bandaids on him, even on his head. But as time went on, the game started to get scary. He started doing regular checks to make sure that I didn't have any toilet paper stuck in me – he would pull my legs apart and look for ages. One time he made me touch him, but I got really scared because his private parts went different and I thought I'd somehow hurt him. I didn't understand what I had done.

There were other games too, that started to give me a really weird feeling in my tummy. I remember him putting things into me, like marbles. He used my favourite teddy, Cutie, to abuse me. Cutie would get curious because my body was different from his, so he would explore it. First he'd look at my hair, my fingers. Then he'd take my shirt off (with a bit of help) and touch my tummy with his nose. Then I'd have to take my pants off and he'd touch me with his nose and try to stick his arm in to me – what a curious little bear...

I am still not really sure how the abuse because so serious, but the games stopped being fun at all as I got older. He started telling me that I was sexy, and I would try to act sexy because I liked the attention. I was only about 6 or 7. He started talking to me about sex because I was a 'big girl' and he wanted me to be prepared. I remember one time he put a texta in me and kept pushing it in and out for a while. I nodded when he said "that doesn't hurt" and I didn't cry. I would have only been about 6.

Another time, when I was about 7, he did the same thing, but with a bottle of roll on deodorant. He did that twice actually. The first time he did it, I got really scared, and said "I don't want to play this game anymore" before he could try pushing it in. He stopped talking to me for what felt like weeks after that (it was probably only a day or two) and started being really nice to my sister and ignoring me. After that I was practically throwing myself at him because I missed the attention and thought I had lost him and that I was going to be all alone in the world. So the next time we were alone I said I was ready to play that new game now. So he grabbed the deodorant bottle and really had to force it into me because I was so small. I remember him spitting on it so it would go in easier. It was sooo incredibly painful and I was trying not to cry. When he said "feels great, doesn't it?" I just nodded. There was very dark blood on it, almost black, and I was terrified. I didn't understand what was happening. I didn't understand why he would do something that hurt me. When I tried to move away because it hurt so much he just rammed it into me, then he kept pushing it in and out and he seemed really happy about it.

Twice (when I was a bit older) I had to suck on his penis. The first time I cried and didn't finish it, but the second time he went as far as covering my mouth to make sure I swallowed. I was 11 years old and still in my school clothes, I remember it so well. I started choking – I thought I was going to die. He let me go and I ran to the bathroom and threw up. He apologised and asked if I wanted some ice cream. I never had to suck on him again after that.

When I was about 8, the bad stuff started happening at night. The first one was during a storm – he was checking that I was okay. From then on he'd come once or twice a week. I would pretend to be asleep while he played with my hair, kissed me and told me how much he loved me. I would lie as still as I could while I waited silently in fear, because I was never sure what was going to happen. Sometimes he'd spend ages molesting me. Sometimes he kissed me. And sometimes he would HURT ME. Rape, rape rape rape rape rape rape rape rape rape. The word drives me insane but I can hardly bring myself to say it to you. I don't have a problem with you saying it though. I just cannot understand why he did that to me when I was so small. As soon as I realised it was about to happen (he'd hook my legs over the sides of my bed because I was so small), a horrible, piercing scream would fill my head and I felt like I was suffocating. It honestly is like using every bit of energy you have to scream, but I never managed to make any sound except once, but he didn't listen to me. I just gave up after that and I would try to tune out, by playing music in my head or pretending I was at the beach with a friend – anything to get away. I suppose that as time went on I got better at removing myself from the reality, but I would always feel the sharp pain at the beginning. I was just a little girl, and I hate that I was forced into the adult world at such a young age. I hate the fact that I was used for someone else's dirty pleasure, and I hate myself for being so compliant. I tried so hard to be a good girl (I still do), and look where it got me.

This letter has taken me hours to write, but probably only took you a couple of minutes to read. Sorry if it's boring or doesn't make sense. I've always wanted to tell you this stuff, but writing's easier. I'll call when I can.

From Jessie the crazy girl.

28th October 2005

Today was the last ever interschool athletics carnival. I only ran in one race and didn't do that well, I probably could have tried a bit harder but I don't really enjoy running anymore. I haven't for a couple of years now.

I've now officially graduated from high school! Our final exams start in just over a week. I'm not worried too much about the exams because it doesn't matter to me anymore – I won't get good enough to get a scholarship because my marks this year haven't been high enough. I tried, but not hard enough.

We had our graduation assembly at school on Wednesday, and then valedictory last night. I got the Diligence Award (with a cheque for $150) for being involved in everything and being nice and caring and studious blah blah blah! Whoever picked me for that award is a total fool because I'm so fake. It's such a joke.

Half of the stuff I've been doing is to keep my mind busy so I don't go outwardly insane.

I don't understand how people can't see me for what I really am – a dirty, disgusting, fake girl.

9th December 2005

It's Friday night and everyone's going on schoolies tomorrow. I was meant to be going with Cassie, Nat, Jason, Dirk etc. but now I'm not going. I have different priorities. I'm staying here to work – I've got a high paying job at a childcare centre and I'm not going to risk losing it. I need the money, every cent of it, so that I can move out as soon as possible. It's short term pain for long term gain and there's no way I'm wasting precious money on schoolies. Fun? Who needs it! I've been working 6 days a week and I'm exhausted. Long hours too, because Monday to Friday I'm leaving the house at 7am, and getting home after 6pm. On Sundays I've been working at the shop like last year.

Is it all worth it? Well I guess so. They say money isn't everything but it's pretty damn important to me right now. I've definitely got a goal – to get me outta here! I just have to work, work, work, save lots of money, and get the hell out of this place.

(**Author's note:** I would no longer call $8 per hour a 'high paying job', but glad to see I was happy with that back then! It definitely did beat my paper round pay rates!)

13th December 2005

Letter to Mrs Stanley (which I never sent)

Dear Mrs Stanley,

I hope you have a really wonderful Christmas and a happy new year. I'm doing okay at the moment, well sort of. Actually, I'm going a bit crazy. But I've always been crazy so that's nothing new.

This week I'm a loner because all my friends are on schoolies. I've been working in the 2-year-olds room and have a sore back from having to lift them all the time.

You probably think I'm dumb for writing a letter. But as I said, I have no friends right now and my sister is away too. I wish I could just pack up and leave like her but I've got to think long-term if I want to survive. It's very frustrating for me though because I've been trying to convince her to move out with ME and then she goes and wastes money on stupid holidays. I NEED her to move out with me but she only ever thinks of herself. Each time I've talked to her on the phone I've reminded her, "We're moving out soon, right?" just to make sure. But she's all talk and no action. As annoying as I find her, I'd much rather move out with her than stay here. And none of my friends are ready to move out – they like their families.

16th December 2005

(Another letter to Mrs Stanley that was never sent)

Dear Mrs Stanley,

I really wish I could talk to you right now because I have nobody to talk to. I'm so lonely, every day's a struggle.

In the last few days, I've really missed you, it's been a really tough time for me because I feel like I'm losing a lot of people, all at once. And as I said before, I don't really have anyone to talk to.

I miss you Mrs Stanley, so so much. I'm not sure if you actually care about me at all but even if you just pretended you did, that would be good enough for me. I just wish someone could give me a big hug right now and tell me that one day everything will be okay. I'm so lonely. I feel like I'm living in hell. I just want to cry. I'm crying now. Help me please, I need so much help.

18th December 2005

I've been having nightmares every night lately. I'm trying to work up the courage to go and see Tanya again in February, because I'll be working every day in January.

2006

3rd January 2006

I started work again yesterday after the shutdown over New Year's. I don't mind work because at least I know that it's worth it – just think how happy I'll be when I'm free!

I don't think I'll ever be free from what's happened to me because I don't know how I'll ever get rid of it. I've already started trying to deal with it but don't really see an end in sight. Will I ever be able to move on, or is it just going to control me forever? I guess I'll only know for sure once I've moved out. It would be wonderful if I could just empty that part of my mind into a little box and never have to look at it again. But I suspect it's going to take a bit more effort than that.

How the abuse has made me feel about myself:

- I feel like I'm different from all my friends, like they'd never understand me if they knew me well, and they don't understand me now.

- I feel superficial because I always try to pretend to be happy around my friends but I'm not at all

- I hate myself for being so submissive and not putting an end to things.

- I feel invaded when people get too close to me or touch me – but I do seem to be getting better at figuring out who isn't a threat to me.

- I find it hard to trust people

- I always get suspicious when I see men with children – especially fathers with their daughters. It gives me a sick feeling in my stomach.

Well that's enough for tonight, I'm pretty drained.

22nd January 2006

I'm quite exhausted today after having Nat stay for the week – her family went away for a week but she stayed here to work. We got sick of each other by the end of it because we spent 24/7 together – we worked together, spent our day off together, slept in the same room etc. After all these years I think she's finally realised how little sleep I get. I slept on a mattress on the floor and let her sleep on my bed, and she was surprised to discover that pretty much anytime she got up to go to the toilet during the night, I was wide awake. But hey, for me it was a safe week so I can't complain. He'd never be dumb enough to try anything when I had a friend in my room.

25th January 2006

Mrs Stanley called today to see how I went in my exams but I missed her because I was at work. She had said she would call, but I didn't really believe that she'd bother, so it was a nice surprise. She said to come down and visit her at school sometime when the new term starts.

I did alright in my final exams — I got a university entrance rank of 96.25. I was happy enough with that because I'd realised ages ago that I wasn't going to get good enough to get a scholarship to go interstate. You need to get at least 98 to get a scholarship.

I've decided that when I'm older I want to work with kids with disabilities, as a teacher. I've been doing some volunteer work with kids and love it. My dad made the worst joke ever once — he said that he can make me mentally handicapped if I like. He was kidding. You know what? He actually is a nice person but like everyone else he has his flaws. I try so hard to be good most of the time because when he gets angry, he gets ANGRY, and will use any pathetic reason as an excuse.

4th February 2006

I get a day off this Wednesday so I'm going to go and visit Mrs Stanley. She's the only good adult in my life right now (apart from Kids Helpline) and I need any support and guidance I can get. It's not as if she's helped me very much but at least she's shown that she cares about me a little bit. The sad thing about Kids Helpline is that Lindy has left! And it doesn't look like she is coming back. But she said if I can, to try and talk to another counsellor called Leah, who is actually the one I talked to in May last year when I gave them my real name. It is weird to talk to her but I am trying to give it a go.

I don't think Mrs Stanley and the other adults I've tried to confide in over the years have ever had any idea of how much hope I've pinned on them. Ever since I was little, I've been clinging to any adults I think might listen to me and support me and I always had this hope that they'd adopt me and I would live happily ever after. Unrealistic I know, but that's what I wished for. In primary school I used to always dream that Mrs Jacobs would adopt me. I think I was about 10 at the time. She didn't have any kids of her own yet and I always tried to be extra good around her and find reasons to go and help her with things. I wanted her to know that I would be a really nice kid to look after – I wouldn't cause any problems! I even used to daydream about her bringing me on holidays to meet her family, and being really proud of me. Then when she got pregnant I was really sad! She wouldn't need me anymore! Then when she went and had a daughter, and went on leave for ages, I was even more sad. She had her own daughter now, and would never need me.

It's like I've always been trying to replace my mum with other mother figures, to get the support I've not had from her. I've never really clung to anybody as a father figure because I find older men kind of creepy. And I really don't know how to act around them because I'm always paranoid, you know?

6th February 2006

I was meant to be seeing Tanya this Friday but I have cancelled. Surprise, surprise hey?

7th February 2006

I got my uni offer but I'm not sure about whether I should defer it or not. I haven't quite saved enough money to move out of home yet. I don't have a solid plan yet about how or when I'm going to move out, right now I'm just saving like crazy so that once I've left I'll never have to come crawling back for anything, ever. I want to be totally self-sufficient.

I might talk to Leah on the phone and see if she has any suggestions for me. She's a counsellor at Kids Helpline and I started talking to her in December because Lindy left. Lindy thought she'd be the best one for me to talk to because she's very nice. I think she's nice too, and easy to talk to.

15th February 2006

This morning there was an assembly and morning tea at school for last year's graduates who won awards. The new principal, Mrs Matthews, made the most random speech ever – going on about Michael Jordan and how inspiring he is...

People were trying not to laugh because it was sooo irrelevant and went on forever.

I finally saw my German teacher Frau Strauss, she's so nice! I love her, she's the cutest granny ever. I also saw Ms Fisher, she actually looked happy to see me and Cassie. I don't know how she can still like us when all we ever did in her class was talk, talk, laugh and talk but there you go. I think in general our year was a good year compared to some of the other years – even though we talked lots, almost all the people in our grade were genuinely nice people.

16th February 2006

We had the actual award ceremony last night. Mrs Sampson (year coordinator) and Mrs Evans (school deputy) were there. Afterwards I went to say bye to them but Mrs Sampson had already left so I only got to talk to Mrs Evans.

It turned out to be such a weird conversation... She told me to stay in touch, then asked me if I've gone to see Jan (the school psych i.e. Ms Lynch) yet, which I haven't... and wasn't planning on doing. Apparently they were expecting me to go and see her after my final exams, thought I'd get help and sort things out or something like that. It was strange because it sounded like they'd talked about me a lot, with me having NO IDEA. Apparently Ms Lynch told Mrs Evans that she had reason to be concerned – legally she had to tell Mrs Evans. I didn't know that, I didn't think she'd told Mrs Evans anything because she promised me that she hadn't and would tell me if she did.

So yes, Mrs Evans knew more about me that I would ever have thought, and here's the funny thing. a couple of years ago, I went to her to ask about a 'friend' of mine. Mrs Evans knew that I was talking about myself. I'd forgotten about that completely. Once when I was at school I went and asked Mrs Evans about what happens when a teacher reports stuff, because I had this 'friend' who was being abused but didn't want anything bad to happen if she told anyone. I can even remember her saying "sounds like you know this friend very well..." God I was such a dumbass, how obvious can you get? But at the time I was panicking and wanted information from her. Last night Mrs Evans said she'd learned the most about my situation from that conversation I had with her about my 'friend'. She said, "I wasn't born yesterday..."

Anyway, she then went on to tell me how she was never good enough for her mother and how much it affected her. I didn't know what to say. She's always seemed like such a tough lady to me, so I was taken aback. She even told me that she's started seeing a psych about it, because it's affected her so much. She always worked too hard trying to please people, I think.

She was telling me such personal things, which I'd never have expected someone like her to tell me. She's the deputy principal! She said that I have to start talking about things now because until I sort them out, they will continue to affect my life. She even said I can talk to her anytime if I want. Now that is really nice of her but it might be a bit strange. I'm not sure if I'd ever be brave enough to talk to her but it's not as if I have much support. So I probably will talk to her. I do want to.

23rd February 2006

Had my orientation day at uni today. I was put in the same group as other students in my course. There was a guy in my group that I really liked, I don't remember his name but he went to Northgate Senior High and knows my friend Anne. I hope I get to know him better.

26th February 2006

I was meant to be seeing Tanya this Friday but I cancelled the appointment because I don't feel like I'm ready to go back to her. It's probably better to focus on enjoying my first week of uni instead of thinking about the bad stuff.

4th March 2006

Uni's fine, it's never really worried me and I'm taking it all in my stride. My favourite new friends are Carlie, Tim and Tanya. They all went to different schools from me. I also spend a fair bit of time catching up with my old school friends – I do units with Nat, Jason, Emily, Anya and Jack.

In other news, I'm going to be a godmother! How exciting is that? But so random – I've only seen Karen a couple of times in the last few years but used to see her and her husband Dan quite a lot when I was younger – they brought me to the football with them which was really fun. I bumped into Karen a few weeks ago, and she realised how much I love kids. Her little girl is called Kelsey and she has bright red hair! She's a few months old now and sooo cute. I really think it's a privilege to be her Godmother, and I'll do what I can to be a good role model for her. The christening ceremony is in 2 weeks.

7th March 2006

A lot's been happening lately. My sister is having the time of her life overseas and is spending all the money that she was supposed to use to move out with me. I keep telling her to stop spending but I just got an email from her saying that she's planning to be away until at least June. I should be happy for her but I'm not – I'm so mad!

22nd March 2006

Mrs Evans asked me if I want to meet up with her for a coffee in the school holidays. Even though it's a bit random I said yes because I really need someone to talk to. I've felt like I haven't really had adults in my life since finishing school. I hope I can talk to her, I really do.

I've been keeping pretty busy but I'm not doing too well. I thought starting uni would make me happier but it hasn't at all. I don't even like it, which is surprising. It's not that the work's too hard, I just can't be bothered. I feel totally burnt out. I need a break but I can't have one. I was looking on the Centrelink website and I can qualify for Youth Allowance in May next year (you have to have been out of school for 18 months to claim) provided that I've earned $18,000 by that time. So far I've saved $6500 which is a great start but I've got a LONG WAY TO GO. After this semester I think I'll take time off uni to make sure I get the $18,000. I know it's worth it, I know it's worth it – I just have to stay on track.

27th March 2006

I sent Tanya an email today suggesting that it might be best for me to see a different counsellor because I'm not really making any progress with her and we've had such huge gaps between appointments. I thought she would get offended, even though it was just because I feel like I need a fresh start. But she took it really well and was so nice about it. She's trying to set me up with a different counsellor there.

29th March 2006

My new counsellor is called Gabbie and I'm seeing her THIS FRIDAY!

31st March 2006

I liked Gabbie but I was so, so dumb. She figured it out straight away by asking:
"If your parents split up, who would you live with?" and I straight away said
"Mum!" It just came out and she could tell by my face, I went bright red. I don't
know why I let myself tell her that, especially when I'd only just met her but
I can't keep this to myself much longer. She knows that I still live with him.
Luckily though, I had the sense to tell her that it has stopped, so she's not going
to have to tell anyone. But still, imagine if my parents found out about this.
They'd go PSYCHO! I have to stop letting my guard down all the time. I'm falling
apart.

9th April 2006

I saw Gabbie again on Friday, and will see her again in 2 weeks time. I don't
know why, but I trusted her straight away and wish I could tell her everything.
It's probably just because I'm so desperate to actually be able to tell someone
this stuff.

10th April 2006

I'm drained, and I'm really struggling right now. I can't keep this up forever.
My attitude has gotten so bad. I'm sick of this. It all seems too hopeless to me.
I really don't know what to do, there's no way out.

7:45pm (Same day)

I'm not getting anywhere. Will I ever get better? I hope so. I want a better life than
this. I wish I could be happy.

The thing is, it's never ending. Think of it this way. If someone was raped by
a stranger in a park or something, yes, the experience would be terrible and
yes, it would affect them for the rest of their life. But at least they would be able
to move on to some extent. They would probably try to avoid the park where it
happened because they wouldn't want to remember. And they would probably
find it really upsetting if they ever again saw the person who did it to them.

So imagine what it's like LIVING with someone who did that to you. Not once,
not twice. Repeatedly, over many years. Taking everything, over and over again.

It's too disgusting for words. Imagine living with someone who did that to you and having to pretend to the world that nothing was wrong. And sleeping in the bed that's the site of all your terror and pain, and knowing that you will never be safe there.

It is a living hell and I truly cannot stand it for much longer.

12th April 2006

I'm writing a letter to Angela Bates* (a politician). I saw her on the news talking about child abuse.

Dear Angela,

As you are an advocate for people who have been abused, I would like to tell you my ideas about how things could change for the better. I think I'm one of the kids who slipped through the cracks.

We need better education about abuse in our schools. I was never taught about sexual abuse in primary school, so I really had no idea. It was all about stranger danger. We were basically taught that strangers are BAD. If you ever have a problem with one, run to a yellow 'safety house' or get home as fast as you can, because nothing bad will ever happen there... But what if someone is doing scary things to you within your own home? Someone who is supposed to be protecting you?

We need to be more open with kids. Tell them how important they are – every single one of them. Make them realise that they can talk to adults about problems. In schools, we really need to move away from the whole stranger danger thing. It makes it so hard for kids in abusive home situations to not only talk about it, but even just realising that there actually is a problem and you're not just imagining it. It makes sense that a kid who doesn't know what abuse is (and what their rights are) isn't going to understand what's happening, so is likely to pretend (even to themselves) that nothing is happening.

Anyway, I'm sorry for wasting your time with this letter, but it's just something I feel very passionate about.

Keep up the great work in the fight against abuse.

Yours sincerely,

Hannah Baker
*Name changed

13th April 2006

I actually wrote up a good copy of my letter to Angela Bates, and posted it. Since writing it, I've been thinking a lot about the education system and how little I learned about abuse. It's pretty surprising.

In Year 3, I was very unhappy and in hindsight, was trying to get some help with my problems. I remember writing really mean notes to myself then going and showing them to the teacher. But he instantly assumed that someone else had written them, because they were so horrible, and I was 'such a good kid'. So then our whole class got in trouble, and the principal got called in. Trent ended up being the one that the teacher blamed for it, and I didn't fess up. I would cry a lot and when asked what was wrong, I would say I was sad "because of the notes". I remember it so clearly.

Later that year, I remember going to the local library and stealing a book about sex. In hindsight it's obvious why – I wanted to understand what was happening to me. But I knew that I shouldn't be seen looking at the book, so I slipped it under my jumper and stole it. Luckily this was before the days of metal detectors in the library!

In Year 3, I also vividly remember making a little picture book, in which I tried to draw pictures of the abuse. I remember pulling my friend Lindsey aside when nobody else was around, to show her the booklet I had made. She looked confused and said "what is that?" She didn't understand it at all and thought it was weird! It was at that moment that I knew that I should not tell anybody else about this, because it was weird and not something that was happening to my friends. After that, I felt very, very alone and depressed. I started considering drowning myself.

In Year 4 I again REALLY wanted to tell my teacher, Mrs Waskiewicz about my problems. I liked and trusted her – she'd also been my teacher in Year 2. The only thing was, I had no idea what to tell her. As far as I was concerned, I was strange. I didn't know why. I didn't make the connection between what Dad was doing to me and the way I was feeling. I just knew that I was different from other kids. That I needed help. At school that year, I painted a lovely picture screaming out for help but of course nobody noticed. I was a good student from a 'nice family' so obviously nothing was wrong.

I definitely would never have told Mrs Waskiewicz about the bad stuff that was happening because I didn't know how to describe it. And I managed to convince myself that I was crazy, imagining it, and that nothing was happening. For years, I believed that I was having nightmares about a giant coming into my room and lying on top of me.

If I had been taught about abuse in primary school it's WAY more likely that I would have told because I'd at least have had a starting point. It's the kind of thing that you should be taught over and over again until it becomes ingrained in your mind. I don't mean teaching kids explicitly about rape or anything. I mean teaching them simple things such as the idea that their body is theirs and that nobody has the right to touch them in a way that makes them feel uncomfortable. That there are some places that adults shouldn't touch. That adults shouldn't hurt you. That it's not your fault. That it's okay to tell someone. You're not imagining it. You're not the only person this has happened to.

I was never taught any of that stuff. I feel really let down by the education system.

15th April 2006

I talked to Leah last night, it went well. I talked to her online (Kids Helpline has online counselling too) because I really needed to talk to her and she doesn't have any other phone shifts for a while. I've never talked to her during one of her web shifts and I doubt I will again, but it was still good. I told her a bit about how I've been feeling. She understood. She knows how hard I find it to open up to anybody. I think talking online was a good chance for me to say the stuff that's too hard to say out loud just yet. Which is why I'd really like to try writing for Gabbie when she asks me a question that's too hard to answer out loud. I'll see what she says.

20th April 2006

Guess who I talked to today? Angela Bates! I sent her the letter just last week, and met her for a coffee (well, a hot chocolate) today! Talk about fast.

I think she was very nice. But I think our views are pretty different in some respects. She's very into getting convictions, introducing mandatory reporting etc. On the other hand, I just want better education for children about what their rights are, and I want it to be easier for them to talk. Because a lot of the time, it feels like nobody is listening.

As a kid I struggled so much because I didn't have anybody to talk to. I didn't know I could talk to anybody about this stuff. You always hear adults say stuff like "what's happening to our kids? Why is there a rise in youth suicide?" Well maybe it's because you stupid adults aren't listening to us! Don't assume that our problems don't matter just because we don't have to pay bills like you.

Don't block your ears just because it's easier to not get involved. For once don't put yourself first and try looking at it from the kids' point of view.

It's like how Mrs Stanley was so reluctant to do anything to help me. So many times I asked her for help with moving out of home, told her "I really want to move out". But she wasn't willing to put her neck on the line and provide much help. You're really not very brave, Mrs Stanley. Try walking in my shoes.

Really, all kids want is for someone to genuinely care. To say 'you matter and I'm going to stand up for you instead of turning a blind eye.' Instead of treating us like hindrances, we need people to stick by us, to be by our side because it is SO SCARY. And if you, the adult, think you're scared? Take a minute to imagine what we're going through.

Otherwise, don't be surprised if you start seeing more of us in graveyards.

28th April 2006

I only fully started realising what was happening when I was about 14 or 15. I felt so stupid, betrayed and worthless. I kept on hating Mum. It's only in the last couple of months that I've stopped hating her because I can see that she's trying to get along better with me. I will never be close to her though.

1st May 2006

I saw Gabbie again today. She gave me information about anxiety. I'm going to write down some of my fears:

- I'm scared of older men

- I'm scared that I'll never be able to be real with anyone, that I'll never have any real friends

- I'm scared that I'll never be normal

- I'm scared that I'll never be happy

- I'm scared that he never even loved me at all, that I was tricked all along.

- I'm scared of doctors because they're invasive of my personal space. Even physios, like when I hurt my back in Year 9 – that was invasive

- I want to get married and have kids but I'm so scared that I won't be able to because I don't ever want to be intimate with anybody. I can't think of anything worse and more scary.

12th May 2006

There comes a point where you really can't take anymore and realise that there have to be some pretty major changes if you're going to make it out alive. I was booked in to see Gabbie today, and I knew I HAD to tell it's still happening so that it can end. I reached a point last week where I was seriously contemplating killing either him or me.

But then I realised that murdering someone would do nothing for me but land me a lifetime in prison. I am 17, almost an adult, so would probably get put in an adult's prison. Nobody would visit me or care about me. I wouldn't be able to prove why I did it and nobody would believe me anyway. I knew there had to be a better option, and I'm so glad I didn't give up hope.

So today when Gabbie started asking me questions I just said I was feeling really bad today and eventually just told her that it's still happening.

It was a huge relief to have someone on my side, knowing the full story. Gabbie looked worried but said that she'd always wondered if he's still abusing me. She said that she feels terrible sending me home when she knows now what I'm going home to. She's a mum and would be horrified if that kind of thing happened to her kids.

After the appointment with Gabbie this morning, I was in a strange state of mind. I felt empty... numb. That's the only way I can describe it. Like there was nothing left of me. I had no energy left. I couldn't be bothered resisting the fact that Gabbie knew the whole story. I know there's a chance that there could be some awful repercussions from this (she could report it) but I'm too tired to care anymore. The truth will set you free. I want to be free and I know that Gabbie is going to listen to me and help me. She is the right person to help me because I trust that she will do the right thing by me, and I'm at the end of my rope as it is. I can't see her letting me down the way the school psych did. I think she genuinely cares, it's not just a job for her.

Gabbie is going to help me look at practical ways to move out of home as soon as possible (which is what I really want!). She knows that I want to move out in a non-confrontational way, and that getting authorities involved would cause huge conflict within the family. She's going to help me move out as quickly and peacefully as possible because I am too weak to handle any more drama at home. She said she can help me find out what financial support I'll be eligible for when I move out, and what my accommodation options are. She's going to help me turn my life around and I am so grateful. I am clinging to the bit of hope that she has given me and if she lets me down I'll give up for good. But somehow, I don't think she will let me down. She really wants to help me, and I really want her help. She is a wonderful person.

20th May 2006

I feel sick. My tummy hurts. I hope Gabbie helps me to get moved out SOON, SOON, SOON!

22nd May 2006

I've just had a fight with Mum. I've upset her. She wonders why I can't have a positive attitude for once, why I'm not trying as hard as she is to make things work. It kind of surprised me because I didn't realise that I'd been that bad lately, but maybe she's right. Whatever. Doesn't really matter anyway, I'm not going to be here for much longer.

I have hope again. But if I look back to mid-March or so, life seemed pretty bleak. I wanted to quit uni, I wanted to run away, I wanted to die. It was all too much to handle. It's pretty scary to think how down I was – I'm not usually that extreme. The only other times I've felt that bad were December last year, and in Year 10 and Year 3. Yes I was a suicidal 8 year old – wanted to jump off a boat.

27th May 2006

Gabbie has been so helpful. She checked with Centrelink and is able to support me getting Youth Allowance a bit earlier than I thought I could get it! She is happy to provide documentation to back it up.

Definitely a step in the right direction, don't you think??!

28th May 2006

Gabbie, I'm not so sure about Centrelink. It has the potential to go very wrong. Obviously when I go and meet the social worker, they're going to ask me a lot of questions. And I'm not sure if you've noticed, but I can be really bad at answering questions. I can answer easy questions but not the hard ones. If it's too hard, nine times out of ten I just say "I don't know", because I can't say what I'm really thinking or feeling.

I think the social worker would probably be asking some pretty specific questions about what's happened and why it's not safe to live at home, and I'd really struggle there. I wouldn't be able to say it all, especially to a total stranger. "Bad stuff happened" or "he hurt me" is probably as far as I'd get.

I hope it goes okay.

1st June 2006

Guess what? There might be a room free on campus for me next semester! I'm going to meet the head of the student residence on Tuesday for a kind of interview I guess. I went to accommodation services at uni and asked what is available. Then Gabbie offered to call them up as well so that they could understand how desperate I was. The lady at accommodation services said that she thinks I have a good chance because I've worked a lot (especially in the holidays) and saved heaps. So I'm bringing along payslips, bank statements etc. as proof of that, to show that I'd be able to pay for accommodation for the whole semester upfront if necessary. I've saved over $8,000 now, that's how hard I've worked to get out of here.

Apparently the residence takes academic performance into account when you apply, so it's lucky that I tried so hard at school! And because the interview is next week they won't know that I'm not doing as well at uni this year because I don't have my results yet.

I am REALLY hoping this works. It might really happen, can you believe it?!? I would be very safe there. Safe! Imagine that!

5th June 2006

Tomorrow I've got my interview with the head of the student residence. I really hope it goes well because if I get accepted, I'm outta here! It's at 10am. I'm bringing my portfolio and everything along just in case. I want to impress this woman so that she has to take me. She HAS to!

6th June 2006

I JUST GOT ACCEPTED! I'm VERY, VERY happy. Except, she did ask a couple of hard questions. Like why I wanted to move out of home ('uuuuuum...'). But it all worked out in the end so who cares. I'm moving out! That's all that matters. Moving out! I think my face is going to crack, I'm smiling so much. I'm so happy that I'm about to cry, and I hardly EVER cry.

THANKYOU SO MUCH GABBIE!

12th June 2006

Mr Basel (used to be a teacher at my school) was in the paper a few days ago for all the wrong reasons. He's been charged with indecent dealings with a student (from when he taught at a different school). People seem shocked, saying stuff like 'I can't believe we knew someone like THAT!', and it seemed so ridiculous to me. What did you expect? That he'd have a label on his head saying 'pervert'? Nat even called me to tell me to look at it in the paper. She never had him as a teacher, but was still so surprised that she had 'known' someone like him.

Some people are so naive.

18th June 2006

Dear Gabbie,

Thank you for being the first adult to actually help me to move out and make my life better. And thank you for letting me trust you. I really appreciate everything you've done for me. Not long ago, life seemed so hopeless but now I truly believe that things are finally going to get better. You have made a huge difference in my life, and I will be forever grateful.

Painting by
Sarah Millicent Elliott

13th July 2006

Guess what? I'm writing from my new room on campus! It's 15 minutes til dinner so I'll have to be quick. It's so strange to finally be free, I don't really know how I feel. a bit confused, a bit guilty, a lot relieved. I found it so annoying to have Mum come into my room here, which is pretty selfish of me because she came here specifically to help me carry my stuff... But I hate her coming here and acting all friendly because then people would probably think — what a spoilt brat, she has such a nice mum and she's moving out! Oh well. It's also annoying that Bec keeps trying to give me so much wonderful advice about living away from home. I felt like saying, "Shut up! Let me have my own adventure, you don't have to keep telling me that you've already had yours. Life isn't always about you, you know?!"

When Mum and Bec had finished helping me carry my stuff, they stayed in my room for ages, until I started laughing at the awkwardness. I felt like telling them to go away, leave me alone forever. Let me have my own life now.

Wow I really sound like a bratty teenager now!

I'm so glad I'm seeing Gabbie this Friday because I really need her support. I don't really have any other support at the moment. It's hard with Leah at Kids Helpline because I still haven't been able to tell her that I still was living with Dad. I will when I am ready, just not yet.

14th July 2006

I sent Gabbie an email last night because I suddenly realised the significance of what I've done. I suddenly felt very guilty for turning my back on my family, but I'm doing great now. I had a wonderful day of freedom, a safe sleep in my new bed too. I made friends with an English girl who watched a movie with me last night. It is so easy to make friends here! I also have a friend from Denmark!

Tomorrow I'm going to the zoo with Karen and the kids. I love them. See, that's what my new life is going to be about – choosing who I spend time with. And not wasting my time with morons who hurt me and don't listen to me. They're not worth the time of day. They are fools and I wish I never had to see them again.

21st July 2006

I saw Gabbie today. We didn't talk about much in particular, but it was so nice to see a familiar, friendly face, because I've been meeting so many new people during these past few days.

In more important news, I told Cassie about the abuse. She is the only friend I have ever really told. Not specific details, I was my usual vague self but she understood that it was serious, and that's why I moved out.

You know what? She said that over the years she'd noticed lots of little things about me that didn't seem quite right, but she sensed I didn't want to talk about it. She actually said that she'd suspected for a while that I was the result of some sort of abuse, isn't that interesting? She noticed that there were lots of things that I refused to talk about, and that I never really showed emotion – I was blank. She also remembers how strangely I was acting that day last year when I had to see the psych about the bruise on my arm. She said it was scary for her because even though she was talking to me, I was so distant that it was as if I wasn't there.

Cassie said she'll come with me when I see Gabbie on Friday, so that Gabbie can help her to understand the situation. Cassie's pretty shocked about it all.

29th July 2006

I think it went really well when Cassie came to Gabbie with me last Friday. It was so weird having a friend with me because every single other appointment I've been to has been on my own. It was a nice change! Cassie seems like she understands it all a bit more because I'm not good at talking about these things and left her a bit confused at first.

4th August 2006

I seem to have been really struggling in the last few days, now that the excitement of meeting new people here has worn off. I really wish I had more support. Even though I really like my new friends here, sometimes I just want to hide from everyone. I get really funny about personal space sometimes which doesn't work well here – I can't even stand having people watching me brush my teeth. I've always been very self-conscious and I hate people staring at me.

As I said, I'm kind of desperate for more support. Not friend support because I've got plenty of friends – old and new. I mean an adult's support. Guidance. Someone who will help me to get on with life. I only see Gabbie once a fortnight for an hour, so that's not enough. I talk to Leah when she is on the phones but don't tell her everything. And it's gotten awkward with Cassie. I'm not sure if we'll be able to talk about any of this again. It seemed at first as though she was really interested and wanted to help. But now the drama and novelty has worn off for her and it's almost as if nothing ever happened. It's fair enough because she is young and has her own life, and isn't old enough to give me the support and understanding that I need.

7th August 2006

I've still been feeling like I need a lot more support, and I think I will talk to Dani. She's one of the residential tutors here, and is the person we're meant to go to if we want to talk to someone about any difficulties living here. She seems really nice and she's only about 25, so she wouldn't be scary to talk to. I'm not sure how much I'll tell her.

11th August 2006

Today I saw Gabbie and got so upset. I cried so much. She was talking about how she thinks it might be a good idea for me to take a break from seeing her for a while. Gabbie is pretty much my only support right now and if I lose her, I will drown. I have no family and no friends that I rely on. So I would die if Gabbie abandoned me right now. I would actually want to kill myself.

17th August 2006

I ended up talking to Dani, and not telling her everything, but enough for her to understand that I'm really struggling. She was very nice about it and didn't make me feel dumb at all.

2nd October 2006

Last week, Mum sent a depressing email to say that Muffin (the cat) is dying. I didn't want to go home, but I felt so guilty, that I did. Bad decision.

6th October 2006

Life on campus has its fair share of difficult moments. When I first moved in, I thought my life was going to be perfect. I assumed that no abuse meant life would be fantastic, without realising that it doesn't work like that. After a few weeks of pure bliss (my newfound freedom!), I started to come back down to earth. In a way, leaving home has allowed me to finally grieve for what I have lost – my childhood, my body, my identity, my family, my dog! (To name a few). So although things should be fabulous for me right now, being free and all, it's still pretty tough at times.

Last night at dinner, Krista was talking about her family and showing us the stuff they'd just sent her from Germany (her dad even cut out some newspaper articles for her). Amanda loves talking to her family on the phone every day. I am constantly reminded that I don't really have a family, and it upsets me so much more than anyone would ever believe. Also, as stupid as it sounds, there are things that I miss from home. I miss my doggy Max so much. I love him, he's adorable. I want him NOW. This is making me cry. If I had a normal family, I'd see Max everyday because I'd still live at home. Or even if I didn't live at home, I'd be able to visit him when I wanted to. I wish I could. It's so unfair that I can't visit him because it's just not safe.

To most people, the concept of not being able to go home because it is too dangerous is absurd. Home is supposed to be a safe and happy place where you can relax. Not a place where you have to be constantly on guard, scared that you will get bashed and raped. It's so frustrating! I guess frustrating isn't the right word at all but I can't think of a better one right now. Max is just a bus trip away but he may as well be in the middle of a war zone...

I wish I had a dad who didn't violate me. Who didn't use me. a dad who respected me and cared about me. Who didn't steal my body. Who didn't put bruises on me. Raping your own daughter is beyond disgusting. a little eight-year-old, did you really think that it was okay? That you weren't harming me?

I wish I had a sister who didn't always have to be better than everyone else. Who wasn't obsessed with the sound of her own voice. Who would actually help me instead of just siding with Mum and Dad, to be good.

Every day of my life, I wish I had a mum. a mum to give me a hug and say 'It's okay, I'm here for you'. a mum to protect me. a mum to listen to me. a mum who actually cared.

Well, technically speaking I do have a mum, but I don't really feel much connection to her.

14th October 2006

I told Leah that it was still happening up til I moved out, that Dad is still around. She wasn't mad. Just sad. She was just sad.

17th October 2006

I am in such a bad mood tonight! I was fine before, but then I went out on a walk with Dani and something's snapped in me since then. I'm like that, a see-saw. Up one minute, down the next. I can feel totally in control, on top of the world, and then an hour later I'm wishing I could be dead. Facing the world can be a real struggle, especially when I remember how little back-up I have. It's too much sometimes. Way too much. If I got a dollar for every time I wished I was dead, I would be one very rich person.

31st October 2006

Last night I went along to my first (and probably last) ever group therapy session. It was held at the sexual assault centre where Gabbie works and run by one of the other counsellors. She put me on the list for it a couple of months ago. She suggested I go along and give it a try. As mean as it sounds, the main thing I've gotten out of it is the knowledge that so far, I've turned out really normal compared to some other people who've been sexually abused! There were about 7 other people, all in their 30s to 50s, except for me, and a 25 year old. Apart from the 25 year old (Natasha, who I got along with well), the rest of them seemed so screwed up. Drug and alcohol problems. Histories of prostitution. Mental breakdowns. Failed marriages. Long-term unemployment. You get the picture... The woman sitting next to me had even been to jail! And then there's me sitting there in my little pink ballet flats, thinking, why am I here???

Gabbie had said to me in the past that I've coped really well, and so has her colleague Tammy (doctor at the sexual assault centre), who I have met a couple of times. But I thought they were just saying that to make me feel better. Or to encourage me or something. Now I see their point. Compared to other people with my 'history', I have done pretty well. I don't know why it worked out for me, I really don't but I am so lucky. These women are only starting on the recovery now, a few decades down the track. They developed those other problems because they weren't dealing with the abuse. I am so fortunate to be able to start dealing with it now, so that hopefully I can avoid some of those issues (e.g. drugs!) and have a decent future. I realise now how young I am and how much of an opportunity I have to make thing work.

It's also made me realise that I must have been a pretty strong and determined kid to get to where I am today, at this age. I chose to start working (right from my paper round) to save money to get out of that house. I chose to call the sexual assault centre and Kids Helpline when I realised I couldn't handle it all on my own anymore. Yes, I chose to get help. Nobody did any of that for me. I chose to go to counselling back in Year 11 without any support at all – without anyone else even knowing that I was going. I chose to change counsellors when I realised it wasn't working with Tanya, because I wanted help so badly. I chose to open up to Gabbie and admit to her that it was Dad, and that it was still happening. And I chose to open up to Leah about what has really been happening, so now I have someone else in my life I can be honest with.

If I hadn't done those things, they never could have helped me.

I chose to move out of home because I knew it was for the best, I knew that I couldn't handle any more abuse. Gabbie gave me good advice and helped me a lot but I am still the one who applied to live on campus. The one who had to

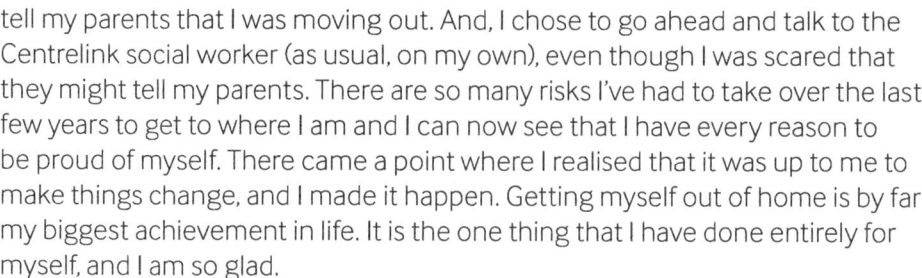

tell my parents that I was moving out. And, I chose to go ahead and talk to the Centrelink social worker (as usual, on my own), even though I was scared that they might tell my parents. There are so many risks I've had to take over the last few years to get to where I am and I can now see that I have every reason to be proud of myself. There came a point where I realised that it was up to me to make things change, and I made it happen. Getting myself out of home is by far my biggest achievement in life. It is the one thing that I have done entirely for myself, and I am so glad.

I'm not sure what the future holds for me but I guess I have every reason to be optimistic. I hope that over the next few years I can deal with the abuse and move on to some extent but I know that I will never be able to forget it. It will affect me forever and that's something I'll have to accept. But hopefully it's affected me in some positive ways too – made me a stronger person.

3rd November 2006

Living on campus is very stressful right now because lots of people are freaking out about exams. It's times like these that I find tough. Every time I'm stressed or something goes wrong (even the little things), I am quick to remember that I don't really have a family to support me. Most people call their mum up if they've had a bad day, and know that they will be listened to and not judged. I don't feel as if I even have a mother. I don't really have any friends who understand me either, so it can be so hard sometimes. So lonely. Lately I've had Dani (the tutor) to talk to and it has helped a lot to know that there is someone who lives near me who I can talk to. I also can still talk to Gabbie, and I call Leah.

Sometimes it seems like when things are at their very worst, I shut down and am never able to talk to anyone. I just go on auto-pilot, like I had to for so many years. Like I did when I went home recently. October 1st. I let Mum talk me into it, she said our cat is dying and that I should come and spend some time with her. And me being the stupid girl I am, I went. And more than a month later, Muffin's ticking along just fine, she's not dead at all! She's probably laughing (great big cat laughs) at the power she has. For the few days after that I felt like the old me, the girl who just gets on with things and tries to forget. But deep down I know that pretending doesn't make things better.

8th November 2006

I finished exams today. I should be happy, but I am so sad. I don't know why. I think it's because my family has been calling me a lot lately, being nice to me.

At a time like exams, having people actually 'care' about you is nice, particularly in a college environment when everyone is so focussed on themselves at this time of year. Sometimes I get a glimpse of what my family could be like WITHOUT the abuse and I long for it. I want a family, it's terrible being all alone. And also, knowing that nearly every single person in college (except a couple of exchange students) will be going home to their families in the holidays – that makes me so jealous! I want to be able to go home to my family too. I sometimes wonder whether I should just move back... especially for the summer. I don't want to stay living at uni over summer even though I'm trying to sound enthusiastic about it. It's going to be like a ghost town. It makes me feel like I'm worth nothing, don't belong anywhere. At least Krista will still be here.

When people ask why I'm going to be staying here in summer I say it's because of where I'll be working. Which is pretty untrue and makes no sense because I'll be working in a shop which is nowhere near here (unless 2 bus trips plus a 15 minute walk counts as 'close').. And it's not as if it's such a great, high paying job that I am planning my life around it. But oh well. I'm prepared to be a bit more honest with people I'm closer to and say that I don't really get along with my family so don't want to go home. But I don't go into the finer details.

I know that next Sunday (last day of semester included in our fees) is going to be really hard... seeing nearly all the people who live on campus go home. I've gotten really sad about it all of a sudden. Yesterday I lay on my bed and cried and cried. I want to go home too.

10th November 2006

I saw Gabbie today. I cried again. I am not much of a crier, so she knew I was upset. But she also gave me a reality check. She said that the reason for my parents' nice phone calls is probably them trying to manipulate me into coming home again. That I can't fool myself into thinking that it would be okay to go home just because I'm jealous of everyone else. The reality is that it never has, and possibly never will be, safe for me to live there again. Also, it would be 100 steps back from the huge steps forward I took when I moved out. It would allow the cycle to continue.

I can't live like that again. That's not even living. But in some ways it was easier. I could live in my fake little world, somehow pretending that the bad stuff wasn't happening and otherwise having everything. That wasn't real though. There's no hiding anymore. Facing the reality is hard, but that's the way it's got to be. My old life seems so far away now, like it was something I imagined. I don't know how it could have been real. How on earth did I put up with that? I have no idea. I don't know how I could stand the fear.

7th December 2006

I wish I could go home like everyone else. And live with a perfect little family, like Nat and Zoe do.

Time to stop whinging now.

Goodnight.

11th December 2006

It's Christmas soon, oh joy of joys... I hate this stupid holiday with a passion. Even more so this year because it will be one of Dad's few opportunities since I moved out, and I'm pretty sure he'll make the most of it. Mum's trying so hard to make me come home for a few weeks and even though I crave having a home to go to, I'm refusing. I can't put up with that anymore, especially having a bit of freedom and getting a glimpse of what it feels like to be alive. Before it was more like just existing.

I've agreed to go home on Christmas Eve and stay the night because Mum is begging me. Apparently it's tradition that we eat breakfast and open presents together in the morning. I don't believe in traditions that are fake and I'm really just going to please Mum. Everything about Christmas in our family is fake and just thinking about it drains the energy out of me. I'm not religious at all so why should I have to celebrate Christmas? I don't even believe in God. And isn't Mum Jewish?

13th December 2006

I have been so homesick that Dani has agreed to come back with me for a visit, so that I can see Max safely. I have told her that Dad hurts me.

17th December 2006

We saw Max! I have missed him so much. Dani couldn't believe how many times Dad called me a 'train wreck' while I was there. He's not usually that mean to me in front of other people. I think he is just really mad at me these days.

26th December 2006

Another Christmas over and yep you guessed it — I'm already back at the uni residence. So much for staying at home for 2 weeks... more like 1 night! After getting over the initial novelty of being at home and seeing Max (!), I soon remembered why I moved out... I am constantly on guard in that house, I can't even walk into a room without figuring out where everyone else in the family is, would I get left alone with him etc etc. And then when it is just me and him in a room I don't know how to react, because there's an unspoken rule between us that I have to act like there is no problem. But there is!

He bothered me a little on Christmas Eve but nothing major. He's actually hurt his leg so can't walk very well.

I was in a very bad mood on Christmas Day but did my best to cover it up. There were lots of people at our house so it wasn't too hard. All the cousins etc.

I don't remember much else, it's all a bit of a blur. a blur of a fake day.

29th December 2006

I've been so awful that I had to go on antidepressants.

I've had the prescription since Gabbie said to go to the doctor a few weeks ago, but had decided not to use it. But now I'm feeling so low that it's my last option.

2007

8th January 2007

My cousins and Aunty from interstate have been here for the last week and a bit. It's been soooooo nice to see them because they moved away so long ago, when I was about 10. Holly has grown up so much, she's 10 now, can you believe?! Not a little baby anymore. And Aiden is as gorgeous as I remember him being. It was so amazing to see my Aunty too, it's been ages.

I won't see them before they go home, which sucks because I only saw them 3 times during their trip! I wish I could have spent more time with them. If Holly lived here I would probably treat her like a little sister, I'd love that! Except a part of me thinks that maybe it's for the best that she lives interstate. She is very petite for her age, the same build I had when I was a kid – thin and small. And I got the sense that my dad had his eye on her if you know what I mean. I could be reading too much into things, I'm not sure. I kept an eye on both of them so that he had absolutely no possibility of getting near her. But the thought of it made me feel horrible. She's a pretty little girl and I don't even want to imagine what was going through Dad's head as he watched her. I am so glad that they're all staying at my Aunty Susie's place during their time here, not my parent's house. I'm pretty sure that he wouldn't do these things to another kid but if he did, I would never forgive myself. And I certainly wasn't about to take any chances with Holly.

18th March 2007

I got so depressed that Gabbie had to get me sent to hospital on Friday because I wanted to die so much. I've been going downhill for a while now, despite being on antidepressants for 3 months. In the hospital it was scary and lonely and I cried so much. I was such a mess, just lying there sobbing. My parents have no idea about this, I'd never tell them that I had to go to hospital. Well I'm out now and trying not to think about it anymore. I'm feeling numb and blank again which is pretty normal for me. Way safer than having feelings because that's when it all gets too much and I want to die. I probably will go through with it one day, if I get in this headspace and can't get out of it. I already know how I'd do it.

25th March 2007

Gabbie and Leah have been checking up on me this week. Leah wants me to stay as safe as possible, she doesn't want me to hurt myself.

Just today I was thinking about how differently things have turned out from what I expected. I thought everything was going to get instantly better the day I moved out, but believe me, there are still plenty of problems. I wish I had a family I could live with. I suppose I could live with my family if I wanted to... But is it better to have a family and pay for it by letting yourself be violated? When I put it like that, the answer seems obvious – stay safe. So I've got to plough through the rest of this mess and keep on being strong, and hopefully one day I'll lead the happy kind of life that I've always craved.

26th March 2007

To my beautiful goddaughter Kelsey,

I don't know you very well yet because you can hardly talk! But I think you are such a gorgeous little girl and I can't wait to watch you grow up. I'm so excited to be going along to your playgroup for the first time tomorrow. And then I can't wait til your first day at school, your birthday parties, helping you with your homework, doing fun stuff with you and Matty on the weekends, watching your school assemblies, going to your sports carnivals, your graduations, seeing what you decide to do when you finish school and everything else! You've got such a bright future ahead of you and I can't wait to watch it unfold.

Kelsey, I've been struggling so much lately. When I was a kid I was sexually abused and it makes me so sad and depressed sometimes. At times I've even wished I could be dead but you know what's helped me to get through? Knowing that there is a precious little girl called Kelsey out there who I really want to see grow up. I love you to pieces! I hope that I become someone that you can trust and talk to if anything ever makes you feel sad or lonely. I will always be there for you, I promise! No matter WHAT, I will always love you and I will always be so proud of you. You've brought so much joy to my life.

Lots of love from,

Your godmother Hannah

5th April 2007

I felt totally fine all day but now I feel terrible again. I'm not sure why – I think I'm just tired and grumpy. I can't be bothered going to the party I was meant to be going to even though I already said I was going. I know I've got lots to live for, but sometimes it's hard to stay on track. I got sent to the hospital AGAIN last week and it wasn't much more helpful than last time. It just makes me feel like I am crazy. I had a social worker talk to me and she was the most boring person to listen to ever. She was pretty ignorant and was pretty much doing her one-size-fits-all 'safety exercises' spiel. It just went on and on.

The hard thing for me is that even though I talk to people like Gabbie and Leah about the impacts of the abuse, I can never quite tell them the details – except for the letter I sent Lindy last year. The memories of what happened keep going around and around in my head.

Anyway, I should go and do an hour study for my test if I want any chance of passing next week. I kind of need to pass since I failed the last test so badly. 7.5%, probably the worst they'd ever seen. I just didn't care anymore.

6th April 2007

Easter break. I hate living on campus at this very moment. Somebody rescue me, please! Pleeeease! I want a home to go to, just like everybody else.

7th April 2007

Dear Dani,

I'm in a really bad mood right now but I'm trying so hard to be happier.

17th April 2007

Dear Tammy,

I'm struggling so much right now. Life is not going very well. I wish someone could help but there's nothing anyone can do. Maybe a brain transplant...

20th April 2007

Dani! I'm still struggling a lot. I'm crying AGAIN – will I ever stop? It's so hard trying to deal with this stuff, I feel like I'm drowning in it. It makes me so sad and the memories can be very overwhelming.

5th May 2007

Dani, I feel so, so sick. Well not really sick, just tired and lonely and sick of thinking.

24th May 2007

After all these years and all this pain, I think I'm finally ready to go to the police. I didn't think I ever would but hey, things change. By the looks of things, it's the only way I'll be able to move on. I want to be safe instead of always fearing the next visit home. I want to be alive instead of being drained and fake. At the moment I don't even feel like I am living. Just existing and somehow making it through each day is all I can manage because the abuse is still a huge dark shadow over my life.

It's going to be so hard and scary, and I have no way of knowing what the outcome will be. But at least it might give me a chance to move on.

I am scared but I know that I am strong enough to make it through. (Actually, terrified is the right word). I have been very brave before and will have to find some of that braveness to get through. But I'll make it, I know I will. I hope the future will be bright.

PEOPLE WHO WILL SUPPORT ME

- Gabbie

- Leah at Kids Helpline – we've talked about it a few times and she is REALLY encouraging me to go to the police.

- Dani

- Mrs Evans

- Deirdre (good friend who lives on campus with me)

- Tammy

28th May 2007

I went home with my sister for dinner at Mum and Dad's place. I knew full well that if I do go to the police, this is the last time I will ever be home. The last time I will see my dog. The last time I will have a 'family'. They'll want to kill me if I tell.

Knowing it was the last visit was comforting and scary, and weird, and terrifying all at the same time.

So goodbye family. I wish things had worked out differently but you made your choices and now I'm making mine. I will be glad to get rid of you from my life.

29th May 2007

I am so scared right now and feel sick with worry. Once I make a statement to the police, there's no turning back. Which would be fine if I knew that what I'm doing is right, but I'm not so sure... Just thinking about it makes me feel so guilty. My family is going to get totally wrecked and I don't think I really want that. I don't think I want Dad to go to jail, not at all. He doesn't deserve that, really he doesn't. He loves me. So does Mum – she doesn't deserve all this pain. She probably wouldn't be able to afford to stay in the house by herself if Dad went to jail. And she would be sooo upset if he did go to jail. He's her husband, how could she handle living a few years without him? And then there's Bec – why should she have to be drawn into this mess?

I don't know, I really don't know what to do. If I go to the police, it means that I'm very brave. It also means that I have no conscience. I'm going to have to block off all my feelings if I go through with this because every aspect is so, so painful. I don't know if I can do it without resisting the urge to kill myself. It's a pretty strong urge right now. My dad is going to hate me so much if this goes to court. He's done good stuff for me over the years too, he really loves me I'm sure. I just don't really understand him sometimes.

30th May 2007

Dear Dani,

I really feel like I want to die right now. If I ever go ahead and kill myself, I want you and Gabbie and Leah and Mrs Evans and Tammy to know that I love you all very much for helping me. But that I just couldn't handle things anymore. I've tried, I really have, but I don't seem to be getting very far. It's just getting harder and harder to cope and I'm not seeing much light at the end of the tunnel.

I hate myself so much. I feel like I'm such a horrible person. I can't believe that I've been thinking about taking my own father to court – what decent daughter does that? I don't want to hurt him and I know he'd be so devastated if I went ahead with it. OHHH I HATE THIS! It's never going to get better. There's no solution for me – well if there is, I'm not seeing it.

HELP ME HELP ME HELP ME MUMMY.

I'm dead inside.

He raped me he raped me he raped me he raped me.

Rape rape rape rape.

I'm not scared of you anymore.

Well maybe I am a bit.

I don't know if I'm doing the right thing but it seems like the only answer.

I hope one day that things will be okay and I will be better.

But I'm not sure that it's possible.

Rape rape rape rape rape rape rape

9th June 2007

I'm really tired right now even though it's only just after 10pm. I've got to wait for the kids I'm babysitting to go to sleep.

I've been getting sick all the time lately, just generally rundown. I've been having vivid dreams and nightmares pretty much every night lately. I had one the other day when we were in our old house and somebody set all around the house on fire. Flames were coming at me from all directions. Then I ran to use the phone but someone had cut it off. Scary!

I'm going to the police on Wednesday – not long now! I wish Dani could come with me but she has exams. But I'm very used to doing things on my own anyway so it doesn't matter.

13th June 2007

I began my police statement today. I don't have much to write now because I am very drained and about to go for a nap. The detective, Jodi, is really nice and tried to make it as easy as possible for me, but it was so hard. So many questions about disgusting things that I find hard to think about – let alone talk about. We still have plenty to go. In fact, we hardly covered any ground in those few hours, so more fun times ahead...

I'm off for a nap now.

Oh yeh and my exam went crap on Monday. I don't have my next one til next Monday, because I failed one of my units so badly during the semester that I'm not allowed to sit the exam. I really don't care about uni right now. As you can probably tell, my focus is elsewhere.

16th June 2007

I'm feeling so depressed right now. I'm not sure if I will ever go ahead and kill myself. I used to think that I'd never take such a drastic step (especially after Ben) but lately it's started to become a more likely option. I don't feel as if I have a lot to live for and I don't have much support. I don't see much hope for the future because I don't see how things could ever truly get better. Everything is so totally screwed up.

I'm really not okay.

I need so much help and I've been given so much help but I'm still not getting anywhere. One of the few things that keeps me alive is my gorgeous goddaughter. I want to be there for her when she's growing up.

But I really don't know how much longer I can fight.

21st June 2007

People are excited here because nearly everyone has finished exams. I finished on Tuesday but I hardly even noticed because I've been so preoccupied with making my statement. Tomorrow will be my 5th day talking to the detective. We hopefully don't have much to go.

I've also decided to ask Mum to come along with me to see Gabbie tomorrow. I was talking to her on the phone on Sunday and I started crying, and I felt like

I had to tell her in black and white, once and for all, so that she fully understands why I'm so screwed up. Not hinting – telling. So that there's no confusion or not listening. Having Gabbie tell her will mean that she'll at least have to think about it because it's more powerful coming from her than me. Also because I wouldn't be able to say it all myself.

I'm so glad that she agreed to come though. The appointment is at 3pm and believe it or not, I'm not actually that nervous. Well I guess I am but as usual I have managed to block out my feelings. It's as if it's been a long time coming and by now I'm too exhausted to really take in the significance of it all. I'd rather mum hear about me going to the police from me, instead of having the police knock on the door. If she gets mad at me it doesn't matter. I've got nothing to lose because I don't have a family now anyway. My family is a lie.

Undated – approx 23rd June 2007

I can't believe what a mess I've made. Dad's gone crazy, he's been stalking and calling and I'm so scared.

Mum finally left him and he went crazy. He's been looking for us at friends' houses, and he came searching at all our relatives' houses.

I've ruined everything.

What a huge mess.

I can't believe I've betrayed him so badly. He's done nothing wrong. He doesn't deserve to be lonely. What if he goes to jail! How could I live with myself? How did I get to be so selfish?

Dad I am sorry, so, so sorry. I'm sorry that I went crazy and got you in trouble. I just couldn't handle things anymore. But I'm sorry, so sorry. And I do love you, I promise! I know you love me too but I'm sorry that I didn't love you as much as you loved me.

I don't think I can ever make this better, I will die with guilt. Dad, I love you and I'm so sorry.

PART TWO:
THE CRIMINAL JUSTICE SYSTEM
(2007–2013)

Painting by
Sarah Millicent Elliott

*Courage doesn't always roar. Sometimes courage is the quiet
voice at the end of the day saying "I'll try again tomorrow."*

(Mary Anne Radmacher)
This quote was sent to me in a card from Leah at Kids Helpline, shortly after the trial.

INTRODUCTION

When I look back at the time I spent going through the criminal justice system, I have feelings of both sadness and pride.

On the one hand, I spent six years in a system that didn't always make sense or care about me. The long waiting periods between court hearings made it difficult to move on; the many appeals I had to endure continued to drag me down. On top of this, I was also dealing with the reality of having my father sent to prison. This led to major feelings of guilt, as well as feelings of loss, because I knew that I would not see my dad again. Despite the abuse that had happened to me, he was still my dad, and I mourned the loss of a parent the way most other people would. The difference was, this loss wasn't really recognised by anyone around me, except the professional people I talked to about it. To family members and friends, it was as though Dad had never existed, and nobody ever dared to mention his name.

The feelings of loss, sadness and guilt drove me to feeling very suicidal and depressed, and at one point I even decided to go and visit my dad in jail. The people around me could not understand why I would want to do this. But I do not regret the visit one bit because it was a huge step for me in understanding how badly Dad was manipulating me, and for accepting that he could no longer be a part of my life.

The time I spent going through the criminal justice system had some positives. Having a compassionate detective who went to all efforts to listen to and help me, made all the difference. I also realised that I had the ability to stand up for myself, to be heard, and to be believed. As hard as it was, I am very proud of myself for enduring the criminal justice system, and for standing up against abuse. I never knew I could be so strong.

THE SPLIT

The afternoon that Mum came to the appointment with me to see Gabbie, she decided to leave Dad. I had not expected this at all. I had always thought that she would stand by Dad even if he did get charged by the police – any other option had not even crossed my mind. After the appointment with Gabbie, Mum dropped me off at my Aunty Barb and Uncle Toby's house, while she went home and got some of her stuff and Max (the dog) before Dad got home. That was pretty brave of her to do. My sister and Mum knew instantly that everything I said was true, which again was extremely fortunate for me. I know that is not how it happens in all families.

The weekend after Mum left Dad sticks in my mind as particularly terrifying. My dad went looking everywhere for us. He tracked down where Mum was, by using online banking records – he could see that she had accessed an ATM near my Uncle Toby's house. He came looking for us there, but by then we were staying elsewhere. Dad's next move was to transfer all of the money out of his and Mum's joint bank account, so that she couldn't access anything. It was a very mean and spiteful thing to do – a real power play. He also changed the locks on the house, so that Mum couldn't get any more of her stuff. I felt very guilty when he did these things to hurt my mum. It felt like it was my fault.

For the next few days, Dad continued to turn up at all the different places he knew we might be. He drove up to where my Aunty Susie and Uncle Roy lived, and parked his car a fair bit up the road, out of view of their house. He then walked up to see if we were there. He also tried approaching some of our friends to see if they knew where we were. Dad also frequently called each of our mobiles. I learned to just turn mine off. Mum had a Mexican Jumping Beans ring tone, and to this day I can't listen to that ringtone without feeling sick. He would call, no answer, then call again. It made me really annoyed that Mum just let it keep ringing, when it was so distressing. I had to tell her to turn her phone off because it was putting me on edge so much.

We ended up having to rent a room in a motel for a few days, just to keep safe. I got quite antsy but at the same time was really happy to have family on my side. I had not expected it at all. I felt relieved.

During the next few weeks and months, I spent a lot of time with my mum and sister. It was almost like a reunion of sorts. Previously I had not considered that they would be a part of my future, because I had assumed they would be on Dad's side if I went to the police. I think this wedge had been built up over the years by Dad, who had always made me feel that nobody else would listen to me or care about me, and that he was the only person I could rely on. He had also spent years making fun of my mum and sister to me (behind their backs), which had made me hate them to a large degree. It is hard to change the beliefs in your head when you've been brought up with them.

As well as my mum and sister, I had extended family rallying around me as well as other friends of the family. Interestingly, practically everyone who knew both Dad and I was on my side, not Dad's. It was ironic, because I had grown up thinking that nobody would believe me over him, but quite the opposite was true.

I started spending a lot of time with my Aunty Susie and her family. It had never occurred to me that I would have such a close relationship with my Aunty Susie. She and her husband Roy had always seemed to get on so well with my dad, so it took me a while to get my head around the fact that they were on my side, not his. I asked my Aunty why, and what she thought of what had happened, and she said "it's worse than murder". Again, I was shocked. Did they really care that much and think it was a big deal? Apparently so. I also got back in contact with my Aunty Jane who lived interstate, who was another great source of support to me in the next few years.

Around this time, a relative on Dad's side of the family, who I had only met twice (the last time being when I was 10 years old), sent a nasty letter about me to my mum. The letter contained the story that Dad was telling anyone who would listen – that I had made everything up because I was failing at uni and needed an excuse. Yes, it is true that I was too suicidal and distracted to care about uni at that time so did start failing. But in previous years, I had been an a grade student who had been holding it together, while still dealing with the abuse. Once evidence started emerging of my long-term contact with sexual assault services, Kids Helpline, and my school's concerns about me, we never heard from this relative again.

In July 2007, I went back to living on campus. I had to repeat some units due to failing the previous semester, which added an extra year to my studies. Despite being very distracted by the legal process and other issues, I did manage to scrape a pass in Semester 2, 2007. My results were nothing to write home about though.

POLICE INVESTIGATION

In late June 2007, I signed my completed police statement. The police officer Jodi knew that I had not been able to tell her of all the incidents that had happened to me. However, I had at least been able to describe a few of the incidents in a lot of detail. To do this, I'd had to become very detached from what I was saying. You would think I would have been very emotional giving my police statement, but I wasn't at all. It was more like a recitation of facts, not a single tear shed. That was all I could manage. I didn't let myself take it all in or have any feelings. I just stuck to the facts.

Soon after I signed my statement, my mum and sister also had to give statements, which clarified and confirmed some of the things that I had mentioned.

Several other people were required to give police statements, including my friends Cassie and Nat, Mrs Evans, the school psych, the school chaplain, and Mrs Stanley. Notes were subpoenaed from Kids Helpline and the sexual assault centre as well.

It also emerged that the state child protection department had a file on me too, because my school had reported me to them without my knowledge. I was surprised that nobody had thought to mention it to me at the time. I requested to see a copy of the file once I knew of its existence, and put in an application under the Freedom of Information Act. In a way it was actually comforting to know that a report had been made. But I was quite disheartened when I read it. It was sad to know that the department had declared "No further action" without even interviewing me, or offering any support whatsoever. How could I recontact the department (as suggested), when I had no idea that I'd been referred to them in the first place?

Here is what the report said (identifying details have been changed):

July 27th 2005

Telephone call from Freda Evans, Deputy Principal of Brookley Senior High School. Freda wanting information logged in relation to Hannah Baker.

Freda advised that Hannah has become close to her physical education teacher, Debbie Stanley, and has told her that she hates her father.

Debbie has sighted a large bruise on Hannah's leg which looks like a hand mark, however Hannah stated that it was caused from a fall. Freda was unable to provide specific information re: location, appearance of the bruise. Freda further advised that Hannah was referred to the school psychologist

Jan Lynch and although she did not make any disclosures, did state "you know what's going on".

Freda advised that any further information would need to be provided by Debbie Stanley.

*Transferred to southern district due to Hannah's home address.

Phone call from Debbie Stanley. Advised that she has had concerns during the past few years in relation to Natalie but had nothing to base this on. She said that Hannah had attempted to hide a bruise on her arm by requesting a long-sleeved upper shirt under her sports shirt but could still see the bruise which was not yellowing yet and was around the soft fleshy part of her upper arm.

Debbie advised that Hannah has incredible coping skills and was not happy when she was advised that Debbie had to report the bruising as a duty of care. Hannah denied that somebody hit her although there are definite finger marks.

Debbie advised that Hannah has never admitted to what is occurring at home and does quite well considering. She is doing well at school and appears as bright not depressed. Debbie said that since speaking with the school psych, Hannah has told her that Debbie's behaviour towards her has changed and that she would like it to be back where it was. Debbie stated that she did not feel that it had but it obviously had as far as Hannah is concerned.

Debbie advised that Hannah has clearly articulated that she hates her dad but this is as far as she goes. She has also made it clear that she is leaving home as soon as she has finished her schooling.

I advised that due to Hannah's age and her not wanting to disclose, there would be no immediate role for the Department. I advised that if at some point she does and wants support/assistance then herself or the psych should recontact.

No further action.

When I published the first version of this book in May 2014, I felt a need to be respectful and not highlight just how terrible this report was. However, I will be honest. It contained a litany of errors.

Firstly, there was a two month lag between the school observing the bruising at the school cross country on May 27th, and actually making a report on July 27th. I don't understand the delay, and it was not referred to at all in the report. I guess the school assumed I would never see the report and pick up on the unexplained lag. Clearly nobody was feeling any urgent need to step in and help me, document things accurately, or, heaven forbid, actually involve me in any decisions.

Secondly, the child protection worker who wrote the report got mixed up about whether the bruise was on my arm or leg – she appeared to use the terms interchangeably in the report. I'm no doctor but last time I checked, there is a difference between arm and leg, and such crucial details are important, especially in a matter that might go to a criminal court. As it turns out, this child protection report was deemed too unprofessional to admit as evidence when my case did go to court. That is unacceptable.

One other error, perhaps the most personally significant, was that the child protection worker had actually gotten my name wrong at one point. Don't get me wrong, I like the name Natalie. It's a beautiful name and I know some great people who are Natalies. But it is not and has never been my name, and I didn't appreciate reading a report that referred to me as Natalie. It was the ultimate kick in the guts, especially given that the child protection worker had not even made the effort to come and meet me. The smallest courtesy she could have given me would have been to get my name right.

The medical exam

The police officer who handled my case, Jodi, asked me if I would be willing to get a medical exam done at the sexual assault centre. I was told that the exam wouldn't come up with any forensic evidence, but might provide evidence of long-term abuse and trauma. Jodi knew this would be a really big deal for me, so she did not put any pressure on me at all. At first, I was very scared of the idea, and in my head I decided that I would not do it. But it weighed on my mind for ages because by not getting it done, I felt like I was letting the abuse (and my dad) beat me.

So, as much as it terrified me, I agreed to get it done. But it was a slow process. Firstly, I called up the doctor who worked at the sexual assault centre, to ask her a few questions. Her name was Eve. Then I asked if I could come in and talk to her about what would happen, stressing that "we're not going to get it done, we're just talking, okay?" Thankfully, Eve was kind and patient and agreed to meet for just a chat. Meeting her helped me to become familiar with the actual setting of the medical examinations room, and she let me walk through and ask questions. She showed me the big bathroom where I would get changed. There was a big cupboard full of spare pairs of underwear and clothes. I asked her, "what are they for?" and she said it was for people who had been assaulted and had to give their clothes up for forensic testing.

Then we went into another room and sat on the couch and she chatted with me a bit. As I later found out, Eve was probably the most specialised sexual assault doctor in the state. For her to be willing to spend this much time to make me feel comfortable about the examination process is a huge compliment to her. I also think it helped that I had previously met Tammy (another doctor at the service) who had always been very friendly to me when I was in there to see Gabbie. This had a positive impact on my ability to trust medical professionals in this service. To them both I say a big thank you.

Eve and I booked in a time the following Thursday morning to get the medical exam done. I asked my Aunty Susie if she could come with me – pretending that it wasn't much of a big deal to me whether she said yes or no, but really, it was. She instantly said yes. I was very relieved!

The night before the examination, I slept over at my Aunty Susie's house and she drove me into the city the next morning. Susie sat in the waiting room reading magazines while I went with the doctor. a part of me wished that she would come in with me because I was really scared, and part of me was too embarrassed for her to come in – I didn't explain that to her at the time though. With the doctor, I went and sat down on the couches where we had chatted the previous week, and she took a detailed history of what had happened to me. The questions were embarrassing but no worse than my police statement, so I coped okay. There was a social worker sitting in as well – she introduced herself but I was so overwhelmed that I forgot her name instantly.

Then, they showed me through to the bathroom and left me to take off my bottom layers in privacy. I think I might have been given a gown to put round myself but the memory is a bit foggy in my head. I remember being in the bathroom and starting to feel very out of it, just like I did when I was being abused as a kid (I know now that this is called dissociation). I sat on the floor in the bathroom for a few minutes and felt very slow and drifty. I finally got changed and came back out to the room with the plinth where I had to lie down.

I don't honestly remember much more of the examination. I remember the social worker talking to me to distract me while the doctor was examining me. I think she might have held onto my hand. It didn't seem to go for as long as I had expected. Suddenly it was all over, but I could barely move, so just lay there and they said to take my time. Then I started to regather my senses a bit, and started crying – a lot. They were very patient with me. When I felt better, I got changed in the bathroom and went back out to my Aunty. I think we went out for lunch or morning tea somewhere. I remember her talking on the phone to my uncle Roy, who was calling to check that I had gone okay. The only things I remember of the day itself are that it was a sunny day, and it was a Thursday.

Charges laid

In September 2007, nearly three months after I'd signed my police statement, Dad was formally charged with over 50 offences of sexual assault, sexual abuse of a minor, and physical assault. He was granted bail immediately. To me, it felt a bit safer knowing that he had been charged (a no-contact order was put in place), but it was still a very unsettling time. I would often freak out when I saw a car similar to his, and would 'see' him everywhere I went, always terrified of bumping into him. The police officer told me that he had shown absolutely no emotion when he was interviewed prior to being charged, that he just sat there with his arms folded saying "no comment... no comment". During breaks in the interview, they watched him from the observation room while he casually made work calls on his mobile — catching up with people, and rescheduling meetings that he wouldn't make it to (without mentioning that he was at the police station!). This is very calm and bizarre behaviour for someone who has just been charged with raping his daughter.

It would be almost a 12 month wait until the trial was held, and in that time, it felt like I was living in limbo.

Lead-up to the trial

In the lead up to the trial, I really cleaned up my act when it came to uni work. From Semester 1 2008, I started working really hard, and getting very good marks. I went from a failing student, to a distinction/high distinction average. It was a welcome distraction for me to throw myself into.

I initially didn't tell lecturers at my university that I was going to have to go to court. However, I got blasted by a lecturer when I asked for him to email me the slides from one of his lectures, and said it was because I had to work (instead of telling him the truth, which was that I would be at a pre-court session). He forwarded my email straight to the head of school, who also blasted me, and said that study should be my priority, not work. I burst into tears at this, because I had been working so incredibly hard at uni. In response, I ended up just telling the head of school outright the real reason for my upcoming absences, and she was apologetic and supportive after that. The course coordinator was my first port of call for the rest of my time at uni, for any personal issues that came up that affected my university studies. She advocated for me several times, and it was one less thing to worry about. To her, I am grateful, and have a lot of respect. I am still in touch with her today.

I was very relieved in May 2008 when a trial date was announced. The trial was to start on Monday 11th of August, 2008. Thankfully, that date did not change, which was a relief because I had been warned that sometimes trials are delayed with little notice. I was very grateful that there were no changes.

I had court support services get in touch with me before the trial, and frankly, they were pretty useless. The main thing they did was give me colour coordinated pamphlets about preparing a victim impact statement, and offered to make me a cup of tea. The most helpful person from Victim Mediation was not a paid employee, but the court volunteer, who sat in with me during the trial when I was giving evidence. She was lovely.

One thing that concerned me a lot in the lead up to the trial was that there was no prosecution lawyer officially assigned to appear in court for the case. When the beginning of the trial was only a couple of weeks away, I became extremely stressed about this. I started to worry that either I would get a really dodgy lawyer, or that the case would be postponed. I frequently called Jodi (the detective) to see if she could get me any further information, and she always did her absolute best to help me and put my mind at ease. The week before the trial, they finally allocated a lawyer. Phew!

I was asked to attend a meeting with the lawyer and junior lawyer that week. Despite having become used to talking to police officers, this was out of my depth. My Aunty Susie came with me, and I'm glad she did! It became apparent quite quickly that the lawyers weren't very familiar with the case at all. We were left praying that they would get their act together by the following week. My Aunty asked a question to clarify their role as my lawyers, to which the senior lawyer sharply responded "we're not Hannah's lawyers, we're here to represent the state". Susie said "oh, okay...", but in our heads I think we were both wondering "so what does that mean?" Basically, in the legal system, the defendant (person who is accused of committing a crime) is defending themselves against the state, and it is the state's responsibility to prove that a crime has occurred. The lawyer is not there for the individual victim as such, but instead to represent the state and its laws. This all makes perfect sense for someone who knows the legal system, but is daunting for someone who is unfamiliar with it.

The junior lawyer was a lady probably in her late 20s. She had really gone overboard with her hair, clothes and makeup, and had the brightest lipstick I have ever seen. My Aunty and I still joke about that lipstick to this day. She came across as very pretentious. When speaking about the work she had done on the case, she added, "I would love to be here for trial. But it's my mum's birthday on Saturday, so I'm going to Melbourne instead!" Just the way she said it made me feel like an insignificant piece of dirt. My Aunty and I looked at each other, sharing a silent "what the fuck?" look. I was wondering how on earth these people were going to have any amount of passion to put together a good prosecution case, that might actually win. It was a relief to get out of that meeting and go and have a coffee in the court cafe.

That meeting, and the frustrations with the lack of preparation by lawyers, made me realise that the court case really could go either way. It is confronting when you realise that a defence lawyer can put in as much time as they like (depending on how much the defendant is willing to pay them!) to work on a case, while the prosecution case can be so disorganised, with no lawyers allocated right up to the week before the trial. I was also warned by Jodi that only a tiny percentage of cases have enough evidence for charges to be laid and to go to court, and a tinier number again actually result in a conviction. When you consider on top of this, that most cases of sexual abuse and assault are not even reported to police – you see how rare it is for an offender to actually be convicted of these crimes. I knew full well that the odds of getting a conviction were very low. I tried not to think about how I would cope either way. I wasn't really sure whether I wanted a conviction or not. I still cared about my dad and a part of me did not want him to go to jail.

Family relationships in the lead-up to the trial

During the lead-up to the trial, I had no contact with my dad whatsoever. Mum had some contact with him as she started launching divorce proceedings against him. This was very stressful for her, and I again did feel a bit guilty, for 'causing' her to need to get a divorce, and for the financial difficulties that she now faced. My sister was very supportive of my mum with the divorce proceedings, but I kept right out of it – I couldn't handle any additional stresses, and the feelings of guilt it gave me.

At the end of 2007, I tried moving in with my mum and sister in a rental house for a while. At first it was really great – spending constant time with my dog, and living with a family. But soon, tensions started to come out. I had a lot of resentment and anger towards both my mum and my sister, which I had easily pushed aside when I first realised they were 'on my side', but that were still bubbling inside me. Mum couldn't seem to understand why things weren't instantly better between myself and her, given that she had now left Dad. But we'd had too many years apart, and I'd been through too much on my own. After six months of living with my mum and sister, I moved back to where I had been living on campus, and then later moved on to share-houses. My relationships with my mum and sister remained rocky.

I found family situations very strange during this time (and to be honest, I still do), because I was used to being in a four person family, but now there were only three of us. Previously, aside from the abuse, I had a shared sense of humour with my dad that my mum and sister did not understand. They were very serious and could talk for hours about politics, while my dad and I could spend ages laughing at a funny video of someone collapsing into a waterbed, or a dog walking into a pole. So I was in some ways grieving the loss of a family member who had at times been a real ally for me, but the grief and loss I was experiencing was not recognised by other family members. Again, I felt alone. When I went to Christmas with the extended family in 2007, I felt sad at how it was as if Dad had never existed – no acknowledgement of him at all, it was as though he was someone I had just imagined that nobody else remembered. So I would not dare to bring up his name but still felt a big emptiness in my heart that took years to come to terms with, and contributed to major feelings of loss and depression.

Over the next few years, I started avoiding situations where it would be me together alone with my mum and sister, because the three-person family thing just never felt right. I would avoid seeing them on Christmas day unless there was a larger gathering with extended family. I know that hurt both of them, but I couldn't cope with anything more. Even as I write this, it has been over three years since there's been a situation with just the three of us together.

Instead, I continued to become even closer to my Aunty Susie and her family. They always made me feel welcome. My cousin Jack became like a little brother to me – and still kind of is (even though he's 20 now!). I would often have dinner with their family and they would come and visit me. My Aunty went out of her way to be a major support to me. Sometimes I think it was really overwhelming for her, because I had so many issues and needed her so much.

Professional supports

Soon after properly disclosing the abuse to Mum, I stopped attending sessions with Gabbie. I had used up my number of sessions for the service – their official limit was 10 sessions though I'd had more than that. It was really upsetting to lose contact with Gabbie because she'd played such a crucial role in my life at a particularly dark time – and helped me to move out of home. The decision to cut my access to counselling appeared fairly sudden to me, with little preparation or effort to build up other supports. I handled the situation badly, by lashing out at Gabbie, even though the decision wasn't really coming from her, it was the policies of the organisation. I was very daunted about what lay ahead with the upcoming trial, and felt that I had been 'ditched'. The timing of them 'cutting me off' was terrible. I had just entered legal proceedings, just lost contact with my dad, and was still adjusting to life outside of home. The lack of support made available to me locally at such a critical time, was to have a significant negative impact on my life.

Despite living and working on the other side of Australia, Leah at Kids Helpline became an increasingly important support in my life. I will forever be grateful to her for 'picking up the slack' of local services and going out of her way to keep me afloat when it seemed like there was nobody else there. It was so vital to have that professional person in my life while I was preparing for the court case. Though I now had unexpected support from immediate and extended family, I still found it virtually impossible to talk to any of those people about my true feelings about Dad, the court case, and the abuse that had happened to me. With friends my own age, I definitely didn't feel like they would understand what I was going through, so I tended to just be fun and outgoing on surface level, without telling them how things really were for me.

I didn't feel up to going and seeing any new counsellors at this time, despite Leah encouraging me to do so. I had so much going on that I couldn't be bothered starting from scratch. There were a few counsellors I saw sporadically for a couple of sessions, but once it got past the initial 'chit-chat' phase I would decide it was all too hard, that the counsellor was not going to be any good, and then would stop going. This was very frustrating for Leah, who termed it "Hannah's cut and run" phenomena. I think a huge part of this was that I felt so burned by the sexual assault centre for so suddenly cutting me off, that I found it very difficult to trust any new counsellor, especially when I knew that there was a limit on how many sessions I could access under Medicare. My finances were limited such that I would be unable to afford many sessions at all. I therefore felt pressure to trust any new counsellor quickly because I was extremely aware of the lack of sessions I could access. Then when I couldn't trust them straight away, I felt it was 'hopeless'.

I was very lucky to have Leah to talk to on the phone during this period. With my permission, she also called up my Aunty Susie to give her information and advice on how she could support me. This was really useful too, because Leah was able to tell Susie about some of the difficulties I had been experiencing that I hadn't been able to tell her about myself.

In the lead-up to the trial, Leah continually reminded me that I was doing the right thing, and that she thought I was brave. It really made a difference. She even started calling me "Hannah the Brave" which I would scoff at and say it was lame, but secretly it meant a lot to me. It was invaluable to have an unbiased person outside of my personal life, who I could talk to about what was going on for me during this time, without fear of hurting or upsetting her.

THE TRIAL

The stress of the upcoming trial impacted on my physical health. My ongoing sleeping difficulties were exacerbated, so in the lead-up to the trial I often took a heavy dose of sleeping tablets which gave me a nasty hangover effect. I also developed an eczema-type rash around my eyes due to stress — I looked like a raccoon! Thankfully this came down with an anti-inflammatory cream. I do not normally have eczema, but during times of extreme stress I do still get that rash around my eyes. I also had several blood noses in the lead-up to the trial, and for several months following it.

Painting by
Sarah Millicent Elliott

The weekend before the trial, I kept busy and did some social things with people close to me who knew what was going on. On the Friday, I decided to skip uni, which was very unusual for me, as I was very studious that year! I went and bought roller skates instead. My old school friend Cassie came over that night and steadied me as I roller-skated down a footpath near the uni. Cassie, true to form, had a mini keyboard with her and played terrible music for me while I was skating. It meant a lot to have Cassie's support. Even though we didn't really talk about the trial, I knew that she was wishing the best for me. She was probably a bit nervous herself, because she had also been subpoenaed to give evidence.

That Saturday, despite being very groggy from the sleeping tablets, I had breakfast with my friend Dani and briefly visited my Aunty Susie's family as well.

On the Sunday, I kept to myself. I became focussed, the way you do when you're about to start a new job. I went into the city and bought a new black skirt to wear to the trial. I laid out the clothes I would wear – a horizontal black and white striped long-sleeved top, black skirt, black shoes. On the day of the trial, Dani drove me into the city and came to the court room with me, which was a good distraction – it would have been hard to go in by myself.

During the week of the trial I had some friends and relatives do lovely things for me. My Aunty Jane from interstate had flowers delivered to me, and my good friend Deirdre left flowers outside my door. These kind gestures helped me to see that important people in my life cared about me.

The trial started on a cold, sunny Monday morning in August 2008, less than a month after my 20th birthday. Dad was on trial for 25 of the charges that had the most evidence, but some of these were dropped on the first day. I was quite oblivious to which charges had and hadn't been dropped – it didn't matter much to me anyway, as all I had to do was answer the questions I was asked. I tried to not think about anything other than sticking to the facts. I wasn't emotional. I tried very hard to forget that it was Dad I would be talking about. I had found that when I 'separated' it in my head, by pretending to myself that it wasn't Dad when I was talking about the abuse, then it was much easier. This 'trick' was a blessing and a curse, because it has taken me years to fully accept that it was my dad who abused me, even though I have always known deep-down that it really was him.

On the first day of the trial, Dani, Aunty Susie, and the detective Jodi sat with me in a separate room while I waited to give evidence. The Beijing Olympics were on, so as I waited to give evidence we watched the swimming on the little TV. I remember watching Libby Trickett win gold that morning which was a good distraction, with Jodi making funny comments to make me laugh. It wasn't until shortly before lunchtime that I started giving evidence.

I was granted permission to give my evidence via video link, which made it much more bearable. I truly think that if I had had to look at Dad when I was giving evidence, I would have felt so guilty and sorry for him that I wouldn't have been able to bear it. You cannot underestimate how much guilt you will experience when it comes to the possibility of getting your parent put in jail.

I wasn't allowed to have any friends or family or even Jodi with me when I gave evidence, but there was a volunteer court support worker who sat with me which was very helpful. During the breaks, she would chat with me and lighten the mood, which genuinely made a difference. During the trial, I didn't step foot in the actual court-room at all, but I did see a copy of the transcripts after the trial.

When giving evidence, I went into 'automatic' mode, like I did when I was giving my police statement. I didn't feel sad or any other emotion, just numb. I answered questions with as many facts as I could. Just as when I was giving my police statement, I had to give specific information, which I really struggled with. I could not say "he hurt me", I had to say "he put his penis in my vagina". I know that might not seem so difficult, but to me it was. In fact, it was mortifying. So I just became very detached because that was the only way I could cope with it. I felt like I wasn't really talking about myself, and it wasn't Dad I was talking about either. It was like it was somebody else's life.

The first day of questioning for me was by the prosecution lawyer whom I had met the previous week – not the junior lawyer, who I sincerely hoped was enjoying her mother's birthday in Melbourne! Not surprisingly, the prosecution lawyer came across as fairly disorganised. I still remember at one point he shuffled his papers a lot, looked at me, and said "Let me put it to you, Miss Baker, that in 2002 (shuffles papers some more), you were 14". To which I responded "uhh, yes". I mean, really!

By the end of the first day, I had finished being questioned by the prosecution. When I came out of court that day, I was surprised by some of the people who had come to watch. There was Anne, the mother of Ben, my friend who had committed suicide a few years ago. I really appreciated that – especially since the trial coincided with the anniversary of his death. Of course there was my Aunty Susie and her husband. And also my Aunty Barb and Uncle Toby. I didn't quite have the same relationship with Aunty Barb and Uncle Toby, and felt quite uncomfortable when I realised that they had been listening to all the evidence.

I hung out with my friend Dani for a while after leaving court, then went home to my dorm room at uni. I tried to get some sleep, in preparation for the following scary day.

I became really nervous the next day knowing that I was about to be cross-examined. I spoke to Jodi about how uncomfortable I had been about not knowing who was going to be listening to the evidence. I was also very, very overwhelmed when I heard that there were random people ('court watchers') who had gone in to watch my case – people who would go from one court room to the next, to see which courtroom had the best show for them to watch.

Doesn't it make you feel sick? Of course, there was nothing Jodi could do to stop those random people from going in, because technically, anyone can go into a court room.

Jodi really looked out for me that day though, and actually went and told my extended family that they were not allowed to go in and watch because it was making me incredibly uncomfortable. That was not pleasant for her to do, because it made them quite annoyed – but nonetheless they did still listen to her even though legally she couldn't stop them from going in. It was hard for me, because I couldn't really say "Oh, well I want Susie to watch, but not Greg because I don't really know Greg very well". So everyone was told that they couldn't go in. Of course, Dad's supporters were still allowed in, as Jodi couldn't stop them. Dad had his brother as a support, as well as a mysterious lady who I will call Gertrude, a.k.a. 'Blondie'. I was to find out a bit more about her in later years – looks like Dad had found it easier to move on than I had expected.

It was a weight off my shoulders knowing that I wouldn't have as many people watching the cross-examination by the defence lawyers. I really had no idea what to expect, but was nervous as all hell. I was wondering whether they would accuse me of causing everything, of being slutty, of making it all up – I didn't know what tack they would go for but had been warned that usually they go for the "slut or nut" approach. I need not have worried too much because the defence lawyer was just as bad as the prosecution lawyer. He would ask me questions about an event that had occurred. I would stick to the facts as usual, without getting emotional. He would then try saying something like "Let me put it to you, that it was just a dream". To which I would say "No, it wasn't." And then he'd start with another line of questioning. I remember on the day thinking "wow, is this all he's got?"

I'm going to include a few excerpts from the transcripts, so that you can see what the legal system is like for victims of sexual abuse. This might shed some light for you on why so few people pursue having charges laid – it all becomes too hard. You have to be very strong to endure the legal system.

Excerpt 1: Focusing on the insignificant details

This excerpt describes the incident when I was raped during a storm as a young child. It shows how the defence lawyer would focus on minor details in an attempt to confuse me and cast doubt on my credibility.

Defence Lawyer: You told us that on that particular night, he moved his hands on your thighs?---Me: Yes.

Inserted his penis into your vagina?---Yes, that's correct.

You say he put the penis right into your vagina?---Yes, that's correct.

Did he have intercourse with you?---Yes, he did.

Did he ejaculate?---I can't remember, sorry.

You didn't mention yesterday that on that same occasion, he was kissing you on the mouth?---Yes, that's correct.

Why was it you didn't mention that?---That's really a minor detail.

You said in your statement to the police, didn't you, that that happened on that occasion?---Yes, and it's correct.

You didn't mention it?---Pardon?

You didn't mention it?---Well, I mention it now and it is correct.

Excerpt 2: Red herring

The defence lawyer tried to suggest that I was unhappy with my mum:

Your allegations there are, that it was in the morning?---Yes, it was in the morning.

About what time?---I was still in bed. There was - - -

Were you still asleep?---No. I think I was lying awake in bed. It was - I was on holidays.

Do you know where your mother was at that time?---No. She could have been at work. She worked full-time when I was - from about the age of seven until about the age of nine or 10, in that particular job.

That was something that you were a bit upset about, wasn't it?---No.

Excerpt 3: Another red herring

Bringing up an incident that was completely irrelevant to any of the charges, to try and paint me as an unhappy child:

Did you have a teacher by the name of Mr Thompson* ---No. He was a computer teacher at the school.

Computer teacher?---Yes.

Did he teach you?---Not as a teacher. He just taught us how to use the computers.

Did you have an altercation with him on one occasion?---Not really. I mean, the things that you think are a big deal in primary school when you get in trouble by teachers, aren't really such a big deal after all.

Did you accuse him of shirt fronting you?---Pardon?

Did you accuse him of shirt fronting you. That's bumping you from the front?---Can you please tell me what you mean?

What's that?---Can you please tell me what you mean by that?

Well. Coming face to face with you and hitting you from the front?---He didn't hit me, no.

What did he do, then, to you?---He just grabbed me by the collar of my shirt.

Grabbed you by the collar of your shirt. Okay?---Yes. Because the reason that he did that was because he was getting my friend Tamara and I in trouble, because we accidentally pressed print about 10 times, because we thought our things weren't printing.

Okay. You complained to your parents about that?---Yes.

Your father went up to the school, I think, to speak to him?---I don't remember. I think my mother did.

Yes, but you were very upset about that, weren't you?---Yeah, for a year 3. I mean, it is pretty upsetting to get in trouble in front of all your friends.

Okay?---It's a big deal in year 3. To get your name on the board. Tamara was upset, too.

Excerpt 4: The saintly father

In contrast, the defence lawyer tried to paint my father as saintly and devoted; a man who went to massive efforts to drive me to cross country training. Again, you will see that these comments are not relevant to the actual criminal charge we were discussing.

Defence lawyer: We then go on to count 9, and you have mentioned in relation to that particular charge, that you were going to cross-country running, training?---Yes, I did cross-country training.

Did in fact your father take you to cross-country training?---I went to two different cross-country trainings. One was at the playing fields, which was a - sort of the club training, and then there was one just down the road, Tuesdays and Thursdays, with my neighbour. So there was two lots of cross-country training.

And sometimes did he have to drive some 30 kilometres to pick you up from cross-country training?---No, it was probably a 10-minute drive, but generally it was mum that did it.

Sometimes it was your father?---Sometimes, yes. I will say a lot of the time it was my neighbour.

Yes. Okay. If we then go on to the particulars in relation to count 9, where you allege that he lay on top of you and put his penis into your private parts, into your vagina. You told us when giving evidence about that matter yesterday.

Excerpt 5: You imagined it!

The main approach of the defence lawyer was to suggest that I had dreamed or imagined the abuse. This tactic just got boring, because he never even had a comeback for me when I said "No, I disagree, it did happen". He would just move on to the next charge. Maybe he had already given up?

This first excerpt is in relation to the storm incident:

And you had been asleep prior to going to your parents' room?---I was asleep until I woke up because of the storm. There was loud thunder.

Are you sure that in fact that incident happened at all?---Yes, I am very sure.

Are you sure you couldn't have dreamt it?---I am very sure.

And you remember it in detail?---Yes, I do.

I would suggest to you that nothing like that happened at all?---That is not true.

And that your father never did any - either of those things to you, or any of those things to you?---I don't agree.

Excerpt 6: You dreamed it!

And you have said in relation to this matter and a whole lot of others, that you pretended to be asleep?---Yes.

Could it be that you just dreamt that this happened?---No, I pretended to be asleep so that I could pretend that I wasn't there, because it wasn't a very pleasant experience. It was easier to pretend that it was a dream, but I know that it wasn't.

Excerpt 7: Still dreaming!

You say that he ejaculated or didn't on that occasion or don't you know?---I don't recall.

Surely you would have known, would you not?---I don't recall.

You don't recall. Could it be that you dreamt that?---No

Excerpt 8: It just didn't happen!

The next allegation, count 18, which is said to have happened in July 2005?---Yes. That's when I had a scratch on my face.

You say that he put his hands inside your legs and touched you on your vagina?---Yes, I believe so.

You say that he also hit you on that occasion?---No. My main memory of that is being scratched on the face. I don't believe I was hit though.

Okay. So you say you got scratched on your face on that occasion?---Yes.

Did that bleed?---I don't remember. Maybe a little bit. I think it scabbed over.

Would that have been fairly obvious to anybody?---Yes. People did notice it. My school psychologist noticed it.

Did you show that to your mother?---Not overtly, but it was fairly obvious. Friends at school noticed it, the school psychologist - - -

What about your sister?---I don't know. You'll have to ask her. I don't know. I can't guess for her.

Then going on to count - again I'll put it to you that that just didn't happen?---Okay. I don't agree with you.

Excerpt 9: STILL imagining things....

This guy is seriously running out of ideas...

Well, could it be that it just didn't happen?---It did happen, I do remember it.

I would suggest - I will put to you that none of those things happened?---Okay, I disagree.

And finally, in relation to all the charges, that none of the allegations of a sexual nature that you made against your father are correct?---Okay, I completely disagree with that statement.

And he never assaulted you in any way at all?---I completely disagree with that and I think that has also been reflected in the way that I approached various people at school and various services for help, from a young age.

We won't go into that?---Okay.

We might be here for a week?---Well, it just shows that I really did - - -

JUDGE: Well, just don't - just answer the questions, thank, Ms Baker?---Okay.

JUDGE: Just disregard that part of the evidence, members of the jury.

The thing that really frustrated me with giving evidence was that Dad's lawyer had found a loophole which made all counselling information confidential, and therefore barred from being used as evidence. This meant that all the evidence of me speaking with Kids Helpline and the sexual assault service was not known to the jury. It seemed really unfair, especially given that I (the victim) had consented to those records being accessed. It was an unfair twist of the rules.

Dad's lawyer was then suggesting that the abuse had not happened because I had never approached anybody for help. I was not allowed to say that I had, which was very frustrating and meant that the jury could not get a true picture of what had been happening. That is why the judge had to ask the jury (in the previous excerpt) to disregard my statement about approaching people for help. I am proud that I managed to weave it in there, because it is incredibly frustrating being told "But if it's true, why didn't you tell anybody?", when I HAD!

Here is another time I managed to weave Kids Helpline into an exchange with the defence lawyer, go me!

How did it come about that you said that?---What happened was, I'd been in contact with Kids Helpline for a few years.

Yeah, well, don't, yeah, okay?---Yeah. I'd told them everything about what Dad had been doing.

Excerpt 10: Maybe I 'misunderstood' it!

DEFENCE LAWYER: You, again, told us yesterday that your father started doing things to you when you were three?---Yeah, pretty much as early as I can remember. But in those first few years it just seemed normal, I didn't really know any different. It's just something I sort of grew up with and at first it didn't seem too abnormal.

Could you have dreamt those things?---No, most of the things when I was younger were during the day. When I was very small, like, the games and stuff, they were all mostly during the day and I was fully, fully awake.

Do you think it could be that you misunderstood what was happening? ---No, I might have misunderstood the intention, but I know that I was definitely touched in a sexual way.

How is it you can remember - well, you alleged, I think, in your statement, that when you were three, that he touched your private parts?---Yes. That's my first memory of being touched in a sexual way.

And you say you didn't think much of it at the time?---I don't think I did, to be honest, because it's just - it was different, it was something that had never happened to me before but at the time I think (inaudible) that's just what dads do. But obviously it did stick in my mind if I remember it, so maybe deep down I did know that it wasn't right.

Excerpt 11: "But you gave him birthday cards!"

This was probably the most ridiculous part of the cross-examination, and went on and on. I was presented with a handful of cards that I had given Dad over the years, and was asked to read every single one of them aloud. Apparently, the fact that I had given Dad cards was proof that he had not abused me:

During the time that you say these things were happening - - -?---Yeah.

- - - on a number of occasions, I think, you sent - or gave cards to your father?---Pardon?

You gave cards to your father?---On what particular occasion? Birthdays?

Yes, on Father's Day?---Yes.

I wonder if you will have a look at this one?---Okay.

Perhaps I will give you all of them?---Okay.

THE SUPPORT PERSON: We have the cards, your Honour.

DEFENCE LAWYER: The first of those cards - - -?---Yes.

- - - and I think you have written on one side of the card. Is that correct? ---Yeah, my sister has written on one side. Yes, it's a birthday card.

Do you remember which birthday that was?---No. It looks like his 50th, because I have written "middle-aged."

No, I think there is one, another one there for his 50th, which is the last of the cards?---Okay. This might have been 49, because it said, "You will soon be middle-aged."

About 2005?---Yeah, probably.

And what have you written on the card?---"Hope you have a great day. a doctor's appointment and meetings with my teachers, the ultimate present. I also hope you have a great year. Enjoy it because you will soon officially be middle-aged. You're a great bloke, dad, and you mean a lot to all of us. Love, Hazza"

And then the next one?---It's a Father's Day card that I made - my sister and I - it's from both of us

Which year was that?---Definitely after 2001, because it has got my dog's name on it.

Okay?---Yeah.

And what did you write on that one?---"Hope you enjoy the day. Thanks for your time that you spend with the dog and your dedication to the poo torch. You're a dog-walker, pooper-scooper, plus teacher and fart-burp evaluator all in one. We're very lucky to have you. Love, Max and Hannah." Max is my dog.

Okay?---Or the family dog.

Then the next one?---Yeah. Father's Day, from my sister and I again.

Do you know which year that was?---No, I would guess probably (inaudible)

2000, I'm sorry?---Well, it says 2005 on the back, so yeah.

Again, I think, the same sort of format. You have written on one side and your sister has written on the other side?---Yeah.

What have you written on that one?---"Thanks for being the kind, helpful and very funny guy you are. I really do appreciate all the maths help, even if I do get a little grumpy. Love, Hannah."

You have mentioned there a couple of times, "Help with maths." Did your father help you with maths?---Yeah, he did. He was good at maths. He helped me with maths.

And the next one?---It's a - it just says, "Dad, thank you so much for putting so much time into teaching me how to drive. From, Hannah."

And so what year would that have been?---2006.

And I think - is there one more, or are there a couple more?---Two more.

Yes. Okay. And the next one?---It's got a picture of a dog that looks like our dog, and it's from my sister and I, again a birthday card. "Dear dad, I hope you have great day and enjoy both of your cakes. Thank you so much for being so patient with Max and taking him on all those walks and thank you for your maths help as well. From, Hannah."

And then the following one, the last one I think, is a 50th birthday card?---Yes. This is while my sister was away. "Talk about over the hill. I hope you enjoy being old. I'm sure I have given you more than a few grey hairs with my far from" - sorry - "Far from perfect driving. Thanks for your time and patience. From, Hannah."

Thank you. If your Honour pleases, I tender those.

Excerpt 12: Use of grainy photos

The defence lawyer tried presenting me with very grainy photos pertaining to one of the charges where I had been physically assaulted and had bruising on my face. The following week, I was in a photograph taken by a friend, in which the bruising could be seen. I had given good copies of the photos to police, but from the defence lawyers I was presented with distorted, grainy copies. Funnily enough, the defence lawyer didn't take me up on my offer to bring the originals. This was a very satisfying exchange with the lawyer for me, because I knew that I made him look ridiculous.

> *COURT MARSHALL: We have the photos, your Honour.*
>
> *JUDGE: Thank you.*
>
> *DEFENCE LAWYER: Are they two of the photographs that were taken on that occasion?---Yes.*
>
> *They're not very good quality, are they?---Not in here, they're not, but if I got them printed on proper photo paper, then yeah, they are.*
>
> *Well, it's pretty hard to tell?---On these ones it is because it's not good quality printing, but if you want me to print some on actual photo paper for tomorrow, I can do that.*
>
> *Well, you can't really point out a bruise on either of those photographs, can you?---That's what I'm saying. The quality is not very good on these, but if you would like better quality, I (inaudible) because I believe that on the other ones, it is good quality and that you can see.*
>
> *Yeah, the colouring is dark colouring in sorts of different places?---That's what I'm saying. This photo, the colouring on it, it's just not very well - it's not very easy to define much on it. Like, even the other people's faces are a bit blurred, but if I actually print you the original, you will be able to see it clearly. Would you like me to do that.*
>
> *No. Your Honour, I tender those two photographs.*

When I read these transcripts now, I feel very proud of how well I stood up for myself and how articulate I managed to be in an intimidating situation.

When I came out from cross-examination, a huge weight had been lifted from my shoulders and I was feeling pretty good. I knew I had done well, and was pleasantly surprised by how straight forward it had been. When I walked out of the room, the first people I saw were my extended family, who Jodi had barred from going into watch my evidence. The looks on their faces said it all

— they were pissed off! Everyone was dead silent — it was a horrible feeling. My mum's brother, Uncle Toby, looked like he had just attended a funeral! It was a very sombre mood indeed. There I was, proud and on a high, not realising how much I had offended them by telling Jodi that I didn't want them to watch my evidence. I had lunch with them afterwards, and again was a bit shocked when lunch break was over, that they all dutifully headed back into the courtroom, while I was left to get the bus home by myself. I was incredibly hurt by this. I have since talked it through with my Aunty Susie and Uncle Roy, who apologised, and I do honestly understand what a tough position they were in — because they were thinking from a strategic point of view, that if nobody from my 'side' was in the courtroom, that it would make Dad and his few supporters look good. Also, my mum and sister were due to give evidence later that day too, so they wanted to support them.

Again, I think all of these upsets could have been avoided if there had been better communication by everyone, including me. On that day though, when everyone else left me to go while they watched the rest of the trial, I really did feel that it was just a 'great show' for everyone to watch, and that they were forgetting the absolute loss of dignity I had and was continuing to experience.

Other people to give evidence during the trial were the doctor from the sexual assault service, as well my friend Cassie (who had seen bruising on me when we were at school), another girl who had seen bruising on me, my mum, my sister, and my teacher Mrs Stanley. There were other people who were subpoenaed but 'dropped' on the day, including my previous school chaplain, and school deputy Mrs Evans, who was in touch with me still and wished me all the best. Prior to the trial, as I've previously mentioned, all counselling evidence had been barred, which meant that Ms Lynch (school psychologist), Kids Helpline, and Gabbie (sexual assault counsellor) were not allowed as witnesses.

I did not watch any of the rest of the court proceedings. I didn't go to uni that week either, instead preferring to hang out by myself. On the Thursday I spent the day playing with my goddaughter and some of her friends which was fun and a good distraction. I wasn't really talking to my mum and sister much during this time. I was still feeling very hurt about being 'left' while everyone went to watch the 'show'. However, my Aunty Susie really pulled through for me, by offering to come round and spend the Thursday afternoon with me while we waited for news of the verdict. While everyone else went to court to watch the proceedings, Susie and I hung around in my room waiting for the news. My good friend Deirdre, who also lived on campus with me, came and joined us for a bit which was nice.

The verdict

I gave strict instructions that the only person to contact me with the verdict was the detective, Jodi. True to form, Jodi called me as soon as the verdict came through.

I can barely remember how she delivered the news. All I remember is that it had come through as a guilty verdict on five of the charges. It took me a while to take it in. The memory is still blurry. I felt very overwhelmed and started crying. I was suddenly racked by guilt at the thought of Dad going to jail. I was emotional and exhausted. In that moment, I really, really appreciated having Aunty Susie by my side.

Dad had been acquitted of most of the 'indecent dealings' charges, while being convicted of the more serious rape charges. It was suggested to me by Jodi that this is because there was just not enough evidence to convict him of the more minor charges. Either way it did not matter much — and it was good that he was convicted of some of the rapes.

I started receiving text messages of support from family and close friends that evening. They were lovely and thoughtful. I remember one of them said "closure at last", which unfortunately for me was far from the reality.

One of the first people I wanted tell about the verdict was Leah at Kids Helpline. She was on the phones the following day, and was very happy that there had been a guilty verdict. But she was also happy to speak with me about my mixed feelings. I was able to tell her how guilty and scared I felt about Dad going to jail, and how I wasn't sure if I had done the right thing. However, at the same time, I was glad to have gotten a guilty verdict, and did feel that I had done the right thing. It was all very confusing.

The sentencing hearing

The following month, my dad was sentenced to 8.5 years jail, which I was told would have been 12.5 years in truth in sentencing. Again, I wasn't really sure what that meant or what truth in sentencing was. However, I later had it clarified for me that Dad had been sentenced to an 8.5 year term, with the possibility of parole after 6.5 years.

I did not attend the sentencing hearing, again, to avoid the 'circus' that I had felt the trial was. I am extremely glad I did not go. a long-lost uncle on Mum's side of the family, Uncle Simon, had heard about the trial through his daughter (who I had contact with). Simon decided that there was no better time for a family reunion than the sentencing hearing. Talk about inappropriate!

He just turned up at the hearing without informing anyone of his intention to do so, without checking that it would be okay. The last contact he had had with the family was in 1997, when he'd had a massive fight with other family members and never spoken to them again. There is a time and a place for a family reunion (especially when you are the one who has cut contact with the family), but a sexual abuse court hearing is not the place. I felt this was very disrespectful of what I had been through, and in some ways I wondered if he merely just wanted to hear the gory details of what had happened. It was definitely not done with my best interests at heart. I have it on good authority from a non-family member who was at the hearing that it was 'quite a scene' and ridiculous – people hugging and crying, a very emotional reunion. Again, I wanted to remind them what the hearing was about – a little girl who was raped by one of the people she should have been able to trust most.

POST-TRIAL

Painting by
Sarah Millicent Elliott

To be honest, the next few months were a blur. I remember that my close school friends had a picnic the weekend after the trial which was nice. It was down by the waterfront, and it was a warm and beautiful sunny day. Other than that I don't remember a whole lot of that period. I was living at uni which was probably the best thing for me – sometimes I could be very sociable, outgoing and funny, which helped distract me from how I was feeling on the inside. I became involved in things going on including a uni play – that was a lot of fun.

I also immersed myself in my uni studies. I went back to uni the Monday after the trial ended and was on a mission to get really good marks. Within a week of being back, I had caught up on all the work I had missed in the lead-up to and during the trial. My hard work continued to pay off – I did really well, getting distinctions and high distinctions that semester. The course coordinator, who was aware of my situation, expressed her surprise to me about my brilliant marks. I explained that it was just my way of coping. I also continued to work part-time, as a way of supporting myself through uni on top of getting Youth Allowance. I never went into debt or spent outside of my means – I was always very responsible when it came to money.

Towards the end of the year, however, the cracks started to show. I started to become increasingly suicidal again. I was overwhelmed by constant feelings of guilt for my dad, and always worried about him. I worried that I had ruined his life and hurt him. I worried about how he was coping in jail. I felt terrible that he was all alone, not realising that he actually did have a lady friend ('Gertrude') who was visiting him regularly. I started having horrible depressed patches where I could barely get out of bed for days. I became negative and reclusive. At the same time I still tried to maintain a happy-go-lucky personality on the outside, but it definitely failed me at times. Sometimes I was downright mean, and very unhappy. About a month after sentencing, I had to go to hospital for a short while because I was very suicidal. My Aunty Susie and Uncle Roy knew about it and came and tried to help me, but soon after this, I started lashing out at them and distancing myself from them too. Nobody could reach me anymore.

Around this time, a girl who lived on campus with me claimed to have been raped. When I became aware of this, I set about trying to help her. I told her everything I knew about the legal system, and even brought her to meet Jodi. I laid myself bare to her because I so badly wanted to help her. I convinced myself that this was the 'good' to come from my experience – that I could help other people. However, it later emerged that this girl had made up the story as a way of getting attention. She had made up several other big lies, including a fake pregnancy, pretending a relative had passed away, and there was a life threatening illness thrown in the mix too. When I found that she had lied about all of these things, in particular the rape, I was really crushed. I was so angry at the extra emotional roller coaster I had been dragged through, less than three months after the trial. I had even offered to take her to get a medical exam but funnily enough she had refused – probably because it was not true! I was very honest and vulnerable with her, and had it all thrown back in my face. However, I was not alone in my anger, which helped. I had other good friends who were also duped, and who understood my absolute rage at this girl.

Professional support during this time

I stayed in close contact with Leah from Kids Helpline following the trial. I was still not up to seeing a face-to-face counsellor consistently at that point – I didn't have the energy to build up rapport with someone new. However, at the recommendation of a friend, I found a brilliant General Practitioner, Dr Camden, who worked very well with Leah to keep me safe over the next few years. The very first time I went to see Dr Camden, I instantly liked and trusted her, and was able to tell her about the difficulties I was having. At the time, my body was under a lot of stress and I was having constant nose bleeds, headaches, and major difficulties with sleep. Dr Camden helped manage my medications (I had stayed on antidepressants since December 2006), and she also put me on a medication to help me sleep. It took me a while to get used to this new medication, because it initially made me feel very groggy in the morning and also made me put on some weight which at that age does make you feel bad about yourself. However, in hindsight I can see that the benefits outweighed the negatives. Getting more sleep helped me to cope better.

Dr Camden remained my GP for the next three years until she left to have a baby. She went above and beyond her role as a GP to provide support to me – she once even helped me with a scholarship application because she knew I was stressed about money. When she knew I was really suicidal, she did everything she could to check up on me and maintained contact with Leah at Kids Helpline so that they could support me together. Do you know many GP's that would do such an amazing job? I was very, very fortunate.

Running away from my problems

After finishing another semester of uni in November 2008, I started to struggle even more. Uni and getting good results had been a great distraction for me, but now with a three month break ahead of me, I suddenly had way more time to think about what had happened during the trial. I decided that I needed to get away from my home city for a while, so I took off for about six weeks, staying with random friends and relatives in different parts of Australia. Part of my reason for running away was that I did not want to be around for Christmas – the first Christmas Dad was in jail. That was very upsetting for me, and I felt really sorry him.

The first person I stayed with was my Aunty Jane and her family, who lived interstate. I stayed with them for two weeks. It was very nice of them to put me up for so long, and Jane knew that I was very fragile. It was great to get to spend some time with her and my cousins Holly and Aiden. I also had an old school friend (Jade) living in the same city as them, so spent some time hanging out with her too.

Next up, I went and caught up with some of the exchange students who had been living at uni with me, who were travelling around Australia. I hung out with them for a few days in Brisbane which was fun. Then I went to visit a friend who lived in a regional town, and stayed with her family for about five days. Again, it was really lovely for her family to put me up like that.

After that, I flew down to Melbourne and stayed by myself in a backpackers – in my own room, because I have trouble sleeping in new places and trusting people in general. This is where it all really fell apart, because finally I had no distractions, and the trauma of the court case really started to sink in. I started to become very, very suicidal. I wrote a suicide note then took an overdose of sleeping tablets, but ironically didn't fall asleep at all. I went into a state of paranoia and hysteria and at around 6am ended up calling an ambulance.

I realised that I didn't really want to die. I just didn't want to feel like this anymore. I talked to Leah at Kids Helpline the next day and she was worried sick, and sounded very angry. I had never heard her like that before and felt really guilty. Leah had been trying to keep in contact with me since I had left on my trip, because she knew that I was in a really bad headspace and was not acting like my usual self.

I eventually got back to my hometown early 2009 and prepared for another year of uni, and part-time work. Uni was probably the only thing that went right for me that year. I worked really hard and continued to do well. At the end of the year I was even offered a place in the honours program, which I accepted. It meant a lot to me, because it was very competitive to get into the honours program, and despite everything I had been through I had been awarded a place, fair and square.

However, it was a difficult year full of suicidal periods and many days spent largely in bed. I was so miserable, and constantly racked with guilt whenever I thought about my dad. I felt so responsible for him ending up in jail, and for ruining his life. I wanted to apologise to him. I wanted his sentence to be cut. But at the same time, deep down, I knew that I would have also been pretty devastated if he had not been sent to jail – I would have felt very invalidated. So I was really confused and found it difficult to live with myself. I decided to change my surname to that of family members on Mum's side of the family, so that I did not have to think about Dad every time I wrote my name. I liked my new name, and in some way it helped me in forming a new future and new identity.

In the midst of all this, I managed to have a great 21st birthday party. Everyone came, even my goddaughter's family, and my mum and sister put in a lot of effort too. Most of the people there did not realise that I had spent the day of the party considering suicide. I was in a terrible headspace at the time. But as usual I covered it up and acted like I was happy. It was clear that people in my life still loved and cared about me. But I had become so full of self-hatred and disgust that I felt very cynical about it all. I would often think, "Can't they see what a horrible person I am?"

I am lucky that I made it through 2009 alive because it was such an excruciating year and there were so many times that I considered killing myself. I often wrote suicide notes and even picked which cemetery I would like to be buried at. Some days it felt too hard to get out of bed. a diary entry I wrote that year which sums it all up is as follows:

"I do not want to feel so disgusting anymore.

I don't want to have nightmares.

Don't want to feel guilty.

I don't want to feel like I am still being controlled by Dad.

I don't want to feel so ashamed".

I was also having really bad nightmares as I tried to process my thoughts and feelings about Dad going to jail. I worried that he was really angry at me. In another diary entry in 2009, I wrote:

"I'm not sure if he would kill me.

I used to be very scared about it, especially when he was free on bail before the trial.

I had one scary nightmare where he got out of jail, tied me up and I tried screaming but nobody listened. I think he was about to kill me but I woke up."

During this time, my great GP Dr Camden continued to work well with my Kids Helpline counsellor to try and keep me safe. Dr Camden tried to get the local sexual assault service to start seeing me again, to offer support following the trial, but was informed by them that I wasn't eligible for services. Firstly the manager said that I had already used up my allotment of sessions. Then when my GP contacted her to say that I really wasn't coping and was suicidal following the trial, the manager said that I no longer fit their service criteria if I was suicidal, and needed to see a psychiatrist.

I doubt I am the first person who has been sexually abused to feel suicidal, particularly if their father has just been jailed.

What I needed most was to be able to talk to people who knew what I had been through and had been a part of my journey, and it really hurt to be so badly 'rejected' by the sexual assault centre. I felt like they had washed their hands of me and that nobody cared about me. To this day, I do not understand why they were so unwilling to provide any follow-up support, when they spent just as much time telling my GP that they couldn't support me, as it would have taken for a counsellor to offer some support on the phone. I have recently given their service feedback about my experience so that hopefully things will change. They are now under new management which I believe might help.

Under my GP's guidance, I had to go to hospital for a while in 2009, which I think did help me a bit. This was the last time I ever had to go to hospital, thankfully. Of course, I didn't tell people about this – I was very ashamed about going into hospital and tried to pretend I was doing fine. However, I did tell my old school friend Nat about it, and she was quite upset that things were still so hard for me.

She had not realised and said she was so sorry for not being there for me more. She didn't need to apologise because she had done nothing wrong, but it was nice to have an honest moment with her — when usually I would be fake instead.

On the other side of the coin, I found that some of the people who had been really interested in me around the time of the trial, started dropping off like flies once the drama had worn off. It's kind of like when you have a relative die, and everyone turns up for the big event (the funeral), and gradually they lose interest in you if they're not a true friend. That is exactly how it was for me, and I learned to not bother with 'fair weather' friends and relatives anymore. Interestingly, I never again heard much from Uncle Simon, the long-lost uncle who had turned up at the sentencing hearing!

The share-house experience

From 2009 to the end of my time at university (end of 2011), I lived in share houses. This added to the instability in my life, but at times also provided me with plenty of distractions.

In the first share house, I lived with two girls who wouldn't have noticed if I disappeared for a month. They spoke a foreign language to each other and largely ignored me, which felt terrible! The house also had rats which was disgusting at night and only added to my sleeping difficulties.

I then moved in with Sadie, a girl I had known since I was a kid, and a couple of her friends. They were all a couple of years older than me, which was initially fine. Though I still remain very close friends with Sadie, we had some very interesting housemates and it did make life more difficult than it had to be sometimes. However in hindsight, I can honestly say that my time in that house was character building!

Initially it had been all girls when I moved in, and I felt quite uncomfortable when it was decided that we were getting a new housemate, a male who was in his 30s. I felt quite powerless when I tried to speak up about this, and ended up having a major fight with one of my housemates. I just had to put up with it, because as a student I had pretty limited options with where I could go.

Anyway, this male housemate, Robbie, turned out to be quite interesting in the end, and he only lasted about 3 months. He was a pharmacist who had major drug issues. He would bring home the spare drugs that people had brought in to the pharmacy to be destroyed, and use them himself. I couldn't believe that a pharmacist would do this! The highlight of Robbie's time in the house was one night when he was completely off his face on something, and acting completely irrationally. He grabbed some bananas, and started smearing them into the bathroom floor. Sadie walked in and said "Robbie, what are you doing??!" In his drugged up stupor, Robbie then tore off the plastic on the nine-pack of toilet paper that we'd just bought, and started attempting to wipe the bananas up with the full nine pack of toilet paper, in large sweeping movements. What a waste of our precious toilet paper, which would have cost a whole $6! Sadie was irate by this point and like a frustrated parent, had to say "Robbie, GO TO BED". Ha!

Through living at uni and living in sharehouses, I learned to always sleep with earplugs and that was a very good move. There was only one occasion where I heard Robbie bring a girl home to have sex with her, and that in itself caused me to have flashbacks.

Robbie ended up leaving the house quite suddenly, without paying all of his outstanding bills (surprise surprise!), and then we got another new house mate called Emma, who could be a real bully. Being older than me and also being a very insecure person, she would try to get the other two girls (who were also older than me) to gang up on me and make fun of me. I really hated it! The worst thing was that most of this was behind my back – in my own home! How ridiculous. It was a very unhappy home in the end, and I tended to just keep to myself because I felt very disrespected. Emma would often call me a 'prude' because of the way I avoided any conversations about sex, and was never the kind of person to bring guys home with me from the pub.

However, Emma was clearly a very unhappy person. I actually think she had bipolar disorder, because she would have times where she would seem as high as a kite, then major lows, where she would drink heaps and lash out at everyone. I remember one time when she was on a "high" I woke up about 2am to the smell of burning. Turned out that Emma had decided on a whim to make cupcakes, then forgotten about it and gone to bed. Yes, on top of everything else going on in my life, my share houses added a fair bit of drama. I feel like I should have been given an honorary psychology degree for my time in shared and on-campus accommodation – I sure learned a lot about people!

APPEALS

I was warned by the detective, Jodi, to expect appeals following sentencing. Well, she was 100% correct about this. The first appeal was lodged within two weeks of the sentencing hearing. It wasn't heard in court until some 15 months later, which really dragged it out for me. In the meantime, it again felt like my life was in limbo. I didn't know what grounds the appeal was on, how likely it was to succeed, and whether it would mean a retrial.

In early 2010, my friend Dani accompanied me to the appeal decision hearing at the Supreme Court. My mum also attended, but I didn't want to sit with her. The way that the hearing was conducted was completely different from what I expected. We went and sat in the public gallery, and within a space of less than five minutes, the judge rattled through the decisions for about five different cases. Dad was not present in the courtroom, but some other people were in the public gallery, waiting to hear the results of other hearings. It was all so fast compared to the way things were done in the trial. Very abruptly and matter-of-factly, the judge announced that my dad had had a two year reduction in sentence, because one of the rape convictions had been overturned. The other four convictions still stood. As a result, Dad would now be eligible for parole in February 2013, after serving just four years and six months.

To find out what had led to this decision, I had to wait for the written explanation to be released. It was 100 pages long, so I will be honest, I did not read all of it.

Here is an excerpt from the decision, outlining Dad's main areas of appeal:

> *The gravamen of the appellant's complaint is twofold. First, the verdicts of guilty on counts 6, 8, 19, 22 and 23 are said to be inconsistent with the acquittals on the remaining counts. The appellant contends there is no logical or rational explanation for the different dispositions of the various counts. Secondly, the complainant's evidence as to events is said to be inherently improbable. Her account of events was unreliable and incapable of sustaining convictions due, in particular to:*
>
> *a. her lack of complaint to any family member or to anyone in authority at or near the time the offences are said to have taken place;*
>
> *b. the lack of evidence of signs of distress or physical injury observed by third parties at or around the time of the alleged offences;*
>
> *c. the continuation by her of participation in an otherwise unremarkable family situation over a long period, including after she turned 18 and moved away from home; and*

d. evidence of affectionate cards sent by her to the appellant from time
   to time during the period when the abuse was said to have been
   perpetrated.

This was all explored in more detail, but inevitably it was decided that the arguments raised by Dad's side did not stack up. For example, there was evidence of physical injuries, and there were people who I had spoken to.

The judge made a brilliant statement in summing up why it is reasonable to accept that I continued to live at home and gave affectionate cards to my dad as a child. It showed that there are people within the justice system who have an understanding of sexual abuse and the confusion it causes.

Judge:
I do not accept the appellant's proposition that the matters on which he relies, individually or collectively, render the complainant's evidence of the offences improbable. That is, these matters do not cause me to experience a reasonable doubt as to the truthfulness or reliability of the complainant's evidence.

On the State case, the abuse commenced when the complainant was a very young child. There is evidence of the appellant grooming the complainant. There is no reason to believe that a young child would know or understand that his or her father, a person expected to provide protection, guidance and love, was acting inappropriately or wrongfully. By the time such a child victim reaches an age where, perhaps with gradually developing awareness, he or she comes to know that the conduct is wrong, it is reasonable to expect the victim to experience deeply conflicting emotions, one of which is likely to be guilt.

Conflicted feelings of love or affection for the offender are not necessarily inconsistent with intra-familial sexual abuse. Even when a person comes to eventually accept that they are truly an innocent victim of a criminal abuse of a position of power, it would be a difficult step to potentially destroy the family unit and expose one's father to the criminal justice system.

The one conviction that was overturned was for an offence where there simply was not enough evidence to prove beyond reasonable doubt that the incident had occurred. This did not particularly bother me. You see, I still had very conflicting emotions, and a small part of me was relieved that Dad's sentence had been cut, and that his suffering in jail would be lessened. If I am being truly honest, a part of me had secretly been hoping that he would be acquitted on all charges, so that I would no longer have to carry the guilt of having "gotten my dad put in jail". Even when people said "you didn't put him in jail, he put himself in jail by abusing you", I would put blinkers on and not want to hear it. I had been on tenterhooks waiting for the result of the appeal. And now that I knew Dad was going to stay in jail, I started to feel dreadful again. It didn't make sense to friends or family, so I mainly spoke to Leah at Kids Helpline and my GP, Dr Camden. Having objective people to talk to about how I really felt, was very helpful.

Guess what? The appeals did not end there. In 2010, Dad also tried lodging an appeal to the High Court of Australia. He decided to represent himself in this appeal, because the lawyers who had worked on his case appeared to have given up on him. The appeal was dismissed instantly.

PRISON VISIT

2010 continued to be a very difficult year for me, even once uni had gone back. I continued to maintain very good grades, and was working hard in the honours program, which went over a two-year period. But the guilt about Dad being in jail continued to eat away at me. I was overcome by a need to 'face up to Dad' and let him tell me how I had ruined his life, and how angry he was at me. It was sort of like I needed to accept responsibility for causing such major disruptions in his life. I felt like I had been a coward for giving evidence via video-link, and that I needed to see him face to face.

I spoke to both Leah at Kids Helpline and Dr Camden about wanting to go and see Dad. I didn't feel comfortable talking about it to friends or family. At this point, I was also seeing a counsellor. Although I never fully trusted her or talked about the actual abuse (and she left the job just as we were building up a relationship), she was a good sounding board. None of the professionals I talked to thought it was a good idea for me to visit Dad. So I really was on my own with the idea.

I very bravely called up the prison and asked the man who answered the phone what the visiting hours were. He asked who I would like to see, and I said my dad's name. The man informed me that prisoners have to approve visitors before they come, so he would have to get back to me about whether Dad would allow me to visit.

I then spoke to my good friend Dani about my decision to visit Dad, and she offered to come with me on the visit, even though she really thought it was a terrible idea. Her offer to join me was a massive relief to me and very generous of her. Two days before the visit, I called up the prison to confirm the details and that it would be okay for my friend Dani to accompany me. It was relayed to me that Dad had said this was fine.

On Saturday 26th June 2010 (the date is still etched in my mind), Dani and I drove out to the prison. I remember it was really cold out there. We went through the metal detectors and it was kind of sad, seeing lots of children and families there to visit a family member. You forget about how it impacts on young children, to have a parent in jail.

Then Dani and I walked into the room — it was like a big mess hall with lots of tables and chairs. a very skinny man walked towards us. I didn't realise at first — it was my dad! He was all skin and bones, he looked like he weighed about 60kg. His face had many new wrinkles on it, and his eyes had sunken in to his head. It was very confronting to see him looking like that — it was like he had aged 10 years and developed anorexia. I instantly felt very, very guilty.

Instead of a nice greeting, Dad instantly barked orders at Dani in an aggressive voice: "I will not see Hannah with you, I will see Hannah on her own, I will not see Hannah with you!" He then caught himself by adding, in a falsely nice voice "Oh, but Dani, would you like a cup of tea?"

Dani looked terrified and walked away – she had no real choice. In hindsight I can see how Dad had it all figured out – he had agreed to see me with a friend because he knew I would definitely come – and then gotten rid of the friend when I was actually there.

Dani stood nearby with a female prison guard, and they watched me carefully while I spoke with Dad. Dani said it was terrible to watch, because they could see that Dad was just talking at me, and I was sitting there crying, not saying much at all. I can clearly remember some of the things Dad said that day. Firstly, he tried to get me on-side with him again by saying that I had "always been the black sheep of the family". He also made several nasty comments about my mum, making fun of her as usual. He added "I won't tell your mother about this visit, she doesn't need to know". Ah, another secret!

I asked him how he was going and he told me that on his bad days he had considered killing himself because he hated being in jail so much. I told him that I too had considered killing myself many times. I said that I had been really depressed. Dad started to casually ask me questions in a caring tone, "Oh, so are you on any medications? Which medications are you on? Have you been in hospital?" I didn't realise that he was asking me all these questions to use the information against me later, in yet another appeal.

The worst thing that Dad said to me that day was that on his "dark days", he wished I was never born. This was a really shocking thing for me to hear. For someone who had grown up being told they were 'special' as part of the grooming process, I was now being told that it would be better if I hadn't been born. I started bawling my eyes out. I asked Dad "Do you think I should kill myself?" and he said no, that I shouldn't, but that there were things I could do to make the situation better. He said that the best thing I could do would be to go to the police and tell them that I had been confused. He promised that he would make sure I was okay if I did that, and that I wouldn't get in trouble, because I was clearly mentally unstable and confused about the allegations anyway. I felt so guilty hearing him talk, that I said I would think about it.

At some point around then, the female prison guard came over to me with a box of tissues and said "Are you alright sweetie?" and patted me on the arm. I really appreciated that she and Dani were keeping such a close eye on me, and they could see how badly I was being manipulated. We decided that it would be best to leave it there. Before I left, I wanted to ask Dad about "Blondie", aka Gertrude.

I said "Dad, do you have a girlfriend, because everyone saw that blonde lady at the trial, and she was living at your house when Aunty Susie and Uncle Toby went to get Mum's stuff". He looked me square in the eye and said he would never have a girlfriend because now, because of what I had "done to him", he found it so hard to trust people. As usual, I believed him. I asked Dad if there was anything else he wanted me to send him, and he said maybe some books, and a photo of me. When I told Jodi from the police this, she said to never, ever send a photo.

It was time to go. Dani and I drove back to the city and that evening I spoke to Leah on the phones at Kids Helpline. I was very distraught at the skinny, old-looking man I had seen, and felt a tremendous amount of guilt. I seriously considered going to the police, just like he had asked me to.

Painting by
Sarah Millicent

However, within a few days, something major started to shift in my brain. I started being able to pick-apart what had happened during the visit – the manipulation and guilt-tripping, the lies and inability to take responsibility for his actions. I started to see that he was very clever and that he was only looking out for himself. I ended up telling Mum that I had gone to visit him and she was quite shocked. I told her about some of the things he had said to me, and about her. Mum then started reeling off many awful things that Dad had said about me over the years to her and other people – mainly that I was "strange" and "mentally unstable" and "there's something not right about her". I have to admit, I was stunned to hear all these things, and it just made me feel even more betrayed. I also wondered why Mum had been willing to stay with someone who said such awful things about their own daughter.

I think that week was the turning point in my recovery in lots of ways. I cried, I expressed the grief of 'losing' my dad, and started to accept that he was actually quite a nasty, manipulative person. It was much needed closure that could only come from a face-to-face meeting. Within a few weeks following the visit, I started exercising regularly, and lost the weight I had put on due to my medications. My confidence increased and I didn't tend to have those awful periods in bed where I would wish Dad wasn't in jail. I started to see that he probably needed to be there, and that he was not nice.

LETTERS FROM DAD

Shortly after the prison visit, Dad started to send manipulative letters to Mum which were clearly meant for my eyes. I am still at a complete loss to understand why my mum felt it would be a good idea to pass these letters on to me! They were very upsetting and confusing to read and made me feel terrible. I would have appreciated being protected from further psychological abuse and manipulation by my dad.

Here is the first letter.

12th July 2010

Toni (Mum),

After seeing Hannah on the 26th June, I am extremely concerned about her state of mental health and the high chance that she will seriously harm herself.

For Hannah's sake, I believe we should have a meeting to discuss Hannah's wellbeing and the meeting should take place sooner rather than later. To this end, I will ensure that I have no visitors booked in on Saturday 24th July. If you wish to meet on the 24 July, you will need to ring the prison between 19th and 22nd July between 9-11am or 1-3pm to book in.

Regarding our different positions as to guilt (i.e. your position that I am guilty and my position that I am not guilty), for the purpose of the meeting we should accept that our positions are different.

The purpose of the meeting is not to change either of our guilty/not guilty positions. The sole purpose of the meeting is to discuss Hannah's future wellbeing.

Thank you

Peter Baker

Mum didn't respond to the letter and a few weeks later Dad sent another one, as follows.

15 August 2010

Toni,

Hannah's wellbeing – Without Prejudice

As a follow up to my letter on 12 July 2010 and in the absence of a meeting, I wish to outline for you some of my concerns regarding Hannah's wellbeing.

As you are aware, I met Hannah on 26 June. We had a wide-ranging discussion. It was clear to me that Hannah is totally uncertain regarding whether the events, detailed in the allegations she made against me, occurred or not. Given this uncertainty, she is struggling with the fact that I am in prison as a result of her making the allegations. Hannah also mentioned that she has and is being treated for depression and suicidal thoughts and that you do not support her in her wish to explore her uncertainties.

Prior to 26 June 2010, I had not been in contact with Hannah for over three years. Given the nature and severity of Hannah's allegations and the outcome of the court case, it would be expected that Hannah would have moved on with her life by now. But she is totally at sea/ totally uncertain whether the events outlined in the allegations occurred or not. Am I surprised? No! As you know, I have stated from the start that the events outlined in the allegations never took place. Hannah knows this deep down (consciously or subconsciously) and hence her current situation.

Hannah knows she is responsible for the imprisonment of an innocent person, her dad. She also knows that she has the power to change the situation. But there are family and state organisations (e.g. DPP) discouraging her from changing her position. How does she feel? At best she would feel very bad and she finds herself in a terrible situation which is almost impossible to sort out.

Given my comments so far, I am not surprised that Hannah is being treated for depression and suicidal thoughts. This is a result of the pressure that she is under. Hannah's desire to explore her uncertainties will never go away. They will need to be dealt with by Hannah sooner or later.

What will the future bring for Hannah?

If things remain unchanged, I have grave fears for Hannah's wellbeing. She will have more severe episodes of depression and suicidal thoughts and could harm herself seriously. I don't want this to happen to Hannah.

The alternative is to encourage Hannah to investigate fully her uncertainties. This would involve arranging appropriate unbiased psychologically trained counsellors to help Hannah. Upfront, you would need to fully support and encourage Hannah with her idea to investigate her uncertainties. Hannah would also need to know that you would support her in the future no matter what final decision she makes.

By taking this route, Hannah will address her issues in a more structured and stable manner. After the investigation, hopefully she will be in a position to move on with her life in a positive manner.

If Hannah does decide to withdraw her allegations, I understand that there is a way she can do it which would give her immunity from charges being brought against her by the DPP.

If we had met, I would have discussed the above concerns in greater detail and raised some further concerns. I am still available to meet.

I am extremely worried about Hannah's wellbeing. I ask you to consider carefully the points raised in this letter and to do what you think is in Hannah's best interest. Hopefully, the right environment can be provided so Hannah can sort out her issues in the near future.

Thank you,

Peter Baker

(Hannah's dad).

I had many thoughts when I read this second letter, which was clearly aimed at making me feel guilty about Dad being in jail. Why else would he have felt a need to sign it off with the words 'Hannah's dad'? I found it interesting that he felt so confident in saying what psychological help I needed when he has absolutely no professional training or skills in that area.

To me, the sentence which highlights his complete lack of insight the most, is this one:

"Given the nature and severity of Hannah's allegations and the outcome of the court case, it would be expected that Hannah would have moved on with her life by now."

I'm not sure which trial Dad was sitting in on, but last time I checked, a child being repeatedly raped by their parent is right up there in terms of 'severity'. His callous disregard for the seriousness of his crimes and their impact made me feel nauseous.

A couple of months later, I was contacted by the Victim Offender Mediation Unit who informed me that Dad was trying to get a letter to me via their office. They asked if I would like to see it but I refused, and said that I would not accept any correspondence from him whatsoever.

CRIMINAL INJURIES COMPENSATION

I was informed by court support services immediately after the trial that I was eligible for criminal injuries compensation. Accessing this would help me to pay for the ongoing counselling and medical treatment that I required. It wasn't until 2010 that I actually put in my application – it was just one extra thing to think about on top of everything else. I think like most victims of crime, I didn't feel that I deserved compensation, but in hindsight I really did. If my application was successful, I would be allocated a payout amount, with specific allotments for medication, psychiatrist care, or psychologists/counsellors.

I was asked to seek submissions from professionals and people in my life who could accurately report the impact of the crimes on my life.

When I finally did go to fill out the application a couple of years after the trial, I felt quite overwhelmed by the paperwork, but did not feel sure about who to turn to. So I found myself searching for the contact details of a local victim's advocate. She herself had been abused and had been awarded a compensation payout. I asked her how to go about the paperwork and she recommended that I get a lawyer. So I ended up approaching a law firm that dealt with compensation matters.

I was young and naïve and if I had my time again I would not recommend going to a commercial law firm. When the final compensation payout came through, the law firm took $7000 of it! This could easily have been avoided if there had been more support available to me. However, at this point I was no longer connected with the local sexual assault service that had abruptly closed my file before the trial, and my Kids Helpline counsellor was based on the other side of the country so was not familiar with local departments and policies. My General Practitioner was great but rarely dealt with criminal injuries compensation so felt out of her depth. I had sporadic contact with Victim Mediation services.

I approached the sexual assault centre, who had known me since I was 16, to see if their counsellors could write a report to support my compensation claim. I received a terse letter back from the manager stating that it would cost me $770, payable regardless of whether or not I received any compensation. This was emphasised in bold print as follows:

Details of payment are:

$770.00 being payment for counselling report

$770.00 = TOTAL PAYMENT

*I understand that if **NO COMPENSATION** is awarded to me, **I am responsible for the payment as above** and will forward to SARC total payment without further delay.*

Signature: _____

Date:_____

Talk about a slap in the face! At that time in my life, I rarely had $770 in my bank account so I decided to just leave it and not get a report from them, even though I knew that it would have been very useful.

Fortunately, I was able to think of other people who I could approach to write reports. My General Practitioner Dr Camden, my friend Dani, my Kids Helpline counsellor Leah and a psychiatrist all offered to write a supporting report for free. I felt grateful for their generosity.

Here is what two of the reports said.

Submission one: From Leah at Kids Helpline

To whom it may concern,

My name is Leah and I have been Hannah's counsellor at Kids Helpline (the national counselling service for young people aged 5–25 years) since December of 2005, through her first disclosure of abuse, the subsequent disclosure to family and other counsellors, the reporting process to police, the court case against her father, and now during the aftermath of this process.

Over this time I have seen many reactions and traits in Hannah that are consistent with the effects of long term familial sexual abuse. As with many survivors of this kind of abuse, there are significant and at times disabling psychological, emotional and physical effects. In Hannah these effects have shown themselves to be:

- *Depression – ongoing and persistent feelings of self-loathing and hopelessness. Hannah sees herself as an "evil" person who has no redeeming qualities*

- *Suicidal ideation and actions – Hannah thinks about ending her life frequently and has researched and experimented with a number of methods.*

- *Self-harm – Hannah habitually hits, pins and chokes herself in an effort to block out memories, guilt, shame and overpowering feelings of being out of control.*

- *Dissociation – Hannah frequently 'drifts away', meaning that she finds herself distracted, heavy, unable to focus and physically paralysed. Her body and her mind seem to separate. It is a common coping strategy that children enlist when being sexually abused; while the body is being hurt, the child no longer feels it because their mind manages to escape to a safe place.*

- *Social isolation and relationship problems such as an inability to trust and a reluctance to disclose details. Hannah doesn't feel she is close to anyone.*

- *An underlying sense of anger, sadness and loss – Hannah feels intense anger against the perpetrator (although this is repressed significantly), and also against other family members and workers who she sees as failing to protect her. She also feels a great sadness and loss in her life, grieving for her loss of a 'real' family and a safe father.*

- *Suspicion and trust issues – Hannah finds it very difficult to trust anyone, particularly men. She believes that all men are likely to sexually abuse their children. This is likely to cause significant problems in forming friendships and romantic relationships with men for some time to come.*

- *Flashbacks and nightmares – Hannah often re-experiences the abuse in nightmares and flashbacks, and also has dreams and guilt and loss about her father being incarcerated. At times, these dreams can feel like being raped all over again.*

- *Guilt and shame – this effect can be paralysing for Hannah and is often the trigger for suicidal ideation and actions. Hannah feels intense shame and guilt as a result of a) the actual abuse, b) the messages told to her by her father for a long time i.e. that she wanted and deserved and lured him into a sexual 'relationship' and c) as a result of the incarceration of her father Hannah feels guilt as her father had always told her that she was the one at fault, that he was innocent and that she 'made him do it'.*

- *Powerlessness – echoing the common feelings of children experiencing abuse, Hannah often feels powerless to effect change in her life. Her peers are moving on into the adult world and Hannah feels she is being left behind. Developmentally, in relation to trust, sexuality, male and female roles and relationships – she is.*

- *Sensitivity to perceived rejection, criticism and abandonment – this sensitivity often manifests itself with Hannah being aggressive, judgemental, conflictual and sarcastic. Hannah can see any disagreement or change in a relationship as a rejection or criticism – confirming her worst fears of being the "evil child" her father convinced her she is. This can cause significant challenges in all relationships and keeps Hannah at arms' length from any intimate or close relationships or friendships.*

- *Physical ailments – again common effects of long term abuse are physical ailments such as headaches/migraines, insomnia, digestive problems and extreme tiredness/lethargy. Hannah is suffering and has suffered from each of these physical effects.*

Hannah is an extraordinary young woman with remarkable resilience, intelligence and strength of character. She has made remarkable and significant steps forward in the healing process. However, as well as attempting to deal with all the above effects of the abuse, Hannah has been trying to support herself financially. She has been supporting herself financially since she escaped from the abuse. Hannah has sought counselling and other medical services at her own cost. The criminal injuries compensation would go some way in assisting Hannah to access and pay for the help she needs to continue her recovery, which includes; ongoing counselling, medical interventions and psychiatric treatment.

Yours sincerely

Leah (Counsellor, Kids Helpline)

Submission two: from my good friend Dani

To whom it may concern,

I have known Hannah Baker since July 2006. I met her on campus at (name of university) in my role as a residential tutor. We have since become very good friends.

I believe that Hannah has been significantly affected by the offences committed. The following information aims to capture some of this.

Psychological: I believe Hannah's emotional development has been impacted. Although very strong, brave and independent, she possesses some child-like tendencies. I believe she finds peace in child activities such as colouring-in and fairies. She is revolted by violence and adult intimacy, to the extent that she is unable to watch television shows or movies which contain such themes.

In addition, I believe that Hannah shows signs of depression. She has said that it would be better to kill herself than keep going through the motions – but has also said that she is afraid of killing herself. It also appears that she despises and blames herself for everything that has happened. At times Hannah has been completely broken and just cried and cried.

When discussing the offences and related issues, she often seemingly separates herself from her environment and becomes vacant.

She is unable to cope with sudden changes and experiences substantial mood swings.

Financial: Before Hannah moved out of home in 2006, she worked and saved all of her earnings, so that she could support herself and move out. Since moving out of home, Hannah has received Youth Allowance, and supplements her earnings with the savings and income from part time work/ holiday jobs. She has managed to pay her living expenses. In addition she has sometimes had to pay for medical or counselling expenses. Her financial position has impacted on her ability to pay for the care she requires. When her HECS falls due, she will also have to pay for additional units which she failed when legal proceedings commenced.

Impact on relationships with family, friends and colleagues

Immediate family: Hannah has a very strained relationship with her mother and sister. She is not able to trust her mother and finds it difficult to relate to her sister. As a result, neither relationship has been able to provide Hannah with support during the period when the offences were committed, or during legal proceedings. Hannah has not seen her father since 2007 and continually blames herself for what has happened, including his prison sentence.

Friends: Hannah often finds it difficult to relate to friends her own age, most of whom have boyfriends and are engaging in adult activities. She also has difficulty trusting friends and does not want to be a burden on them. In addition, she pushes people away to protect herself as she does not want to become heavily dependent on others who might:

- *let her down;*

- *cause her harm; or*

- *unsettle her routine (routine and planning provides her with some stability)*

Daily activities: Since I have known Hannah, she has had difficulty sleeping (especially in unfamiliar places). When she eventually falls asleep she almost always has horrific nightmares.

The medication prescribed to Hannah to help deal with the emotional/psychological impacts has caused her to gain weight which has further affected her self-esteem/self-hatred.

Hannah has trouble seeing people who look like her father. There are also some locations that remind her of the offences. Subsequently, she tries to avoid seeing such men and avoids going to these places.

By having to save all her money to support herself, Hannah has not been able to live the life of a care-free teenager. She has not been able to afford many new clothes, or go out or on holidays like other young girls around her.

Dani Whitley

These reports were sent directly to the criminal injuries compensation department, not me, so I only read them during later appeal hearings. It was difficult to read them but they were completely accurate – I think that was what made them hard to read. There are not many people in the world who knew me and my difficulties as well as those two people.

With criminal injuries compensation, at least in my case, the state was meant to pay half of it, and if he was able to, Dad was supposed to pay the other half. My dad was clearly capable of spending bucket-loads of money on defence lawyers for himself, so it didn't seem that it would be too hard for him to pay half of it. However, he simply did not want to.

I remember it clearly – coming home on a Friday afternoon in the first week of September 2011, to a rather sinister looking envelope in the mail. Hmm. I opened it and saw it was from a government legal department. I quickly scanned it, initially not thinking much of it. I couldn't quite take in what I was reading. The letter stated that there was an appeal filed in the district court and that I was the defendant. I put the letter away for a few minutes, then pulled it out again. The letter even contained links to legal websites about "Representing Yourself". I just couldn't quite get my head around it.

Here's what had happened: Dad had found a way to appeal the Criminal Injuries Compensation by launching civil legal action against me. A convicted paedophile was given the right to attempt to sue his victim. To this day, I do not understand how this was allowed to happen.

I was informed that I would have to appear in court. Dad had also managed to attach a letter to me, as an 'Appendix' of the appeal documents he lodged. Talk about sneaky. I was shocked that he got away with it.

Here is what Dad's letter said.

24 October 2010

Hi Hannah,

At the outset, I do apologise that the letter is very formal. It has to be unfortunately, as the letter is going through formal channels. This letter is a follow up to our meeting on 26 June.

I received a phone call from your mum on 1 July, which was about five days after our meeting. No doubt, at that time, you were recovering from your wisdom teeth operation. During the call, your mum told me that she knew about your visit to me. I presumed you had told your mum about the visit. Therefore, I decided to communicate with your mum regarding your wellbeing, as it concerns me greatly.

I sent the enclosed two letters to your mum regarding your wellbeing. To date, I have not received a reply to either of the letters.

I have also received a letter from the Criminal Injuries Compensation Board regarding your claim. This was a surprise to me, given the discussions during your visit to me on 26 June 2010. During the visit, you told me, amongst other things that

a. I was a good person.

b. You were not certain whether the allegations you made against me had happened or not.

c. Some days you were certain that they had happened and some days you were uncertain that they happened.

d. You had discussed these doubts with your counsellor.

Can you please confirm in writing to me that this is, in essence, what you told me?

I have written to the Criminal Injuries Compensation Board requesting that they defer consideration of the claim, until I receive an answer from you to the above questions.

If you wish to see me regarding any issues, I am available to meet.

I await your reply.

Dad.

Dad's appeal was nonsensical. He had attached several rambling appendixes with his personal opinion on how the compensation process should be carried out, and used legal language to try and make himself sound official. Statements included:

> *"I request that you suspend processing of the claim until I receive a reply from Hannah to my letter."*

> *"If the Respondent is not certain whether the allegations she made against me took place or not, she can't make a compensation claim".*

> *"I have not received a reply to my letter of 24 October 2010."*

> *"Final payment of the compensation claim is to be deferred until the Respondent replies in writing under oath to my letter to her dated 24 October 2010."*

The court documents gave a pretty good insight into my dad's controlling nature.

As I began to fully grasp the situation, I felt sick. It was about 4:30pm on a Friday afternoon, so I attempted calling the government department that had sent the letter, the State Solicitor's Office. I was answered by a very uncompassionate woman named Andrea who clearly did not want to help anyone this late on a Friday afternoon – she wanted her early knock off! There was nothing I could have asked her without receiving the same response: (*Exasperated sigh*) "I am not able to provide further information". It was amazing how quickly I had gone from being the victim of a crime, to the defendant.

With a complete lack of information at my finger tips, I was left with many unanswered questions until the following week. It was a horrible weekend. Ironically, on the Sunday it was Father's Day. I developed a terrible migraine, as well as sharp stabbing pains in my stomach that made it difficult to move.

The following Monday I went into action with phone calls to get as much information as possible so I could understand what was going on. I was surprised to discover that the appeal had actually been sitting in the system for close to a year before I was even alerted to it. When I dared to ask Andrea at the State Solicitor's Office about this delay, she actually blamed me, for not ensuring that their office had my current contact details. I remember thinking, "I'm sorry, I didn't realise it is my civic duty to ensure that a government department I have never even heard of, has my current contact details just in case someone decides to sue me." It also highlighted to me the lack of communication between departments, because the Victim Offender Mediation Unit always had my current contact information and would have seemed a logical first port of call for an appeal in a criminal matter.

I went through all my phone credit in a day trying to figure out what was going on and realised that I would have to sign up for a different phone plan! One of my first ports of call was Jodi, the detective who had originally handled my case. I went in to see her, which was very reassuring because she helped to put me in touch with the right people. I also spoke to my friend Dani, who put me in touch with a lawyer friend of hers who worked for a large commercial firm and amazingly agreed to be my lawyer pro-bono. It was so very generous of her, and I really appreciated it.

I then sent an email to the State Solicitor's Office, as I'd had no luck whatsoever on the phone. In my email, I CC'd as many important people as I could – including Jodi; a lady from corrective services; and a senior lawyer who had handled the original appeal and been approachable. This senior lawyer emailed me back very quickly to say that he was on leave but still had access to emails, and also gave me his mobile number in case anything urgent came up. This was very generous, and showed me that there are some extremely kind and compassionate people working within the legal system.

If push had come to shove, I would have gone to the media at this point, because I firstly think it is disgraceful that criminals are allowed to appeal against their victims being compensated, and secondly, that he was able to attach correspondence to me with the appeal. I also think it is shocking that a victim of crime can be forced to get a lawyer and defend themselves in a civil case brought about by someone who has committed a crime against them – a convicted paedophile, no less. This is just outrageous. I was very relieved to speak with Leah at Kids Helpline, a familiar person who knew me well. She was as shocked as I was, and tried to do some ringing around to government departments to find out how this had been allowed to happen. She had never heard of a criminal appealing a victim's criminal injuries compensation claim. Jodi said that she had never heard of someone successfully appealing against their victim's compensation claim, and that usually appeals were simply because the criminal couldn't afford to pay the costs. This was much more malicious than that – Dad was appealing on the grounds that he didn't think I deserved compensation.

Once I had gotten a few people involved and alerted them to the situation, things started to roll in my favour. It's sad that sometimes you need to involve powerful people to be listened to, but I was lucky to have enough 'powerful' people willing to stand in my corner. Jodi offered to come and sit with me in the hearing which again was very generous of her. The lawyer working pro-bono on the case put a lot of effort into making sure that the appeal would be quashed as soon as possible. The whole thing dragged on for three long weeks and was due to be heard in the District Court in late September 2011.

Submissions had to be made by both sides a couple of days before the hearing. Dad submitted an outline containing his personal opinion on what compensation money should be awarded to me. Here is an excerpt from the court documents.

> *In his written submissions filed in support of the appeal, Mr Baker sought the following orders:*
>
> *1. Hannah be given 28 days to confirm whether or not she agrees with statement (a) to (c) of my letter of 24th October 2010.*
>
> *2. If Hannah replies under oath within the time limit, either orally or in writing,*
>
> *2.1 and agrees with any of the statements (a) to (c) of my letter of 24th October 2010, then the total compensation amount and the amount payable by me should be reduced, or,*
>
> *2.2 and disagrees with all of the statements (a) to (c) of my letter of 24th October 2010, then the total compensation amount payable by me should remain as is.*
>
> *3. If Hannah does not reply under oath within the time limit, then the total compensation amount payable by me should be reduced to zero.*

My lawyer put in a submission which simply stated that my dad had been convicted of several offences, and that I was therefore entitled to compensation.

Dad was probably a bit surprised that I had gotten a lawyer, and realising that he was pretty well screwed and never going to win this one, he tried to withdraw the appeal the day before the hearing. I think he must have realised that this malicious behaviour towards me was not going to look good on his file when he applied for parole in 18 months' time. However, the judge would not allow him to withdraw it, and made sure it went down on his record.

On the day of the hearing, it was lashing rain as I went in to the city on the bus, by myself. I had gotten to the point of not wanting to ask my Aunty Susie or close friends to come with me to anything like that, because I had been through so many hearings and difficult things that I felt I was wearing those few trusted people thin.

The appeal was dismissed in just a few short minutes. Dad was not present. I had a coffee with Jodi and the lawyer, Bree, in the District Court cafe – the same cafe I had been at during the original trial in 2008. I felt I was becoming an 'old hand' at this court stuff. I was so blasé about it that I caught the bus home, then headed to a tutorial at uni that afternoon.

The timing of the appeal had been really dreadful, because my honours thesis was due in mid-October. By late August, everyone was already incredibly stressed — now try throwing an unexpected court hearing into the mix! The honours thesis was to be followed by an intense two months of course work and a final exam. It was a very stressful year for everyone in my course. Of the 12 of us doing honours in addition to our regular coursework, three people needed to get extensions. I am proud to say that I was not one of them, despite the legal hearings and their impact on me. I still managed to get my thesis in a couple of days early, and put in a great effort for the rest of my uni work. I am proud to say that I ended up graduating uni with "First Class Honours".

However, it was at this time that I decided that there was no future for me in my home state, and started making plans to leave. I applied for jobs interstate, and had signed on to a new job before I even finished my course. Less than 10 days after my last day of university, I chucked as much stuff in my small car as I could, and left my hometown. I literally moved to the other side of the country. If there were any more appeals I was expected to attend, I would do it at the state government's expense, thank you very much!

A NEW LIFE

In January 2012, I was a uni graduate, embarking on life in a new state. I did not know a single soul when I arrived in my new hometown, and that didn't actually bother me. I was so exhausted and burned out from the previous few years that I just needed to veg out.

I had a few weeks to settle in before starting work, and it's fair to say that these weeks were very lazy. I was renting a small unit by myself – I had had enough of share houses and really needed some peace and quiet. The only furniture I had was a bed, and I had brought a TV with me. I set to work on putting together some flat pack furniture, including a table and a bedside locker (which I'm ashamed to say took me hours to put together!). I soon decided that a priority for me was to buy a couch. So I did that and voila – endless days of lazy lying on the couch, watching old and comforting movies and TV shows. I decided that this would be as good a time as any to come off my antidepressant medication so I did – I tapered off it gradually, and did pretty well for someone who had been on antidepressants for six years. I was proud of myself.

By this point, I was still talking to Leah at Kids Helpline, but not as often as I used to because Leah's role at Kids Helpline had changed and she wasn't on the phones much anymore. Since September 2011, I had gradually started speaking with another counsellor there called Brooke. It came about quite randomly. Leah had had several changes in her shifts, and when I called up yet another time only to be told she wasn't there, I was really upset. Brooke was the counsellor who had answered my call, and instead of dismissing me or telling me to wait until Leah was back, she let me talk it through with her and explain why I struggled so much with all the changes in Leah's shifts, and the feelings of rejection that came with them.

Learning to trust Brooke worked out really well for me, because over the years I had come to trust and rely on Leah so much that I found it hard to talk to other people. Leah shared all my information with Brooke, and in time I found that I felt more and more comfortable with her. Within six months, I tended to speak to Brooke more often than Leah, and was able to talk to her about the exact same things that previously would have been too embarrassing to talk to anyone about, other than Leah. It was a great team effort, and in the long-term has been very beneficial to me.

After my success with Brooke, I felt confident enough to 'really try' at face-to-face counselling, no cut and run this time. So I started seeing a counsellor called Libby, who I felt comfortable with instantly. Leah at Kids Helpline provided Libby with a thorough handover of information so that I didn't have to start from scratch, and throughout my time working with Libby, Brooke and Leah stayed in touch with her to make sure they were all on the same page. It took a few months for me to really trust Libby, but after that, we were able to talk about all the things that had happened to me, right down to the really embarrassing details. I had never before gotten to that point with a face-to-face counsellor, where I felt comfortable enough to talk about the details of what happened. And for me, that has been an essential thing to do, to be able to move on. It is very different to sit in a courtroom and recite the facts of what happened, compared to telling someone what happened and how you actually feel about it.

I saw Libby once a week or fortnight over a period of 18 months. We achieved so much in that time, and I will forever be grateful. In Part 3 of this book, I will go into more detail about the things we worked on, because I think this information would be useful for others who know someone who has experienced trauma. Though Libby and I have now parted ways, I do hope to bump into her in the future, or even to drop her a line every now and then. Even better, it would be great if I could tell her that my life has worked out well

Painting by
Sarah Millicent Elliott

Life chugged along for me fairly well in my new life interstate. I quickly made some great new friends, many of whom were also from other parts of Australia. I had lots of people to go with on weekend road trips, to go for a walk or run after work, or go to the movies or anything else. As my confidence in my abilities at work increased, I started to have more energy to do things outside of work. I joined a sporting club, and then started learning a new language. I became part of a pub trivia team on Tuesdays, and regularly went out for Friday night or weekend drinks. I even went to tennis lessons for a while – which I had never tried before! I was really starting to enjoy life and make the most of things. By about September 2012, I was the happiest I had been in.... well... ever. I really felt like I was blossoming.

PAROLE

On Friday October 26th 2012, I was out having after-work drinks, to celebrate with one of our colleagues who was moving away. I came home feeling happy and relaxed. On my way in, grabbed my mail from the letter box. And there it was – a letter from the parole board. The letter informed me that on January 23rd 2013, a hearing would be held to determine whether or not my dad would be granted parole in February 2013.

To me, this letter was a complete bolt out of the blue, especially since I was reading it late on a Friday night. I couldn't get to sleep that night, and the next day I was very nauseous. I had been planning on doing some things with friends, but cancelled out on everything. I just wanted to recluse and be by myself. It was a real mix of emotions for me. Here is a diary entry that captures it:

> *"If he gets parole, he will get out on February 10th 2013. That is soon and will mean he's served 4.5 years. I suppose that's okay. The sooner he's out, the easier it will be for me. I hate thinking of him being in jail because of me. I know I was doing the best I could when I went to the police – it was that or kill myself. I don't always think I made the right choice."*

The following week I spoke to Brooke at Kids Helpline. I talked about the letter I had received, and said "I'm not ready for a parole hearing!" She had not really heard me cry before, but this day I was sobbing, telling her how overwhelmed and suicidal I was feeling.

It really felt as if I had only just 'gotten out' of the legal system – the last appeal had only been thrown out 13 months earlier. For all of those years, I had been dragged through an unforgiving and difficult system, and now I had to face even more? It seemed too much. It really began to get to me, and made me physically ill, to the point that I had to take a day off work.

On my day off, I decided to be proactive and try and help myself to feel better, by arming myself with information. I tried contacting the parole board to get more information about the parole process and to try and find out how likely it was that Dad would get parole. I had no luck getting through to the board so instead spoke to a couple of people at victim's services and the prison authority. Both said that from all accounts it appeared very unlikely that Dad would get parole, because he had not shown any remorse and had refused to do the sex offender's treatment program. This was a relief to me, and the next day I returned to work feeling happy and reassured. I put in an application for annual leave for January 23rd, so that I would have the space I needed to cope with the parole decision. I knew that it was a day that would bring up some emotions for me, even though it was unlikely that he would get parole.

In early December, as usual, on a Friday afternoon, I got home from work to a letter in the mailbox. With the O.H.M.S. stamp, I immediately recognised who it was from. I could barely bring myself to open it – I stalled for about 10 minutes. When I opened it, the letter stated abruptly that the hearing date had changed, and would now occur 'on or about January 30th'. This might not seem like a big change, but to me it was a really big deal. How could they change it? It felt like the rug was being ripped out from underneath me. Now I would have to wait even longer to find out whether he was getting parole or not, and I would have to go to my boss at work and have my leave dates changed. I tried calling up the parole board (again, no response), so spoke to someone in the prison services who was not very compassionate at all: "To be honest, they deal with many cases each week, yours is one of many, so changes can and will happen". I ended up writing a letter to the board saying how extremely anxious I had become, and they did in fact respond, saying that they would try to not change the date again.

The hearing was held on Wednesday January 30th. I had been so anxious in the lead-up to it, that I couldn't wait for it to be over. I was fairly certain that I knew what the outcome would be – that Dad would not get parole. How could he? He had shown no remorse whatsoever – as evidenced by his appeals. There was no way he could get parole.

At about 4:30pm, I got the much anticipated phone call. I was at work, and went into an empty room. I hadn't bothered to bring anything to write on, because I really expected a simple call to say 'Nope, he's not getting parole'. However, it soon became clear that it was not so simple. The lady from Victim Services, Pam, called me and said that the decision had been postponed until March the 6th. My heart sank. More waiting. The legal system is all about waiting, isn't it?

I searched around the room for something to write on, and started scrawling messy notes on a tissue, with a coloured marker.

I asked why they were postponing it and this is when I got the biggest shock. Pam said that it was because Dad's accommodation plan was inappropriate. "Okay... what does that mean?" I asked. She explained that Dad had applied to move in with a woman (the one who I referred to as "Blondie", aka Gertrude). The problem was that she had children and a person with a disability who visited or lived at her home (the information was limited). I was lost for words. In my head, I had always been worried about Dad having nobody in the world who cared about him, and here he was, apparently quite comfortable moving in with this lady friend of his. I couldn't understand why she would want to live with him. She had been at the trial, so she knew the nature of his convictions.

She had visited him in jail. She had never met or spoken to me. So why did she stand by him like that? I will never really know. One thing I do know is that I feel very concerned for the children in her life, whoever they are.

Over the next couple of days I felt like I was in mourning again. I am not sure why. I was just gutted that Dad had found it so easy to move on, while here I was still with all these problems. It didn't seem right! I could never easily move on and set up a new life! So why was it so easy for him? It was really hard to deal with. I was barely sleeping, but still forced myself to go to work the day after the hearing, because there was to be a farewell lunch for a much loved staff member and I didn't want to let my workmates down. Thankfully, I was able to take annual leave on Friday the 1st of February.

The next five weeks waiting for the board's decision were sheer hell. I was holding it together at work, but at home collapsing in a heap and feeling really, really depressed and anxious. The time went so slowly, other than the one weekend I went away with a few workmates — we stayed in a small cottage near the beach and it was a nice distraction for me.

During the week of the hearing I was incredibly anxious. Things that wouldn't normally have stressed me out too much became a major issue. a good friend asked me if I could drop her at the airport at a time that would have been easy and convenient for me to do so, but I said no. The thought of it was too stressful, too much planning for my already exhausted brain. I could manage to get myself to work every day but that was about it — I wasn't eating or sleeping properly, and didn't want to do anything social.

Finally, Wednesday March 6th rolled around. I had to work the day of the hearing, and also the following day (the Thursday). I was due to be flying back to my home town that Friday (March 8th) — it was to be my first visit in 12 months and had been booked in December, well before I had any idea that a parole hearing would be occurring that very week. I had booked a week of annual leave, and made plans to catch up with friends and relatives during this time, as well as attending a course that was relevant to my work.

Again, at about 4:30pm on the Wednesday afternoon, news of the decision came through.

The news was completely unexpected... Dad was going to get parole.

He was to be released from prison on the morning of Friday March 8th, the day I was flying back to my home town. I could not believe how unlucky the timing was. It was just awful.

I was then informed that the reason for parole being granted was that Dad had amended his accommodation plan – he and Gertrude had promised that the children mentioned in the previous plan would never visit her house. Shockingly, this plan had been accepted. Dad was to be a free man in less than 48 hours. This was despite not completing the sex offender's treatment program, showing no remorse for his crimes, and appealing against and harassing his victim.

I was absolutely stunned by this decision, and went into shut-down mode. I went to work on the Thursday but may as well not have been there, because I was very distracted (and had diarrhoea). It was very difficult to even contemplate going back to my hometown because I wasn't in the headspace to see family or friends – I knew that I wouldn't tell most of them what had happened with parole. I realised that my visit to my hometown would be exhausting, that I would be glossing over what was really going on, and pretending that everything was fine. But my annual leave, flights and course had been booked ages ago, so I really had to go.

I did end up going, and just tried not to think about Dad and the parole situation too much. I stayed at my Aunt's house which was good because it did give me a chance to debrief a bit about what was going on. During the week I experienced nausea, poor sleep and other anxiety symptoms, and I was relieved to get back on the plane at the end of the week.

After that it took me several months to really process the fact that Dad had been handed parole so easily. I don't think 4.5 years in prison is a very long sentence for the crimes committed, but I am relieved that I am no longer being thrown around in that awful legal system, waiting for hearing dates and appeals.

THE END OF PAROLE

Life during Dad's parole period ticked along without too much drama. I knew which agency to contact (the Victim Notification Register) if I had any questions about him and generally if I was proactive and went and asked them the right questions, they would answer them. Generally, I did have to push them for information. I am a proactive person so I was able to make it work, but for others who are less confident at reading or speaking on the phone, I do not know how they would navigate the system.

For example, in early 2014, I received a letter from the Register to state that Dad was still on parole for another year and that his reporting station had changed. I did not realise that the sentence about the 'reporting station' was significant so did not think to chase them up for further information. Eight months later, I had to call them up to ask them another question and thought I would query them about the reporting station. As it turned out, my dad had moved and was now living in the area that I had been living in until the end of 2011. They couldn't confirm the exact suburb of course, because as I was constantly told, offenders have a right to privacy. When I had visited my home town recently, I had actually stayed at a friend's house in that area, without realising that Dad could have been living next door! I could easily have bumped into him at the shops. I don't understand why the Victim Notification Register does not give transparent information to victims instead of making them chase up the details. Not everybody has the capacity to read between the lines, be extremely intuitive about what questions to ask, or advocate for themselves.

As I sit writing this now, it is February 2015 and my dad's parole period ends in just two days. I am fortunate enough to have a great memory for dates because I certainly have not received any information in the last few months from any government departments to confirm this date or what it will mean. I expect that I will receive a formal letter at some point to inform me that the parole period has ended but there have been zero offers of preparation or planning for how I will cope once Dad is finished parole. I have very little idea what his rights are or what monitoring will apply to him. As far as I am aware, he is free to travel interstate as he pleases once the parole period ends. I am assuming he will be placed on a Sex Offender's register but again, this has not been clarified for me and I don't know what his reporting responsibilities will be.

I also have no idea whether I will receive any information about my dad from now on, for example if he passes away or is terminally ill. While he was on parole I knew that I would receive that sort of information, but now I will have no idea. This is really significant to me, because he is still my parent after all. I again feel a huge sense of grief and loss as I start to comprehend that I really won't know what happens to my dad from here. If you haven't been in this situation I suppose it is hard to understand. But despite everything that has happened to me, I would feel devastated to know that my dad had been in a car accident or had a stroke, and that I hadn't provided any support. I would feel like a horrible person. I guess this shows you just how confusing abuse is when it happens in families. It is impossible to completely stop thinking or caring about someone, no matter how much they have hurt you.

I have also suddenly become very anxious as the parole period comes to an end, as evidenced by the nightmares I have been having. I have been letting my dog sleep on my bed every night to help ease my fears. For the last few years I have felt safe knowing that I live interstate and that Dad was unable to travel while he was on parole. Also, while he was on parole there was an automatic no-contact order in place. However, this expires the day that his parole ends. There is no protection in place for me, and I have not had anybody from my home state make any effort to support me to find a solution. Once again I find myself grappling with fear and uncertainty. I recently spent a Friday afternoon talking to local police in my new home state about restraining orders, but as it turns out, there are no national orders. Restraining orders only apply in the state of which you are a resident. So, if I were to go and get a restraining order against Dad now, I would have to get it signed off in a court house in my new home town, which would be a dead giveaway to Dad about which town and state I now live in, because the order would come via the police in the state I now reside in. If you ask me, this totally defeats the purpose, and the police officer I was speaking to could see my point of view. Off the cuff, I was advised that the best approach would be to wait until Dad contacts me or until I feel sure that he knows where I live, and then get a restraining order done here. Talk about a flawed system.

Once again, I feel alone and unsupported, to deal with the legacy of the abuse and the systems that do not seem to offer much protection or humanity.

Addition: a luke-warm farewell from the criminal justice system

Two weeks after Dad's parole ended, I finally received a much-anticipated letter from the Victim Notification Register, which is part of the Department of Corrective Services. I had hoped that it might contain some information for me about Dad's reporting requirements, protection in place for me, even some offer of support. Instead, I received a letter which failed to give me ONE useful piece of information, and reeked of political correctness ("We value your feedback…!).

Here is what the letter said:

Dear Miss Baker,

Please be advised that in relation to Peter Baker:

Mr Baker has now completed the term of his Order and as such your registration with this service is now concluded.

I trust that this service has been of some value to you and I would appreciate it if you would complete the attached short questionnaire and return it to the Manager VNR in the enclosed self-addressed envelope. This is so that we can monitor the service we provide to victims of crime and work towards improving it.

Yours sincerely,

Karina P.

Registrar

Victim Notification Register (VNR)

17/02/2015

And with that, a letter as callous as what one might expect when they cancel a gym membership, I was out of the system. Eight long years in that dehumanising system had taught me to not expect much more.

There is nothing wrong with surveys and self-addressed envelopes, but when they're attached to such a pitiful, uncompassionate letter received on the back of an horrendous journey through the criminal justice system, I can't imagine that they really expect many responses.

The thoughts running through my head when I read this letter included:

"Do you have any idea what I have been through? How many years of my life I have lost to these systems, years in which I should have been living a young, carefree life?"

"Do you have any idea how much pain I have endured? How much indignity I have suffered?"

"Do you actually care?"

I showed the letter to a friend of mine who has also experienced sexual abuse. She referred to the writer as 'Ms Ice-Cold' which gave me a giggle.

It took me a few days to process the upset feelings I had after receiving that letter. Thanks to some helpful contacts and persistent questioning, I then did my best to follow up with government departments including the Sex Offenders Management Unit to get information about my dad. The police officer I spoke to there was very nice, however, she simply was not allowed to provide me with any information. I could tell that she genuinely wanted to help me, but answering my questions would have been in breach of the very strict laws which protect a sex offender's right to privacy. If she had answered them, she herself would have been committing an offence.

My questions included:

"So can you confirm for me what area Dad is now living in?" No

"Can you confirm for me whether Dad is working and where?" No

"Will you tell me if he travels interstate to where I am living?" No

"Will you tell me if he passes away?" (long pause)... Probably not

"So what can you tell me?" We're unable to release any information about the offender.

The police officer was really making an effort to be nice to me and said to please call her back if I had any questions and I couldn't help responding bluntly: "But you won't answer my questions, you won't tell me anything, so why on earth would I ever call you back?". She conceded that I was right.

I've heard professionals say in my home state of Western Australia (WA) that the state is "at the forefront" of victim support services. After all that I have been through, I am extremely unconvinced. I think it is great that there is now a Commissioner for Victims of Crime in Western Australia, and I've met her and think highly of her. However, it is going to take so much more than one person to create system change. There needs to be a stronger commitment from the government to improve the experiences of vulnerable victims of crime – particularly children and young people.

PART THREE:
ONGOING DIFFICULTIES

Painting by
Sarah Millicent Elliott

On and on you will hike
And I know you'll hike far
And face up to your problems
Whatever they are

(Dr Seuss, in *Oh the Places You'll Go*)

INTRODUCTION

Despite the abuse ending a few years ago and the legal process now being complete, I face many ongoing difficulties. I have sought professional support where possible to help me to overcome these issues, to give myself the best possible chance of having the future I want. But at times, I feel depressed and hopeless about how many things I still struggle with.

Some of the ongoing difficulties that I will explore further in this section include:

- Sleep difficulties, flashbacks and intrusive memories

- Dissociation

- Anxiety and depression

- Intense feelings

- Relationship and trust difficulties

- Impact on my work and living situation

I am also going to include information about some of the things that have helped me to reduce these difficulties, that I have worked on in counselling.

It is my hope that some of the very honest information I have included will help those who have experienced abuse, and their supporters.

I also hope that by reading about these ongoing effects, you will again see the importance of helping to prevent child abuse and providing adequate support when it does occur.

SLEEP DIFFICULTIES, FLASHBACKS AND INTRUSIVE MEMORIES

One of the nasty impacts of the abuse for me has been ongoing sleep difficulties, flashbacks and intrusive memories. These can have a major impact on my ability to function, and can come from completely out of the blue.

Sleep difficulties and the impact of ill-informed comments

Ever since I was a kid, I have had major difficulties with sleep – which makes a lot of sense, because what child is going to fall asleep easily when they know they might be abused in their own bed? At night, I am still extremely sensitive to noise, which was a major difficulty in the unit I was living in until recently – I could often hear neighbours walking around on the shared floor boards, and people coming in and out of their front doors. Because of this, I needed to wear earplugs most nights. You wouldn't believe how much money I have spent on earplugs over the years!

For several years I have been on a medication that I take each night to help me sleep. This medication does have some side effects, including that it initially made me put on weight which I've had to work hard to keep off. It also makes me very slow and lethargic in the morning, and generally knocks me out to the point of needing nine hours sleep per night. This means I usually have to get to bed quite early, otherwise I can't function the next day. However, the benefits do outweigh the costs, because without proper sleep, I become extremely depressed and struggle to function.

I have had people make comments about me being on sleep medication and give their opinion ("haven't you tried camomile tea?") which is well meaning, but not really their place to do so. They do not understand the severity of my sleep difficulties. I went to a General Practitioner in mid-2013 who said that "a young girl like you shouldn't need to be on this sleep medication". Despite me trying to explain to her the trauma I had experienced, this GP did not seem to want to hear it. I felt major pressure to come off the medication. She had really hit a sore spot for me, which is my hatred of feeling 'different' from other people my age. Of course, I wanted to be normal! I wanted to be like other people my age! Hell, I was going to come off the sleep medication, no problem! What followed was a disastrous few months.

Firstly, I tried coming off my sleep medication by halving the dose. I had a lot more difficulty getting to sleep than usual but persisted, until I got a really bad cold due to being so run down. I went back to my full dose for another week, until I was better. After that, I really persisted with cutting down the sleep medication again. I was on a mission – I was going to be normal! I even made a chart to record the amount (or lack) of sleep that I was getting each night and dutifully filled it out every day for almost three months. Talk about commitment to the cause! The problem was, it was taking me hours to fall asleep each night, and I was waking up really early. Usually I would fall asleep, wake up again after an hour, then wake intermittently throughout the night, before fully waking up at 4:30am or 5am. My body just did not know how to sleep without medication to help it.

Within a month, I was so run down that I was extremely depressed. I ended up being put on anti-depressants again (which I had proudly been off for 18 months) but it was a new antidepressant which did not agree with me – I became extremely nauseous over a period of weeks. It was particularly bad at night when I wasn't moving around. I felt so sick that I had to have crackers beside my bed to nibble on during the night. I had to have a day off work due to nausea, but other than that I pushed through, albeit being very distractible. I lost weight during this time and felt absolutely dreadful. I had to come off the antidepressants after five weeks because they continued to make me really sick, and had other side effects including muscle spasms and heart palpitations. Coming off the antidepressants made my mood even worse. I became incredibly suicidal, partly due to sheer exhaustion. I was snappier than usual with my colleagues. I would literally go to work, hold it together, then collapse onto the couch as soon as I got home. I was unable to do anything social or attend my sports club. I started dissociating heavily, which I think was largely due to the lack of sleep.

In the end, after going and seeking the opinion of another General Practitioner and having conversations with a very concerned Leah and Brooke at Kids Helpline, I decided to just go back on my original sleep medication. Within a few days I was feeling much, much better. It was a horrendous three month journey, but at least it has made me realise just how much I do need to be on that sleep medication for now. I will just have to ignore other peoples' ill-informed opinions on that.

Nightmares

Nightmares are another difficulty that I continue to face, but they have eased up over time. After first moving out of home, I tended to have nightmares all the time. But now, they are more sporadic and I tend to have only a couple each week, with an occasional bad patch where they are more frequent.

Nightmares can range from seeing incidents that happened during the abuse, to having confusing situations where Dad comes to see me (as an adult) and I suddenly realise he is really angry at me for getting him put in jail. I have also had several nightmares where I am back living with my parents in the original family home, and am scared about what is going to happen to me when I am left alone with Dad. All of these nightmares are unsettling but they happen so often that I have learned to cope with them.

One thing that I have found impacts on nightmares is medication. When I am on a high dose of sleep medication, I find it harder to wake up from nightmares and can therefore get 'locked in' to a scary nightmare, unable to wake myself up. It is a terrifying sensation of not being able to open my eyes and having to keep experiencing the nightmare. When I do finally wake up, I often feel very confused – for a while I forget how old I am, and even which state I am living in.

When I wake up from a nightmare in the middle of the night, I try to get up or put a bedside light on for a bit, re-orient myself to the present day, then go back to sleep. Sometimes, it helps to have a little notepad by my bed, so that I can write the bad dream down and get it out of my head. Then I can discuss it later with a counsellor if I need to. Embarrassingly, I still sleep with a stuffed toy. Even though I know that's immature for my age, it helps to get me through.

Intrusive memories and flashbacks

Intrusive memories and flashbacks are also ongoing issues for me. Generally, I have a lot more intrusive memories than flashbacks.

In my experience, people tend to use the word 'flashback' a bit loosely, and don't understand its true meaning. From my experience, there are major differences between intrusive memories and flashbacks. I will try to explain them to you.

To me, an intrusive memory is similar to a nightmare, but occurs during the day. It is when you can see the abuse (either snapshots or a 'film'), or hear the sounds you heard during the abuse, but you are still able to ground yourself in the present day and know that it is just a memory. For me, these happen quite regularly (most likely every day) but again, are so normal to me that I have learned to cope with them. They can happen at any time – at work, when I'm out with friends, or when I am by myself. I have learned to re-focus my attention and not get too stuck in them.

In contrast, flashbacks are much more severe, and have a major impact on my ability to function. a flashback is when you re-experience the trauma, to the point that you really feel like you are back there, and that you are the age you were when the incident occurred. You lose track of the present-day, and find it hard to move or open your eyes. This is when heavy dissociation occurs, which will be explored in more detail shortly. In the past 12 months, I have had two bouts of major flashbacks, which were both horrible.

For me, situations that are likely to trigger intrusive memories or flashbacks include:

- Noises that remind me of the abuse e.g. heavy breathing, hearing people having sex, footsteps at night

- People I don't trust getting really close to me or breathing on me, particularly males

- Movies or TV shows with sex scenes

- Comedy with crude sexual undertones

- People talking about sex

An example of flashbacks and the impact on my life

To give you a real picture of what flashbacks are like and how much they can impact on a person, I will give you an example of a bout of flashbacks I experienced in late 2012. I had decided to spend a long weekend in a different town, by myself. I opted to stay at a backpackers, reasoning that this would be good practice for me, because for years I had been dreaming of doing a big overseas backpacking trip around Europe.

Shortly after arriving at the backpackers, I used my regular earplugs and sleeping tablets to try and settle to sleep. However, before I had a chance to fall asleep, I could hear people on the other side of me having sex. I knew that I was unable to drive anywhere or leave, because I had already taken my sleeping tablets. I was trapped. It was a horrible feeling. What followed was a night of zero hours sleep, and seven hours worth of horrendous flashbacks. I felt like I was raped several times over that night. I felt like I was about 10 years old, and was having flashbacks of a particularly bad incident. In my head, I could see, feel and hear myself being raped. It was very, very distressing.

At 6am the next morning, I packed up my stuff and left, instead of staying the extra two nights I had planned. All I wanted was to go home, and forget about what had 'happened' – because I really did feel as if I had been raped. When I got home, I washed everything I had been wearing and that I had brought with me. I needed everything to be clean.

It took ages for those flashbacks to go away. For about six months, whenever I heard a creaking noise that reminded me of the creaky bed in the backpackers, I would again be stuck in the flashbacks. I went back to needing earplugs every single night in my own home, to block out any noises outside such as a shed creaking in the wind. Earplugs weren't always enough, so then I got some heavy duty ear muffs to wear as well. The ear muffs were good at blocking out sound but not good for sleeping, because you can't roll over when you're wearing them without waking up. I then also tried getting a white noise app on my phone which gave me soothing music or rain sounds to fall asleep to, and that helped a bit. I had to increase my sleeping medication, and it was several months before I could reduce it again.

The unfortunate thing I realised after this incident was that it is possible to have flashbacks of flashbacks. How unlucky is that? The next time I tried staying in a motel in a different city, I started having flashbacks of the backpacker's place I had stayed at, and what had 'happened' there. I had to completely knock myself out with my regular sleep medication, plus Temazepam and earplugs to be able to cope. For good measure I even threw in some Dimetapp, which was stupid of me but at the time I was desperate. I may as well not have bothered going away, because I was so knocked out just to cope. I was so relieved to get home in the end. Even now, it is very difficult for me to stay anywhere new for fear of the flashbacks coming back.

Okay, so I don't like sleeping in new places much... no big deal right? Well, for me, it was. For about four years, I had been planning on working and travelling overseas for an extended period of time. Suddenly, I realised that this was not a very realistic goal for me while I was, and still am, so prone to flashbacks. If I can only cope by knocking myself out with medications, what is the point in going? All I would be achieving is 'coping', I would be too stressed to really enjoy myself. It has been very, very hard to admit to myself that at the moment I am unable to do what I have always wanted to do.

However, I am learning to find ways around my difficulties. I am okay staying in new places when I am with people I know and trust. For example, in early 2013 I went away for a weekend with a few friends. We stayed in a small holiday house, so there was nobody unfamiliar nearby. This made a difference, and I actually felt really safe there. I also can cope well if I am staying in a room that doesn't have a shared wall (so that I can't hear other people as much).

I am determined to not let the flashbacks and difficulties stop me from living a happy life. In 2013, I went on a trip overseas to do volunteer work, with a group of people who I knew would look out for me. I was very anxious about how I would cope on the trip given my recent bouts of flashbacks. However, despite experiencing sleep difficulties, I still managed to enjoy myself. Hopefully it was a good stepping stone to build up my confidence for more travel in the future. Life is all about finding ways to overcome the obstacles that come your way, which for me for a long time will include nightmares, flashbacks and sleep difficulties.

What's helped me to work through flashbacks, nightmares and memories

Short term strategies

In counselling with Libby, I came up with a plan for how to ground myself if I experienced intrusive memories or flashbacks. The plan included:

- Acknowledging early warning signs that a flashback or memory is occurring, and taking action as soon as possible

- Removing myself from the situation if possible

- Moving around or looking out the window

- Drawing/writing/colouring

- Reminding myself that I coped as well as possible with the memory or flashback, instead of getting annoyed at myself for not coping better

Sometimes it helps me to write down what I have seen or heard in the flashback or memory, but in some situations this isn't practical. What is important is to remind myself that the flashbacks and memories are not my fault, they are simply my brain's way of trying to process what happened to me.

Long-term strategies

In recent years, I have really pushed myself to stop avoiding some of the situations that cause memories and flashbacks. For example, hearing men's breathing has always been a big trigger for me. This made it very difficult for me to go to a gym or participate in sports with males – so I tended not to. But in 2012, I really pushed myself to join a sports group where I would regularly be running alongside men. I learned to overcome the trigger by initially wearing earphones to block out the sound; then progressing to running with only one earphone in. Gradually I managed to desensitise myself, to the point that I can now cope better with the sound of a man's heavy breathing, though it is still not something I enjoy listening to.

In the long-term, the most useful strategy for me in dealing with the flashbacks, nightmares and intrusive memories has been to talk through them with counsellors, in detail. This was done with Leah and Brooke at Kids Helpline, and my face-to-face counsellor Libby. It was a team effort for all of us. Firstly, I would call up Brooke or Leah, and talk through a memory with them. It was easier to talk about a memory for the first time on the phone, without someone looking at me. Usually I would send an email to them prior to our phone call to tell them what the memory was, and the most distressing details that I knew would be too hard for me to say. I found it helpful to send this email, because it prepared me for what we were about to talk about. The written information in the emails also helped Brooke or Leah to prompt me when I tried to tell them difficult details, without me needing to initiate it all myself. When I called them, they would ask me questions about the memory, and help me to talk through it with them from start to finish.

One thing that Leah and Brooke did that I found really useful was that at the end of the memory, they would help me to make a different ending, where a trusted adult would come to pick me up and keep me safe. Alternatively, we would go back to the beginning of the memory and have a trusted adult come and rescue me before the abusive incident took place. Then, that adult would take me away to a safe place, and look after me, and we would do something fun and happy. Creating an alternative ending was very helpful, because the next time I had flashbacks about an incident, I could make myself remember the new ending which was very comforting.

I will give you an example of one of the new endings I created with Brooke:

It's evening and nearly time to start getting ready for bed. You're getting anxious. And then Jenny knocks on the door and Dad answers. Jenny says: "Hannah's staying with me for the rest of the week". She says it in a very matter of fact voice, not in a friendly way. Dad says "No way" and then Jenny says "Yes she is, you are not allowed to rape her anymore or you'll have to go to jail".

You run past Dad to Jenny and give her a big hug, you are so happy that she has come to get you. You get to go in her car and drive far away so you know you're nowhere near home which makes you feel safer. When you get to Jenny's house she asks what you need to feel better. You ask if you can have a shower and a bath just to get really clean. And then you get to put on clean clothes that Jenny has bought for you. Then you get to sit on the couch with Jenny and watch your favourite movie. Jenny wraps a nice rug around you and lets you snuggle up to her and you feel very safe. She even has a little puppy called Belle, and the puppy sits on the couch with you too.

When it's time for bed you start getting a bit scared, but Jenny's got a nice little room for you with a pretty pink flower bedspread and a nightlight. She lets the puppy sleep on your bed. Jenny sleeps on a mattress right next to your bed so that you know nothing bad will happen.

In the morning she lets you sleep in, to make up for all the sleep you've missed lately. And then she brings you to the beach and you have the best day.

After working through a difficult memory on the phone, I would go and see Libby the following week. I would go through the same memory with her, only this time face-to-face. Sometimes we would write down the main points as I talked about them, because we found that writing helped me to keep my eyes open and to stay grounded. When I didn't have something in front of me to keep my eyes open, I would sometimes become very dissociated and not be able to move or talk properly.

Early on in the memory recall process, Libby got me a long piece of butcher's paper that we turned into a timeline, so that I could write each of the incidents at the correct age. When we were finished, I could see everything that had happened to me in chronological order, which helped it to make more sense to me. We also stuck some pictures of me onto the timeline at different ages, which again helped me to realise how small I had been when some of these things were happening to me. I think this helped me to not blame myself as much, because the photos made me realise that there wasn't a lot I could have done to stop the abuse.

With both Kids Helpline and Libby, I would go over the same memory as many times as I needed to, until it became easier to talk about. Eventually, once I had gone through a distressing memory a few times, it no longer tended to cause as many flashbacks or nightmares. The process of going through all the memories took us about nine months, with some further revisiting of a handful of 'stubborn' memories that took longer to go away. We also worked very hard on getting me to use the correct words such as "rape" which I found very difficult to say. Brooke worked with me for ages to help me to be able to say "Dad raped me". It's still not a sentence that easily rolls off the tongue for me, but I can say it.

Going through the memories was gruelling, but also a crucial part of my healing. The memories have lost a lot of their power over me. I don't struggle quite as much with the details of the abuse now, and have fewer flashbacks.

DISSOCIATION

Both when speaking on the phone and in person I can become very dissociated when talking about memories of the abuse. If you don't know what dissociation is, it's the feeling of being cut off from your body, as though you're not really there. When I first started talking about it to Leah as a teenager, I tended to call it 'feeling drifty' which is what I still usually call it. But the correct term is dissociation. It is actually a symptom of Post Traumatic Stress Disorder (PTSD), which I have.

Painting by
Sarah Millicent Elliott

With my face to face counsellor Libby and some help from Leah and Brooke at Kids Helpline, I put together a 'driftiness scale' to track how I progress from being fine, to completely dissociated. We created this in September 2012, because I was becoming heavily dissociated during my sessions with Libby, to the point where I couldn't keep my eyes open or head up.

Hannah's driftiness scale

Level 1

Looks like: Joking, smiling. I make sense and can follow the conversation easily. Acting my age, talking about current things such as work. No problem with eye contact.

Feels like: Being a normal, functioning person, and I don't feel exhausted. This is where I want to be more often.

What you or I can do to help: Enjoy it, acknowledge it and appreciate it ... Helps me feel more hopeful and normal, so help me to recognise that I am doing well.

Level 2

Looks like: Less eye contact. Still making sense. a bit quieter. Still have my eyes open and head up.

Feels like: a bit uncomfortable/ embarrassed/ ashamed – usually when we start talking about something a bit harder.

What you or I can do to help: I can try and just say how I feel, like "I'm really embarrassed and scared you think I am gross".

Level 3

Looks like: Might start doing repetitive things like messy scribbling (just to keep myself awake) or fidgeting or playing with my toy dog. Often will start swinging my head, and saying things that don't quite make sense/are a bit odd/start getting obsessed with talking about dates of peoples' birthdays or the weather.

Feels like: Starting to feel a bit tired and light headed. Feeling a bit younger.

What you or I can do to help: Help me keep doing stuff to keep my eyes open like colouring or writing. Try to get me to stand up or move around a bit e.g. walk over to the window. Ask me to explain how I am feeling and what is in my head because if I don't explain it then I kind of shut down. If that means writing it down first then that's okay. I can remind myself or be reminded of some of the improvements I have made recently so that I don't feel so hopeless.

Level 4

Looks like: Eyes closed. Put head down or resting it in my hands. Speaking slowly. Sounding younger.

Feels like: Feels like I am starting to not be there. Head feels heavy. Body starts feeling numb. Sometimes my tummy feels weird.

What you or I can do to help: Helping me to write a summary is useful (similar to level 5), but I might also be able to open my eyes or start colouring/writing again with some encouragement. Try to get me to open my eyes — if you put something in front of me to look at, that will help. I could also probably answer some questions about everyday things without needing one word answers. Tell me a lame joke (by level 5 I am probably too out of it).

Level 5

Looks like: Head down (with Libby) or lying down unable to move if I'm on the phone or at home. Eyes closed. Not talking, not moving much. Can't seem to follow conversation.

Feels like: Frozen, moving is too hard. Exhausted. No energy. Trying so hard to follow what we're talking about but it seems impossible. It's like I'm not really there, disconnected. Disoriented.

What you or I can do to help: You can tell me or ask me what you see/hear because that helps me to be more aware (and has helped me to write this) e.g. 'I can see you're finding it hard to keep your head up' or 'Are your eyes open?' Ask me easy yes/no questions. Ask me if I am having flashbacks (often I do but feel too frozen to say or explain that). I can read or write a summary later of what we were talking about so that it makes sense again. I can also try to not be angry at myself for 'being out of it', and make sure I eat properly and go to bed early that night.

As a result of Libby, Brooke and Leah really getting to know when I was becoming dissociated, they put in place good strategies to help minimise it where possible. Libby would pull out some colouring pencils and colouring sheets the second my head started swinging, and put them in front of me. If my head started to drop towards the table or my hand, she would make me get up out of my seat to look out the window. Sometimes I would say "No I can't get up!" because I would be getting too stuck, but even just looking out the window and answering questions about what I could see was helpful.

Having something to play with in my hands has also been useful. With Libby, I would sometimes wear a bracelet so that I had something to feel in my hands. When I forgot mine, she would lend me one of hers to play with for the session which really helped because it made a rattling sound which helped to keep me alert. I also sometimes brought in my babushka doll and would rearrange the dolls methodically throughout the session — another helpful strategy. There's no real science to it, it was just trial and error to find what worked for me.

On the phone, it's a bit different, because the ability to become completely out of it is even higher. When you see someone in person, you do at least try to 'appear normal' but on the phone I have been completely out of it many times. Leah has known me since I was 16, and thinks that over time I have stopped dissociating as frequently and as severely as I used to, and that in the past sometimes it was as if I was 'on another planet'. However, in 2013 I had a couple of weeks where I was heavily dissociating, which even Leah said was worse than I had been in several years. It was pretty depressing for me to be dissociating so badly, but there were several factors involved – mainly a complete lack of sleep (this was when I tried coming off my sleep medication), along with workplace and personal stressors in my life. I was so dissociated that it wasn't really safe for me to drive, and I would get so exhausted just from going for a 10 minute walk because it was taking so much energy to stay present.

When I am really out of it, particularly when going through the details of some of the things that happened to me, I can become so detached from my body that I can't even move or open my eyes. Sometimes I can't even stop myself from drooling, which is really disgusting and embarrassing. I regress in age and just want to play with my toy dog, which I started bringing to counselling sessions with me. When I am very dissociated, it is also harder than usual to talk and to get the words out that you want. It's frustrating, it's like having a road block in your brain.

As the counsellors explained to me, when I dissociate, my brain goes back to the age it was when the trauma occurred. Due to this regression, it has been very helpful for counsellors to allow me to do things that are childish while I am in this state. For example, Leah at Kids Helpline would read me Dr Seuss books which I loved – as evidenced by the Dr Seuss quotes I have included in this book! Brooke would tell me lame jokes and also read me Horton Hears a Who. Libby would let me play with play dough and other games such as Jenga and Barrel of Monkeys. At first I felt stupid about it, but I learned to accept that that is what my brain really needed at the time.

Dissociation is not something I enjoy. Actually, I hate it. It is something I work very hard to mask, and most often occurs when talking about the abuse itself. The only people who fully see it are the people who I feel really comfortable around who I know won't reject me for being the way I am – and usually these are professionals who are less likely to reject me than friends in my life! Generally these are also people who are older than me who I don't feel will judge me as harshly as people my own age. I can count on one hand the people in my life who fully know how I am when I am dissociated.

Alcohol and dissociation

One thing that I have learned is that drinking alcohol is a bad match for someone who dissociates severely. At times when I have already been struggling to 'stay with it', when I've had just a few drinks I've very quickly become very, very out of it. I talked about this to Leah at Kids Helpline, who explained that alcohol dissociates you, so if you're already dissociated and then get drunk, well you are going to completely magnify it and lose control of your body even more. It makes sense to me. In the scheme of things, this does not bother me too much, although it was difficult at parties during my uni years to always be the one not drinking. At this point, I don't really care if I can't drink much alcohol. It saves me money anyway!

Depression after dissociation

The bad thing about dissociation is that when I start coming out of it, I get really angry at myself for being so 'retarded' and 'stupid'. As a joke, Brooke at Kids Helpline said we should set up a 'swear jar' for every time I called myself a retard, and that I would save a massive amount of money in doing so. It's just that I get so sad and hopeless that I am still struggling so much and sometimes not really able to stay in the present, and not able to cope with things as someone my age 'should'.

It is really frustrating to feel like I'm not normal, and to know that my brain has completely slowed down. I am often a very busy and motivated person with a big list of things I plan to get done, and when I become dissociated and can't do a single one of them, I start getting really stressed out. During my really bad patch in 2013, I was in tears one evening knowing I had promised to make soup for people at work the next day, but was so dissociated that I could barely even chop up vegetables. I am learning that there is nothing I can do in those times, other than to just step back and let myself do nothing for a while. Doing jigsaw puzzles has been a good distraction for me that I have gotten into in the past year. Playing with silly phone apps is another good distraction – I've got Face Juggle, Stachify and other silly apps which always give me a giggle. If I have the energy, going for a short walk also helps. I don't tend to do too well trying to watch any TV shows when I am like that, because usually I'll just end up with my eyes closed having intrusive memories, instead of watching what I was supposed to. I need to do something that keeps my mind focussed and eyes open.

I have also learned that after coming out of dissociation I have to be very careful about getting to bed early and doing everything I can to make life easier for myself. So usually, if I knew I was going to a tough counselling session with Libby, I would make sure that prior to going to the session, I had some dinner cooked for that evening, and clothes laid out for work the next day, in case I couldn't do much that evening.

ANXIETY AND DEPRESSION

After reading my diaries and my experiences of the legal system, it will come as no surprise to you that I still experience anxiety and depression.

Anxiety

Anxiety is something I experience on an everyday basis. When unexpected changes occur in my personal life, instead of just accepting them and getting on with things, I can become extremely stressed and upset. As a result, I often try to maintain a fairly rigid routine. It is difficult for me to break this routine sometimes, which has a negative impact on my friendships. For example, if someone asked me spontaneously if I wanted to join them for dinner that night, even if I was free and would be happy to spend time with them, I would start fretting and thinking "But I hadn't planned for that". I often wonder why I get so anxious and so upset by changes, but as has been explained to me, the abuse that happened was sometimes so unpredictable that it is no wonder I seek a bit of structure and predictability in my life.

With the support and encouragement of counsellors, I have been trying to retrain my brain to learn that it is okay to have unexpected changes sometimes. I try to push myself to go along with things when they happen unexpectedly, and have been trying to make myself accept unexpected social invitations. This is an important step, because if you are seen to be someone who never accepts social invitations, then people will think you are disinterested and won't pursue a friendship with you. Whenever I do break my routine, I try to praise myself a lot because it is hard for me to do.

A lot of my anxiety is related to trying to avoid things that remind me of the abuse. There are many things that can trigger memories, some of which have already been discussed. Even situations where I feel physically trapped can cause major anxiety. For example, if I am 'boxed in' on public transport, particularly by an older male, I will start to fret. Being on a plane trip next to an older male is also very uncomfortable, and in such situations I would prefer to be in the aisle seat. Even being in elevators can make me feel claustrophobic and trapped, but it is something that I have learned to cope with.

The anxiety I experience often manifests itself physically as well, in the form of headaches, stomach aches and nausea. I have had all of these symptoms when any court or parole hearings were occurring, and even sometimes experienced these symptoms prior to going to counselling sessions. I also find it very difficult to relax, and tend to always keep busy. I can become fixated on minor things that aren't really a big deal, but to me become a major issue. For example, when

I found out about the last appeal in 2011, I suddenly realised that I had lots of split ends in my hair, and became really distraught, thinking that the split ends were going to take over my hair and that I would have to get it all cut off! I went to the hairdresser nearly crying and said "oh you have to help me, I have so many split ends" and the hairdresser just stared at me, probably thinking "what's her problem?" The problem wasn't really the split ends, it was that I felt the rug had been ripped from underneath me in other areas of my life.

An example of my anxiety

I will now give another example of a situation that caused me to experience high anxiety levels, and how my good friend Grace helped me to overcome it.

I had planned an event for a few friends that involved a bit of a road trip. There were supposed to be five of us, but two people bailed at the last minute. This left just me, a guy I didn't know that well called Rick who was in his mid 30s, and my good friend Grace.

I became very panicky and distressed, with a weird sick feeling in my tummy when I realised that I would have to go alone in the car with Rick, to pick up Grace, who lived 30 minutes away. I didn't feel in control of the situation at all, and didn't quite know or trust him enough. The thought of being in a car alone with an older guy I didn't know made me feel very trapped. What if he tried something on me? What if he said something weird?

I tried changing the plan to avoid the car-trip alone with Rick, which only proceeded to offend Rick and confuse Grace. In the end, I spoke alone to Grace about my anxieties. Instead of laughing at me, she was very empathetic. She explained that she experiences anxiety herself, and has seen a psychologist about it. She explained that when you're scared of something, the more you avoid it, the more it becomes reinforced in your brain, so it gets harder and harder to overcome. She gave me examples of some of her fears.

It was really helpful to know that Grace understood my anxiety instead of dismissing me. I decided to go ahead with the car trip with Rick, but texted Grace when we were leaving my place just to make sure she would be there to meet us. It was a very anxious drive for me, but nothing bad happened at all. Rick and I just chatted and though it was a bit awkward, I was fine. I was exhausted by the time I got home that evening but was proud of myself for doing something that was uncomfortable. a couple of weeks later I went on a short car trip at work with an older guy I didn't know that well either, and again despite being uncomfortable I coped fine. It was a nice supported way for me to start overcoming an uncomfortable situation, and I was very proud to tell Libby about my success! The more I tackle my problems, the more confident I become in my abilities to cope.

Obsessive compulsive tendencies – dates and numbers

Another thing that comes out when I am either very distressed or dissociated is my obsession with dates and numbers. From around age eight, numbers became a great source of comfort to me. I started developing some obsessive compulsive tendencies around that age – I remember for months when I was eight, everything had to be done in 3's – for example, I had to take three steps at a time. I knew it was weird, and I wanted to be able to tell someone about it, because it felt like it was driving me crazy. But I didn't think anyone would understand.

After this, my major obsession became birthdays. If I met someone new, I wanted to know when their birthday was. I would then remember that birthday, and in my head would continually recite the birthdays of people I knew. For example, I can still remember that the birthday of Moya (a girl I went to primary school with) was on May 6th, and that her mother was May 16th. I have not seen this girl in over 12 years and didn't really like her, but still remember these useless facts. I chuckle to myself every year on May 16th when I think 'ah yep, Moya's mum's birthday'. Over time, I think I am losing my knack for remembering dates as well as I used to, but am still pretty good. I am the person who sends text messages to people to remind them of important anniversaries or birthdays. I am a useful person to be friends with!

My good memory for dates actually served me very well during the trial. There was one particular incident that had occurred in March 2000. I was able to pinpoint the exact date on which this incident had occurred, because I knew it was the Monday before the birthday of a relative. I remembered that the day after the incident, I had been home sick from school, and that on this day I had made a birthday card for the relative. Amazingly, the police subpoenaed the records from my primary school in 2007 and found that yes indeed, I had been absent on that particular Tuesday in March, 2000. There were several other similar incidents where I had managed to remember particular dates, and it was often those particular incidents that resulted in convictions, because more corroborating evidence was available.

As a child, in times of real distress, I would also start reciting peoples' phone numbers and addresses in my head. This again provided me with some comfort, but I can't really explain why. I think it was just soothing and predictable. I can still remember those numbers and addresses that I recited repeatedly as a kid! But now I don't ever remember peoples' addresses and phone numbers –

I haven't done that for years. In hindsight and from speaking about it with E
at Kids Helpline, I think these obsessions came from trying to have some (
and predictability in a situation that was very much out of my control.

Another obsession of mine as a kid was the weather. I loved to know what the
forecast would be for the major cities, both in Australia and overseas. I could
recite weather statistics and forecasts. Even today, I must confess that I look at
the bureau of meteorology website every single day, to check the forecast for
my city. I can't really say why, other than that it's calming for me. I can always
tell you what percentage chance there is of rain on any given day. My former
workmate Karla used to always get a giggle out of my frequent weather updates.
These quirks are a bit odd but I suppose they are harmless and hey, at least if
you hang out with me you'll know whether to bring an umbrella!

Depression

I have already discussed the depression I've experienced in the previous two
sections of this book. As you may have guessed, I have a tendency to be very
hard on myself and beat myself up. Brooke, Leah and Libby often had to remind
me not to use the word "should". I still often say things like:

- I should be over this by now!

- I should act my age!

- I should stop being so immature!

- I should stop having flashbacks!

- I should be able to cope better with relationships!

- I should cope better when people talk about sex instead of thinking it is
  the worst thing in the world!

All of this self-criticism gets exhausting, and leads to me feeling really hopeless
about my future.

Now when I am feeling really hopeless, it escalates more quickly than it used
to, to the point of becoming very suicidal. However, it also tends to resolve
itself quicker than it used to, and does not happen nearly as often. I think
the reason it escalates so quickly now is because I have had problems and
difficulties for so many years, that sometimes I suddenly reach a point where
I think "Enough! I can't take this anymore! I want to give up!"

In previous years, I was constantly depressed and hopeless. But now, despite the occasional bad patch, I cope quite well. I work hard to keep my life as positive as possible – in Part Four of this book I have given examples of some of the things that have worked for me. Except for those brief few weeks in 2013, I haven't been on antidepressants since leaving my hometown in January 2012. This is a massive achievement, given that I had been on them for over five years prior to that. However, if it got to a point where I really did need to be on an antidepressant to ensure my safety, then I would be open to that. Medication is definitely a useful tool sometimes, when you find a medication that works well for you.

When I am in my really depressed patches, it is helpful to try and remember the improvements and achievements I have had in the past few years. It helps me to realise that I can keep trying a bit longer, because I have overcome a lot worse in the past. Sometimes you just have to put one foot in front of the other, and just think about getting through the day.

INTENSE FEELINGS

Jealousy

Something that I had to work on a lot in counselling was my feelings of jealousy. It took me ages to feel comfortable in sharing those feelings with Leah, Brooke and Libby. At one point, I started to feel very jealous of the young children that Libby worked with. This really came out when I learned that Libby was working with a young child I knew, who had experienced a once-off incident of sexual abuse by a friend. The child's mother told me about this, without knowing that I also had been sexually abused and was seeing Libby. I held it together during the conversation with the mother, then went home and cried. I didn't know what was wrong with me or why I was reacting in such a way. It took a while to pick it apart, with help from the counsellors.

Basically, I was jealous because this child (aged six) was receiving help far earlier than I did, before the abuse had escalated. The child's mother was very gung-ho about supporting and getting help for the child and diligently making sure that her child attended appointments with Libby. I was left wondering why this child was so worthy of support and help at such an early age. Why wasn't I worthy of such care? I can only imagine how much I would have loved to be taken to see Libby as a child. Can you imagine how differently my life would have been if I had been helped at age six?

In a way, it is really like grieving for the future you've lost, because you didn't get the help when you needed it. It made me wonder if I would have developed so many problems if someone had stepped in to help me, just like they had for this child. I became so, so, sad. It was difficult for me to admit to Libby how I really felt, because I knew it was wrong to be jealous of a child getting help. It wasn't so much being jealous of the child, as feelings of grief and loss. But I still felt like a horrible person. I then took it out on Libby, by deciding that I hated her and didn't want to see her anymore. It took us a month to get back on track again.

The jealousy I experienced with Libby has also been present with other people in my life. At times I felt very insecure when I had planned on talking to Brooke or Leah but they were not available that day because they were busy working with other kids. I would start thinking "Oh, they must like the other kids more than me, why aren't I good enough?" It is a very childish way of thinking, and really does go straight back to the times I was rejected as a kid, and made to feel not good enough. I think it also comes down to not feeling listened to as a kid when I wanted the abuse to stop. I definitely experienced those jealous feelings as a teenager, for example when another girl from my school was sexually assaulted and got help straight away.

When I was finally feeling better, Libby and I picked apart the 'jealous' feeling, so that I could see that it made a lot of sense, and that it did not make me a bad person. We brainstormed all the different situations that bring about the jealous feeling for me, and what other feelings were a part of it. It was a very useful process and opened up lots for us to talk about.

Here is what we came up with.

Situation 1: When other people (especially friends) have close-knit families

Feeling that comes up: Sad, depressed, feeling bad about myself, alone, hopeless, retarded.

What I can do: Remember that families can be a burden sometimes too. Remember that people do care about me. Doing something nice for myself e.g. go for a run. Connect with other people e.g. catch up with a friend.

Situation 2: When Libby/Leah/Brooke talk to other kids

Feelings that come up: Afraid of losing them/losing support. Being scared that I don't matter, then feeling hurt and lashing out. Being surprised. Being scared of change. Feeling stupid and mean. Hopeless, guilty, retarded.

What I can do: Take time out before responding. Look over some of the things I've done with them that show I do matter. Remind myself that I've coped fine with these kinds of changes in the past and still kept in contact with Leah despite years of changes.

Situation 3: When kids have adults who care for them and keep them safe, or when they get help early e.g. with Libby seeing the child I knew

Feelings that come up: Angry that I didn't get that. Guilty for feeling jealous. Hopeless. Grief/loss. Unloved/worthless. Retarded.

What I can do: Write how I'm feeling or talk it through. Try to do something nice for myself or distracting. Try not to be too hard on myself for having those feelings. Remind myself that it's not really about the other kid, it's about what I didn't get. I do want other kids to get help.

Situation 4: Getting jealous of friends who can do things or cope in situations that I can't, or find very difficult e.g. relationships, marriage, having kids, coping with change more easily, being able to sleep in different places without as many difficulties

Feelings that come up: Retarded, sad, depressed. Scared of missing out on things in the future that matter to me. Hopeless/suicidal. Angry at myself. Stupid. Frustrated. Angry that I was abused. Different.

What I can do: Remember that other people do struggle in different situations, I just don't always see it. Remember that I've tried really hard e.g. use my sticker chart. Try not to be mad at myself. Remind myself that I'm still young enough for life to work out okay. Remind myself that I am getting a lot better at trusting guys, and that I have coped well with some major changes, like moving interstate.

I hadn't realised just how complex those jealousy feelings were until we completed this brainstorm. I then spoke about it with Leah and Brooke at Kids Helpline. Leah helped me put together the "jealousy process", so that I could see how it had a predictable pattern. I will show this now.

The jealousy process

1. **Pre-trigger:** circumstances are difficult e.g.: not sleeping, coping with changes, feeling overwhelmed, or sick

2. **Trigger:** often something that reminds me of past rejections or being abandoned. Sick tummy, shock feeling, intense negative feelings, starting to feel paralysed

3. **Paralysed:** irrational thinking, feeling stuck and frozen, aimless and 'flopping around', negative self talk begins e.g. pathetic, dumb, worthless, drifty

4. **Movement:** some energy comes back, very angry, lashing out, still sick in tummy, act in some way e.g. send email or tell someone off, punish someone for feeling of rejection

5. **Guilt:** regretting actions, still sick in tummy, tired, foggy in the head, hopeless, continued negative self talk e.g. 'pathetic, dumb, childish'

6. **Despair:** very tired, want to cut and run, can't sleep, thinking of ways to ditch people, mind racing, suicidal thoughts

7. **Rational thought:** physical reactions start to settle down, embarrassment, start to work out thoughts and challenge negative assumptions, sometimes talk it through with Leah/ Brooke/ Libby

Talking about my feelings of jealousy and gaining an understanding of them has been very helpful for me. Although the feelings continue to arise, I am able to identify them a lot faster, and also to talk about them without feeling like a horrible person. They are no longer having such an impact on me and are occurring less frequently.

Feelings of guilt and shame

I have already explored my feelings of guilt a lot in my diaries and during Part Two of this book. I have continued to experience feelings of guilt, but they lessened a lot after I visited Dad in jail in 2010.

Another intense feeling that I continue to have is shame. This is also something that I have worked on in counselling. With Libby in 2012, I was asked to write a list of all the things that I was ashamed of.

Here is what I wrote (and also shared with Brooke and Leah):

- I am ashamed because I 'had sex with my dad' – so I just blame myself a lot of the time. And feel embarrassed about it/like it makes me a bad person.

- Because I remember some really gross things that I wish didn't even exist in my memory and that make me feel disgusting/bad about myself. It's the gross little details that are the worst.

- Feeling like I'm not good enough/behind in some areas because I still struggle with a lot of things that my friends don't. I want to be normal.

- Feeling like I wasn't good enough for anyone in the end because it was like nobody really cared about me and the person I thought did (Dad), was just tricking me and ditched me.

- For being a selfish/bad person sometimes, and reacting stupidly to things like people not being there, or things changing. I know I am not the only person in the world, it doesn't revolve around me. But I just act like it does sometimes.

- I often feel disgusting physically like I just hate myself and am so ugly and disgusting.

- Ashamed that I liked getting compliments from Dad when I was younger. I liked getting attention.

- Ashamed that I liked playing some of the games when I was younger, before they started to get scary.

- Ashamed that people listened to the details in court, including relatives who I don't talk to very much.

Being able to express all of these things was a big step for me. I was then able to talk them through with Brooke, Leah and Libby, which although very embarrassing and difficult, was the first step in letting go of some of the shame.

RELATIONSHIPS

The most significant and upsetting impact of the abuse has been on my ability to trust people and form relationships. If you didn't know me really well, you might not pick up on this. I come across as a normal 26 year old in lots of ways. It is only once you try to get close to me that you start to see the difficulties.

Trust and friendships

Even with trusted counsellors Libby, Leah and Brooke, I had periods of not trusting them, rejecting them and telling them that I was not ever talking to them again. Usually when I have that sort of reaction in a relationship, I don't know exactly why I am reacting like that, I just feel scared and like I need to lash out. You would think that I would not have had these insecurities with Leah after speaking with her for so many years, but they endured over our nine years of working together. I often asked her whether she really cared about me, how I could know if I could trust her, whether she believed me, and whether she thought I was stupid. I also often accused Leah of laughing at me and thinking I was gross – which was the opposite of the reality. It was amazing that she stuck with me for all those years despite my insecurities, but she truly seemed to understand that it was the abuse I had experienced that made it so hard for me to form trusting relationships with people.

I am always terrified of rejection, particularly by people who matter to me. If you are a 'close' person in my life and I think you disapprove of something I say or do, or I think you are laughing at me, I will go on the attack and push you away. If you don't get back to me about something or answer my phone calls, I might assume that you have stopped talking to me and that the friendship is pretty well over. I am always fearful of being ditched and abandoned by the people who matter to me, so tend to keep most people at a distance. This keeps me safe from being rejected and hurt. It also makes life very lonely for me sometimes, and affects my prospects for the future.

I actually have a lot of friends and am sometimes the person who is organising social events. But I don't have many people in my life who I could truly call a 'close friend'. There are a lot of people who might think they are a close friend, but have no idea of the many difficulties I face. When I am close to people, I often end up having a big fight with them or lashing out, to the point that they don't want to be my friend anymore. I often expect that people I am friends with will ditch or reject me, the way that Dad did sometimes when I wouldn't do what he wanted me to do. I also often feel that friends don't really value me, even when they do. From speaking with counsellors, it seems that a lot of this comes from the feeling of being 'tricked' by Dad – thinking he was caring and nice, but then finding out it was just because he was grooming me for abuse.

One of the closest friendships I have had was with my friend Dani, who I have mentioned extensively throughout this book. She is a few years older than me, so I felt safe enough to be my true self around her, instead of feeling a need to 'act my age'. Sadly, our friendship doesn't seem to have coped well with transitions in our lives, as she is shortly to be married and looking to start a family and have children. I had long valued Dani as the very best of friends, so was really hurt when I found out that she had picked other people to be her bridesmaids. You know that sad, hurt feeling you get when you realise that you value a friendship more than the other person – that they don't really need you? That is how it was for me. Being the confrontational person I am, I told her that I was hurt – which of course was hurtful for her too, and impacted on our friendship. Writing up this book and typing up my diaries has been very helpful for me to put it all in perspective, and to see that my friendship with Dani was truly special, but that it may just have run its course as we move on to very different stages in our lives. We are actually very different people, with different experiences, priorities and values, so I am learning to not take it so personally that we have grown apart. I will always be grateful to her for the important role she did play in earlier years.

I am proud to say that in the friendships I have formed since moving away from my home town, I have made some improvements. I have met new friends who know more of the 'real me' than most of my old friends. Within a year of settling into my new town, I had two particularly close friends, Abbey and Grace, with whom I can be more honest and don't feel a need to lash out. I am able to speak to them about some of my honest feelings and fears, without being laughed at. Grace understands anxiety and how it is to hold it together at work and then go home and collapse in a heap; Abbey knows how it is to feel rejected by friends in your life. These are not the sort of honest conversations I tended to have with friends in the past. These friends are absolutely worth their weight in gold, and they really look out for me. When I was very distressed by parole hearings, they are the two friends who I wanted to be around, so we went and played mini golf and had dinner at our favourite pub. They didn't laugh at me (much!) when I was having a really rough day and preferred to sit and eat lunch alone while looking at pictures of cute puppies on Facebook!

My close friendships are not limited to Abbey and Grace. I have made a good solid bunch of friends since moving, who are like family to me. I feel very loved and cared for. On my 25th birthday in July 2013, I was completely spoilt by all of my new friends. I think I got about three cakes in total, a lifetime's supply of chocolate (almost!), and some very personalised presents and cards. One friend even took me out to choose some nice wool so that she could crochet me some gloves and a hat, then took me to lunch at a chocolate cafe – perfect! It was quite a surprise to feel so valued and made me realise that I really have carved out a new place in the world for myself, and that there are people who like me for who I am. Two friends at work who sat near me were also great supports in 2013 when I was going through a difficult patch, trying to come off my sleep medication. They didn't know the details, but would always ask how I was going and do small kind things to make me laugh or smile. One day I was barely coping, and came into work to find a funny picture Karla had put on my desk, to cheer me up. Jane always managed to give me chocolate at just the right moments, when I needed a sugar hit. They also put up with my distractedness and chatter. These small gestures helped me to get through.

A major step for me in trusting friends was to allow two people in my personal life to read the manuscript of this book. One of those was a close friend, the other was a more distant but trusted friend who I felt could provide objective feedback. Allowing them to read it was a huge risk for me – I have never felt so exposed in my entire life. I was very fortunate that they both responded so well and said that it had taught them a lot. I have found that it's strengthened my friendship with my close friend, who has been willing to be more open with me about the things she finds difficult. It is so helpful to have people in my personal life who fully understand and accept the difficulties I face, and who are willing to share their own difficulties. It helps me to feel more accepted and normal.

One thing I should mention is how difficult it is for me to ask friends for help. This is a result of having learned to be very independent, and not relying on anyone else to keep me safe. When I was moving recently, I could have asked several friends who have trailers to help me, but instead just went and organised a hire-van for myself. The thought of making someone take a few hours out of their day was too much for me, when I 'should' be able to do it myself. a few of my friends saw through this and one ended up helping me with their ute. But I wouldn't have thought to ask for this myself.

I nearly always drive myself to the airport instead of asking someone for a lift. I hate asking anyone for anything, though I am happy to give a lot. I think part of my reluctance to accept help from people is that I don't want to 'owe' them anything. It takes me a while to screen who is safe and who is not. I find it really difficult to accept anything (e.g. a gift) from someone I don't like, because it just feels fake — what do they expect in return? It gives me a slimy feeling inside and reminds me of the abuse and how manipulated I was.

Relationships with authority figures

One other thing that I have noticed recently is that there is often an authority figure in my life who I absolutely hate. Usually, my hate for them is out of proportion to the actual situation, and takes over my thoughts. Most recently, it was a direct line manager in my workplace who triggered this reaction. This lady, Alicia, was one of those people who would be really nice to your face and would pretend to listen to you, while secretly completely disregarding what you were saying. There was an issue in the workplace that was having a negative impact on me, so I continually raised this issue with Alicia over a period of months. She would smile, nod and say all the right things ("yup, 100%, I completely hear what you're saying") — but no changes occurred.

Eventually, when pressed again, Alicia said to me that "as a level one" (junior) staff member, I would just have to put up with it. The use of her power over me continued to upset me further and reminded me of the abuse. The issue eventually came to a head when I brought it up at a wider staff meeting. Following this, Alicia proceeded to say how 'hurt' and 'shocked' she was that I had brought up the issue in front of other people. She went into overdrive being nice to me, speaking in a really friendly high-pitched voice, gave me chocolates, lent me DVDs, anything to save face. This only proceeded to make me angrier, because I could see it as manipulation. My interactions with her were continuing to cause memories of the abuse, and the way Dad would say he was hurt if I wouldn't play a game or do something he wanted me to do. I started having really bad nightmares, and felt like I was going crazy. I decided to take a new job somewhere else, and go to a workplace where I would be listened to. The extreme feelings were directly related to the abuse I had experienced, but it took me a few weeks to step back and realise this.

Family relationships

Family relationships continue to be a major area of difficulty for me. I still struggle with most family occasions such as Christmas and Easter, and tend to avoid them. Moving interstate has been really helpful in that respect, but I still feel that gaping hole in my heart when I see the workplace clear out and it feels like everyone else is going home to their happy families. I often feel like I don't belong anywhere, and that makes me feel really worthless.

My relationship with Mum

I have had periods where I have been in contact with my mum fairly regularly by phone or text, followed by periods where I will barely reply to a text message from her in six months. During visits to my home town, I don't stay with her and tend to have limited contact.

I think a major problem in my relationship with Mum is that I am not able to tell her how I honestly feel about things, and how much my life has been affected by what happened to me. It's like I am always trying to protect her, which in the end doesn't work, because so much resentment builds up in me that I then explode, lash out at her and stop talking to her for several months. It's a lose-lose situation at the moment, and I truly think that reading this will give her so much more insight into my experiences than I have been able to give her in my whole life. I am not trying to hurt my mum and I genuinely do care about her. But I need her to understand how much I have been hurt.

Another difficulty I have with Mum is that sometimes it feels like the issues I experience are glossed over or forgotten by her. An example of this is my major difficulties with sleeping. a few years ago, I was staying at Mum's house for a night, and had forgotten to bring my regular sleeping tablets. Mum said to me "you don't need a tablet to sleep, sleep is a natural thing, you shouldn't be taking tablets". Yes, sleep is a natural thing... But not when you have experienced years of trauma, where your brain becomes hard-wired to think that sleep is not safe. I've talked about it with her a few times since, and she seems to understand it better now.

Another thing I have struggled with is that sometimes I feel that Mum guilt trips me. For example, in about 2009, I won a big award at uni. I decided to bring my good friend Dani and her boyfriend Cale along to the ceremony with me. Mum took this very personally, that I had taken them and not her. But what right did she have? In my head, I thought "well, you're actually just lucky that I'm alive. Since when did you have a right to take ownership of the good things in my life, when I have achieved them against all odds?" We had a big argument after that.

I get that Mum really put her neck on the line by leaving Dad, that she has made major efforts to support me since then and advocated for me, but that does not take away what happened prior to 2007. She is going to have to expect me to remain angry and resentful at times – I think she understands this.

Mum has read the manuscript of this book. I take my hat off to her for doing that, because I know how difficult it was for her. I know she feels really guilty for letting me down, and wishes she'd had more information. I know that life is not easy for her. I don't hate her. I am not trying to hurt her. I still send birthday cards and mother's day cards and presents. There are still times when I talk to her and want to share the goods things in my life. Despite how hurt she may feel, I am not a spiteful person. I am just trying to move on in a way that is healthy for me. I know that reading this book may shatter our relationship even further, or maybe it will make it stronger? I have no way of knowing. I can honestly see how the major fault lines in my relationship with Mum started when I was much, much younger, and how Dad worked hard to build up a wedge between the two of us. It is hard to repair such long-term damage, and I don't tend to have the energy to make it a priority at this point.

Relationship with my sister Bec

My relationship with my sister Bec seems to be improving. Previously, I would feel like she and Mum were such a tight little 'unit' and that they were ganging up on me. I know that sounds irrational, but when you have been brought up to feel that you are a misfit and that only your dad will listen to you, it is hard to break down the barriers with other family members. But my sister has been making a lot of effort to show that she is there for me, and hopefully sometimes I am a good source of support to her too.

I am also learning to be more honest with Bec about how I am feeling. Previously, when she was enthusiastic about wanting to come and visit me and spend time with me, I would end up getting so overwhelmed that I would end up cancelling the whole thing. I felt that there were too many things that I did not want to talk about with Bec. But now I am learning to say to her honestly what I can cope with. In setting these boundaries, we are starting to be able to build up a relationship without me feeling a need to push her away.

To her credit, she is getting better at understanding the boundaries I put in place, even though they must be frustrating for her sometimes. I did have her come and spend a weekend with me in 2013, and it went well. Moving into the future, there will continue to be times when I am really overwhelmed by Bec — sometimes she gets on a roll and rattles off several texts at a time, and if I'm not in the right headspace I will recluse and not answer, or send a sarcastic response. This is just my way of saying that I need some space, and I think she is coming to understand this. At least for the next few years, there will continue to be times when I still need to recluse.

However, I have come to realise that I actually really respect Bec as a person. She has been through her fair share of difficulties, which are not my place to discuss. She continues to maintain a positive attitude, and looks for a silver lining in bad experiences. She doesn't always know how things are for me, but shows more awareness sometimes than I would have expected. She didn't hesitate to believe me over Dad about the abuse — she knew instantly that it was true. And all in all, I think she is a genuinely good person who has a lot of integrity. Despite some of the typical sisterly annoyances, I think we will continue to build on our relationship, especially now that I realise that a large part of the rift between us was created by Dad.

Relationship with Dad

I have not had any contact with my dad since I went and visited him in prison in June 2010. I have no desire to ever have contact with him again. He has proven time and again that he is manipulative and nasty — it just took me a while to see his true colours. I can see why I felt sorry for him though. Nobody wants to see their parent get in trouble or go to jail, particularly when you have been brought up being told that this is the only person in the world who cares about you. I resent that I was put in such a confusing situation and that I was so badly manipulated.

At this point I haven't yet fully been able to process my feelings towards Dad — it is a work in progress. I still get upset on Father's Day, because that is when I miss the good things about my dad. I hear other friends of mine talking about their dads, and that makes me feel really sad. I guess that's the grief and loss stuff again.

Probably the hardest thing for me has been to fully accept that it was Dad who abused me. In my mind, I was often able to separate it, so that even though I was talking about Dad, I was talking about the 'other Dad' or a giant. It was like I was able to separate Dad into the Dad who abused me, and the nice Dad who joked around with me and was fun to be around. I would not have gotten through my childhood if I hadn't been able to separate Dad in my mind from the abuse.

But it has made my recovery difficult at times. I have gone through patches of denying that it was Dad, as a way of protecting myself. I feel sad, shocked and confused that the Dad who did nice things was also the Dad who hurt me. And I feel embarrassed to have done gross sexual things with my dad. So there are lots of reasons why it has taken me a while to process it. When I did start to process it on a deeper level, I went through a period of deep depression and was extremely close to suicide. It was just so painful. I am likely to continue to experience patches of major depression when I deal with what he has done to me.

Relationships with extended family

I have maintained a close relationship with my Aunty Susie. Though we now live in different states, I email her quite often, and try and call her every couple of months. We mean to speak more often but everyone gets so busy in life. I know that if I ever really needed her, she would be there for me in a heartbeat. I think it has often been difficult for Susie, because she is sometimes placed in the middle of my mum and I. Sometimes she probably feels that she has to be the peacekeeper. Despite this, she still manages to be really good to me. Recently, I have started confiding some of the long-term difficulties to her, which previously I wouldn't have told her out of fear of rejection. It took me some time to really trust her again, after an argument in 2009 – which was my fault, I felt a need to push her away. Now I feel that I could tell Susie a lot of things if I needed to, but generally would choose not to have those sorts of conversations with her, probably because I don't see her very often. When we do chat, I tend to feel a need to tell her mainly the good stuff in my life, so that she does not give up on me.

Susie and her family came and visited me interstate in 2013, which was really lovely. I felt very special that they made the effort to come and visit me. It was also really great for me having my uncle Roy and cousin Jack come to stay. Jack is 20 now but will always be like a little brother to me. I felt safe and comfortable having both Jack and Roy staying in my house. Building up positive relationships with males in my life is a really good thing for me. After having Jack and Roy stay at my place, I later agreed to have a male friend from my home town come to stay at my place for a few days. This was a really big step for me in allowing trusted males into my personal space more.

Intimate relationships

As mentioned earlier in this book, one of the things that the abuse has really affected is my thoughts about sex and intimate relationships. The idea of sex is so repulsive to me. I cannot understand why anyone would do that voluntarily, let alone for fun. I know that makes me sound very immature, but that is how it is for me.

There have been guys who have been interested in me over the years, but my absolute fear and avoidance of intimacy has been my downfall. I have never even let a boy kiss me – other than spin the bottle in Grade 7. Is that ridiculous? Yes, a little bit. It shows how immature I am. But it is what it is.

My views on sex and intimacy also impact on my friendships, which can make life difficult. I avoid being reminded of sex to the point of preferring to watch harmless kids' movies and shows, over the movies and shows that other people my age watch. Whenever I am invited to the movies with friends, I will check the reviews before agreeing to it, because I don't want to be stuck in a movie with lots of sex scenes. It's difficult at the movies, because you're trapped – you can't just press 'fast forward' or leave the room for a few minutes.

When I'm talking to people and there is sexual banter or jokes of any sort, I hate it and just want to disappear. I honestly just wish sex didn't exist. I would prefer to pretend that none of my friends ever have sex, unless it's to have a baby – I guess then it is okay, but still gross. It is hard for other people to understand my extreme views, and I've had people think I am very religious (I'm not), or 'a prude'.

Recently, I had a friend get pregnant by accident to a guy she had just met. I was so shocked when I heard this. I am happy for her, because I know she will be a great mum – she is a lovely person and also very mature. But at the same time I was thinking, "How can you 'just have sex', no big deal?" It was brewing in my head for a couple of weeks until I ended up blurting out to her that I knew she had only met him a couple of weeks before she became pregnant. It was terribly rude of me. It is none of my business to worry about other peoples' pregnancies, but it really did get to me for some reason. This friend handled my comment really well thankfully, and I have since apologised about it and made amends. I am hoping to maintain my friendship with her through her pregnancy.

To be honest, I have difficulty with the idea of pregnancy in general, particularly in the last few years as some of my similar age friends start moving towards having babies. The problem is, I desperately want to get married and have children of my own when I am older. I have wanted that for years, probably more so than my friends. But if I get married, I would prefer to sleep in my own bedroom and never be expected to have sex! I know that is not how it works, and I know how childish it makes me sound. But if you had been forced to have sex from such an early age, you might feel the same way too. My body and mind really were not ready for those things to happen, and whenever I think about sex, that is the 'age' my mind goes back to. If I do get married, which I desperately hope I do, I think I will actually need to have a 'safe' bedroom of my own that I can at least sleep in some of the time when I am struggling. I know realistically that I will always have difficult patches where I have flashbacks, depression and nightmares.

If I don't get to have children of my own, I will be absolutely devastated. I would probably blame myself for failing as a person, for not being who I want to be. I think I would also be angry at the abuse for ruining my life from turning out how I want it to. I desperately want that feeling of being in a family unit and I desperately want to provide children of my own with a good, loving home, where they feel listened to and loved. I desperately want a daughter of my own who I can look after and give her a happy childhood. You have no idea how much I want that.

In the last couple of years, it has been really difficult to see the gap between my same-age friends and myself become wider and wider, as several of them have gotten married and started to have kids. Every time I get another wedding invitation I feel a sense of fear. I am scared that in 10 years all my good friends will be happy and married with kids... and that those things will be out of reach for me due to all the problems I've had to endure. If it gets to a point where it doesn't look like those things will work out for me, in 10 years or whatever, I am scared I will kill myself. I've thought that many times. I don't want to be alone. I don't know how that could be a life worth living. I think it is even more important to me than for other friends because I don't feel like I have a sense of belonging in the world, so having a family of my own really would give me something that I so badly would love. Something that so many people seem to take for granted.

That is the main reason why I have worked so hard in counselling to overcome my problems, because I really, really want to have my life work out, with a family and kids. I want to be happy. I can't quite imagine true happiness but I am going to keep trying and maybe one day my life will work out.

In counselling, I have worked hard to try and overcome my negative feelings about intimacy. I did a lot of work with Leah, Brooke and Libby, to help me to understand the difference between sex and rape. You wouldn't believe how long we had to talk about this before we started to make any progress. We also talked about 'consent', and the fact that even if I didn't say no as a child, I was far too young to give consent. I am going to include a summary email that Leah sent me, about the difference between rape and sex. It was helpful for her to send me a summary, because I became very dissociated during our discussion and couldn't remember much of it later.

Hi Hannah,

Thanks for your hard work today. I know you are very tired and it takes a lot of energy to talk sometimes. You did really well :-)

Some reminders of our call:

You said that one of the things that is stuck on repeat in your head is an incident when Dad was angry at you and you let him touch you and "have sex" (a reminder that what happened was NOT sex. It was rape)

You said you get really confused about that incident. You feel like you gave Dad consent to touch you.

We then went through the definitions of rape and consent that you know.

We then talked about the type of situations where consent for sexual touching is not able to be given. These include: when there is a child involved, when the person feels threatened physically or emotionally and is scared in any way, when the person is drunk or under the influence of drugs, when the perpetrator is a lot older or has power over the person being touched.

We then talked about the incident you described again and found that what happened was NOT your fault. It was NOT consent. You were a child, you were emotionally threatened, as your parent he had complete control and power over you. All those things mean you did not and were not able to give consent.

You asked me if I think you wanted to have sex with your dad. I said NO I do not think that, I have never thought that and I won't ever think that. You wanted love and attention (like any child wants) but that is completely different to rape.

I understand these are tough concepts and things to talk about and very confusing. But you are doing really well to talk about them.

Again, what happened was NOT your fault, you did not give consent and I know you did not want to be abused by your father.

I encourage you to talk to Libby about this stuff. If you find it hard to bring it up or talk, maybe print out this email and start from there. See how you feel.

Talk to you in a couple of weeks,

Leah

Talking explicitly about the difference between rape and sex has been helpful for me, particularly since the three helpers in my life (Leah, Brooke and Libby) were consistent in their definitions. It has helped me to better understand what happened to me and to put it in context, which will hopefully make it easier for me to trust other males and create better boundaries in the future.

I should add that my ability to trust guys has slowly been improving in the last few years. I am starting to get better at figuring out which guys I can and cannot feel safe with. I feel very safe around the husband of one of my best friends, Grace — I can very happily hang out with them and feel fine. I also became good friends with a male co-worker in my previous job, and would regularly go to pub trivia with him and his friends. As mentioned, in 2013 I also had my uncle and cousin, and then a male friend come and stay at my house. In late 2013, I even went on a few dates with a guy I hardly knew. Despite experiencing a lot of anxiety, I still pushed myself to have a go, and nothing bad happened. In previous years, those things would have been too challenging for me. I am making huge gains, so there is still a lot of hope for me.

IMPACT OF DIFFICULTIES ON MY WORK AND LIVING SITUATION

I can hear you wondering how all the impacts of the abuse affect my ability to be a functioning member of society. Well, you might be surprised to hear that I am a full-time working professional. If you met me, you would just think that I am like any other recent university graduate, building up their skills. You might even think I am ambitious. In a workplace situation, I manage to pull myself together pretty well. I think to a large extent, this comes from years of having to get myself out of bed and go to school, despite the horrible abuse I was experiencing at home. I learned to just keep going, and this is a skill I maintain today.

I expect a lot of myself professionally, and have a job that requires me to be responsible and mature. I am good at 'switching off' from whatever else is going on in my life, and getting on with the task at hand when I need to. I can 'function' quite well, but sometimes when I am in a bad headspace, I will go home feeling completely zonked and just needing to be by myself, and wrap myself up in a blanket. In this sense, it was really great to have some time living by myself since moving away from my home town, because it really gave me the space I needed to cope.

When I am struggling at work, I will sometimes seek out a quiet space to eat lunch on my own, or eat lunch a bit later when the lunch room is nearly empty. On weekends, I am sometimes so exhausted that I really do just need a day by myself to regather. But I also have the ability to be very social and have a lot of friendships that I manage to maintain. There are many things that I manage to do that are genuinely a part of who I am, despite the difficulties I sometimes face.

Living situation

The difficulties that I have mentioned have a significant impact on my living situation. Living in share houses was extremely difficult for me, due to the unpredictability of lots of people coming in and out of the house. I was unable to switch off because I automatically used to figure out exactly where everyone was in the house. When you have a sharehouse with three or four people, plus their friends, coming in and out at all hours, it becomes very overwhelming. It was impossible for me to cope without earplugs.

For a few months, I also tried renting a room out in a house owned by a lady twice my age. Work colleagues and friends would make comments about it, such as "Don't you want to live with younger people in a sharehouse?", but they didn't understand the difficulties I face. I would love to live with young people, but the fact is, they are much less predictable. At least with this lady, I knew her routine and was generally left alone to have my own space.

However, I have since decided that for the sake of my mental wellbeing, living by myself is the best option. I need my own space to call home, and to feel safe. a place where I can make decisions about who can and can't stay over, and where I can retreat and be by myself when I need to. I have also recently gotten a dog, which really makes it my own safe little home.

PART FOUR:
MY ADVICE FOR PEOPLE WHO HAVE BEEN ABUSED AND THEIR SUPPORTERS

Painting by
Sarah Millicent Elliott

You have brains in your feet
You have feet in your shoes
You can steer yourself
Any direction you choose

(Dr Seuss, in *Oh The Places You'll Go*)

INTRODUCTION

In this section of the book, I am going to give my general advice for people who have experienced abuse or trauma, or are going through the criminal justice system. It is important to remember that I am not a trained professional in this area, I am just giving you information about what I found useful. If you find yourself needing professional support, a good place to start is your General Practitioner who will know of local services available.

I am also going to include my advice for those who are supporting young people who have been abused – whether you are family members, carers, teachers or health professionals. I hope that you realise just how crucial a role you can play in the life of a young person, if you're willing to respect and be there for them. I look at the support I received, especially from Kids Helpline and my face-to-face counsellor Libby, and I am eternally grateful for the difference it has made in my life.

I also think of the informal supports I have had in my life. People who have been willing to walk a mile in my shoes. People who have been willing to put up with me when I've had nightmares without making me feel embarrassed or stupid. People who have let me be myself without judgement. People who have shown me care and compassion and let me say how I feel about everything that has happened to me. People who have humoured my obsession with my dog and other quirks... And the people who have put up with my use of writing as my 'outlet' which unfortunately means there are always trusted people in my life who receive a barrage of emails!

Having people accept me for who I am without making me feel embarrassed, stupid or guilty, has made an immeasurable difference to my life.

Never underestimate the impact you are having on a young person's life, even if they can't articulate it.

MY ADVICE FOR YOUNG PEOPLE WHO ARE CURRENTLY BEING ABUSED

In counselling with Libby, I was asked to write down what I would say to a child who was being abused. I will share it now, in the hope that it will help any young person who is currently experiencing abuse:

I would say, it's not your fault. You haven't done anything wrong. You think you are bad and disgusting, but you didn't start this.

You are a child.

The only reason you know all this stuff about sex is because the adult forced all that on you. That does not make you a bad person.

People will listen and help you. It might take you a while to find the right adult (and some adults will <u>totally</u> let you down), but just keep trying.

Try telling little bits at a time until you can trust an adult. Try Kids Helpline! You are worthy of being listened to. People will care – I care! I am sad that you have to go through such hell.

Please note: I have written two books that are appropriate for kids, teens and young people which provide a lot of information about abuse and coping in the aftermath of abuse. Please visit www.dealingwithsexualabuse.com.au to find out more.

MY ADVICE FOR PEOPLE WHO HAVE EXPERIENCED TRAUMA

If you are dealing with trauma or major issues, I am sorry to hear this. I am not a trained professional in this area, so can only give broad advice on what helped me. But I really do recommend that you seek professional help, either through a counsellor (phone or face to face), or a General Practitioner, who can make appropriate referrals. I will put a list of some useful contacts at the back of this book as a starting point.

I will also include some broad tips about what has helped me to get through my difficulties, and what makes me feel better about myself:

A beautiful place: Find a beautiful place that you like going, and make sure you go there as often as possible. For me, this has always been the beach, which has been a very calming place for me, right since I was a kid.

Look after your health: Try to eat healthily, do regular exercise and get plenty of sleep. You would not believe what a difference those things can make in your ability to cope!

Get involved in the community: If you're up to it, join a sports club or a community group or class that interests you. This will broaden your social network, and also help you to further develop your own interests. Or you could try doing some volunteer work, even if it's a once-off event. This might help you to feel a bit better about yourself, and also you will be around other positive people.

Maintain a sense of humour! Joke with your friends and workmates. Do silly things! Enjoy life.

Be social: Even when you don't feel like it, try to maintain your friendships – even if you just catch up with one friend for coffee, go for a walk, or go along to Friday night drinks for an hour. It will help take your mind off things, and will help you feel more connected.

Indulge in your favourite movie, even if it's the one you loved as a kid. I have learned to not beat myself up too much for watching kids' movies, because I find them comforting.

Seek sunshine and get outdoors! It can really make a difference to how you're feeling.

Music: Find a song that captures where you are at and what you are feeling. For me, I had a couple of songs that I found comforting at particular times during the legal process, depending on whether I was angry or sad.

Favourite quotes: Find a quote that helps to inspire you, or that makes you laugh. I have put a few of my favourites in this book. I will also share one that was given to me by Brooke at Kids Helpline that I like: "On particularly rough days when I'm sure I can't possibly endure, I like to remind myself that my track record for getting through bad days so far is 100%, and that's pretty good" – Unknown.

Seek support: Try to be honest and open with people in your life about the support you need.

Be kind to yourself: Try not to beat yourself up too much... And that includes trying not to use the word "should" too much. I know, coming from me, this sounds very hypocritical. Leah at Kids Helpline sent me a small card a few years ago that says "I release the need to determine how things should be". I have stuck this on my wardrobe so that I see it every day. You are doing the absolute best you can, so just keep going. You have every reason to be proud.

Positive self-talk

No doubt you are going to have days where you feel hopeless and that you are getting nowhere. Your long-term hopes and dreams seem so far out of reach, that you don't know how life will ever work out. I have had many of these days. What helps me is to recognise the little, everyday achievements. With my counsellor Libby, I started keeping a log of all the small things I pushed myself to do when I was struggling to stay motivated, and gave myself a sticker for each one. It sounds corny, but for me it was really effective. Then on a bad day, I could look back on the chart and see the progress I was making.

Examples of some of my little achievements:

- Went out for drinks even though I didn't feel like it
- Had coffee with Jen even though I was stressed about stuff I needed to get done
- Ran my first 5km for the year.
- Went for a walk nearly every day this week to get back into the habit of exercising again
- Went skydiving!
- Went out with Jacinta at short notice despite being tired

- Organised breakfast with three non-work friends
- Went to my sports club training even though I didn't feel like going
- Went to movies with Abbey despite it being a bad weekend (parole letter), and not knowing the movie.
- Went out for dinner at late notice (usually I'd say no), and had fun.
- Went for a run with a friend from work.

Because I found counselling so difficult and sometimes felt I wasn't achieving anything, I also created a sticker chart for my achievements in counselling.

Examples of my achievements in counselling:

- Doing homework for Libby despite feeling crappy
- Grounding myself quickly after being drifty
- Talked to Brooke about something really embarrassing
- Went to see Libby despite not wanting to go.
- Kept my head off the desk and eyes open the whole session with Libby.

Writing a kind letter to myself

Another exercise that helped me to recognise my strengths and improvements was to write kind letters to myself, congratulating myself on the things I had done well. Here is an example:

24.4.2013

Dear Hannah,

I am proud of the way you handled things with Grace. You were feeling rejected by her because she hasn't been coming to any of the social things you have organised lately, and you have really missed her. You were starting to take it as a personal rejection.

Instead of lashing out (which is what you would normally do), you tried to think of things from Grace's point of view. You know that she often gets sick and stressed. You said "Grace, I miss you, do you want to get a coffee sometime?" instead of saying "WHY AREN'T YOU TALKING TO ME!" which is what you would normally say. Grace said "yes I'd love to" and you had a nice catch up on Saturday, then walked into town. Good job! I'm so proud of how you handled that. You sure are growing up.

I'm also proud of how you had Peter and Roslyn (from athletics) over o~~n~~ Monday evening, even though you were a bit nervous.

You don't really feel like going out tonight to see the band play, especially because you know the new guy from work is coming and you don't feel totally comfortable with him. But you are going, so that's a good effort too.

I'm also proud that you have decided not to run away from Libby despite finding counselling really difficult lately and having lashed out at her. I am proud that you are willing to go back and keep trying – and today went really well.

I am even prouder that you are writing this letter and actually being nice to yourself for once. This is rare. So, 'good job!' You do struggle so much to be kind to yourself.

From Hannah

Develop your sense of who you are

One thing I have found is that the abuse can really take over your identity and your thoughts about yourself. The best way to combat this is to actively go about figuring out who you are, and what interests you. What are your strengths? What are your good qualities? You're probably so used to seeing the difficulties and struggles, that you forget to think about these things. I am definitely guilty of that, so I am going to practise what I preach by writing down my strengths. You would be surprised at how hard it is to write your strengths without qualifying them with "but" or "not very'. But I am going to do it.

My strengths and interests

- I am a good godmother. Before Kelsey started school, I used to go to her weekly playgroup sessions. I was also there for her on her first day of school, attended her and her brothers' school sports days when I still lived in the same state, and since moving I have kept in touch with phone calls and letters.

- I care a lot about my dog.

- I am intelligent.

- I am good at writing.

- I am good at some crafty things like scrapbooking, and currently trying to get better at knitting.

- I am hardworking! I got through uni despite all of the difficulties I faced (while also juggling part-time work). I have had no difficulty getting professional jobs and maintaining them. I have also worked my arse off in counselling to try and give myself the future I want.

- I can be fun and cheeky, especially when I am comfortable with someone.

- I have been very brave and strong to face everything the way I have.

- I am proactive. If I am unhappy about a situation, I will actively go and change it.

- I like making cakes and getting presents for people.

- I have made some great friends through the sports club I am in, who really seem to value me for who I am.

- I stand up for what I believe in and have integrity.

- I am very independent and was very good at managing myself (including my finances) even as a teenager.

Find a good General Practitioner

This is so crucial that it deserves a few paragraphs. One of my strongest recommendations for anyone who has experienced abuse or trauma and is trying to overcome it, is to find a good General Practitioner (GP)! I have had both the experience of having a wonderful GP, and having terrible GPs, and seen for myself what a major difference it makes. Although it can be a hassle, I really do recommend asking friends and family whether they have a good GP, and see if you can get in. I strongly recommend going to meet the GP when you are in a good headspace, if possible. By being proactive, you can establish a good relationship with the GP prior to being in a crisis and really needing help. It might take a few appointments to get to know him or her, but it is money and time well spent, because any medications that may be prescribed for you can have a major impact on your life and ability to cope. You need to have a GP who is willing to listen to you, and who will care about you and help you if you have a negative reaction to any medication that is prescribed for you. a good GP can also recommend a psychologist or counsellor who might be helpful to you, and develop a mental health care plan with you.

When I moved interstate, it took me over 18 months to find a good GP, and what a relief that was. For the two years prior to that, I did not have a consistent or good GP, and it had such a negative impact on me. a couple of the GPs I tried had very little understanding of the impact of trauma, and didn't respond to my counsellor Libby's attempts to get in contact with them. As a result, they gave me medical advice that had a detrimental impact on me. One doctor also made very cutting comments which made me feel like I 'should' be able to cope better than I was.

If you find yourself with a GP like this, who shows little understanding of trauma and makes you feel worse about yourself – hold your head up high, walk away, and find someone else. It's not worth your energy. You can find someone better! My fabulous GP in my hometown, Dr Camden, truly understood the difficulties I faced, and it made such a difference. My new GP is also very understanding and keen to listen to me, which is a major relief. She was very happy to receive a handover from the Kids Helpline counsellors who knew me well, to understand my history and what has helped me in the past. When discussing the need for me to have a pelvic exam she was also very respectful of the difficulties this could cause for me, and was keen to find a way to make it as un-traumatic as possible.

MY ADVICE FOR PEOPLE GOING THROUGH THE CRIMINAL JUSTICE SYSTEM

Advice for victims of crime

If you are making a statement to the police, be kind to yourself. It is going to be really difficult, so make sure that you give yourself the space you need. If you can find someone to come with you, then I would encourage that. But it is possible to go through making the statement by yourself – I did. If possible, try and find a police officer who you are comfortable with, because ultimately that is going to make a major difference in your ability and willingness to share information with them. It is distressing enough as it is, so you want to feel as comfortable as possible. For example, if you would prefer to speak to an officer of a particular gender, don't hesitate to ask if this is an option. It might not be – but you have nothing to lose by asking. If it isn't an option, try and find a way around it – for example, if you wanted a female police officer but none are available, think about requesting a female counsellor to sit with you while you speak to the police.

When I decided that I was going to consider talking to the police, I got advice from Gabbie (sexual assault counsellor) about who might be good, and she recommended a female detective. If I hadn't gone to Jodi, I am honestly not sure that I would have gone through the process. If you are considering making a report to the police, don't hesitate to ask to meet the detective to have an informal chat, to discuss your concerns and to get to know them. I did that with Jodi, and it was very worthwhile – putting a face to the name and having a look at the police station can make a big difference.

There is no doubt about it that giving a statement is very difficult. All I wanted to do after making mine was go home, sleep, and eat Smarties! When I had enough energy, I walked to a nearby park and went on the swings there for ages. I know that is a little childish (I was 18!), but that is what I needed. I also wanted to do some colouring in, which again is childish but what I needed to do. It is okay to do the things that make you feel safe and comfortable. Don't beat yourself up over that.

Waiting for court dates is difficult, and it is hard to plan your life with much certainty while you wait. So I would just recommend that you have something that you regularly do and enjoy, to focus on. This might involve being in a sports club, or a social club. For me, living on campus provided me with plenty of opportunities for distraction during this time. Try not to recluse from the world, even when you want to. You'll lose too much of your life if you recluse, because sadly, the legal system doesn't move quickly.

If your case doesn't make it to court – don't be dismayed. You did the best you could, and very often, there just isn't enough evidence. That is not your fault and it doesn't mean that people don't believe you. I can only imagine how defeated I would have felt if charges had not been laid, so I really do feel for you if that happens to you.

If your case does head to court – try and go about your normal routine as much as possible. Make sure you have something to wear for each day of the trial – try to find something that will make you feel nice, or safe, even if you have a favourite scarf or pair of earrings or shoes or anything like that. If you have people in your life who want to support you during the court case, be open and honest with them about what would and wouldn't be helpful for you. This was a bit of a downfall for me, because I didn't have open and honest conversations with people about whether I was comfortable for them to watch my testimony. In fact, I wasn't even aware that some of them were coming to watch. To prevent this from happening to you, I would strongly suggest having open conversations with anyone you know who might be intending to come. If there is a friend or family member who is a good advocate for you, let them know what your wishes are, so that they can also spread this to other people. The main priority should be for you to feel safe and comfortable during your testimony. You have already been really badly violated with the assaults themselves, so try not to feel guilty about hurting peoples' feelings by wanting your privacy. Your feelings matter too.

When giving testimony, keep a level head. I think defence lawyers really do want to make you angry and get a response out of you. I got the feeling that in my case, the defence lawyer would have loved nothing more than for me to fly off the handle and start swearing at him. But I didn't do either of those things. I just stuck to the facts, and rationally explained to him that I stood by what I had said, and that I disagreed with him. If you keep a level head, the defence lawyer will be left with no real come-back to anything you say, and you will come out of the process with your dignity shining through. Stay cool, and stick to the facts. Even if you do not win your case (remember, it is incredibly difficult to get a conviction in cases of rape or sexual abuse), at least you know you have acted with integrity – the rest is out of your hands.

Unfortunately, the legal system is fraught with difficulties, and you may feel like you are being tossed around. My only advice is to just be proud of yourself for doing your best. Advocate for yourself. Chase people up on the phone, and when that doesn't work, put it in writing. If you find someone who is willing to advocate for you within the system, CC them into any emails you send – you would be surprised at how much of a difference that can make. If you're seen as having 'important' people on your side, people tend to treat you with a bit more dignity and respect – this is a sad reality that I have learned.

A final piece of advice I have is to not contact the person who abused you, unless you really feel this is necessary. If, like me, you feel that this is crucial to you getting over what happened and putting the guilt behind you, seriously weigh up the pros and cons. I do not for one second regret going and visiting Dad. But I can see how it complicated my life further, because it gave him more 'material' for his appeals. If you do decide that you want to visit the perpetrator, I would recommend having at least two impartial witnesses with you, and refusing to go ahead with the meeting if the perpetrator shoos your witnesses away, which is what happened to me.

Advice for friends and family of someone going through the criminal justice system

If you know someone who is going through the legal system, it is great that you want to support them. It is important that you keep in mind how stressful it is for them, and that the details they have to discuss in court are very personal and embarrassing. If you want to support them through the process, ask them what is the best way for you to support them. I would not recommend just turning up at court and assuming that they'll want you there. Please don't take it personally if they do not want you there. It doesn't mean that they don't value you and the care you are showing. Try and imagine how you would feel if you had to stand up in a room full of people and answer questions in detail about sexual things that had happened to you. Now add on the extra humiliation of those sexual things involving your dad. Now add on the trauma of knowing that by speaking, you might possibly get a parent, who you still care about, put in jail. It is fair enough that you might not want your great Aunty Jude sitting in the court room listening to those details.

A good piece of advice I have is to give the person options. If you ask them straight out 'Do you want me to come or not?' they might feel too scared to offend you by saying no. But if you give them options such as "Do you want me to come into the courtroom, or I could come and have lunch with you instead if that's easier? Or would you rather catch up some other time once the court proceedings are over?" They will appreciate you giving them power and options at a time when so much of their life is out of their control.

The purpose of going to court should be about supporting the victim, not about hearing the details. To those random people who go from court room to court room to hear all the gory details – have more respect, please.

MY ADVICE FOR SUPPORT PEOPLE

In Part 3, I already included information about how I worked with counsellors to overcome some of the difficulties I have experienced. The recommendations I will include here are more general, and are relevant to anybody either supporting or working professionally with someone who has experienced abuse or trauma.

Team work: For me, it was so useful that Kids Helpline worked so closely with my GP Dr Camden (in my home town), and my face to face counsellor Libby. When any of them had concerns about me, they would work as a team to help me. It also meant that everyone in the team had a full picture of what was going on for me, so that I didn't always have to give the same information twice. When working on particular aspects of the trauma with Libby, this was reinforced by my work with Leah and Brooke. I don't think I would have done such great counselling work without the tremendous team work of all involved.

Consistency: Where possible, offer consistency to the young person who has experienced trauma. Abuse is highly unpredictable, and for me has led to major anxieties when sudden and unexpected changes occur. I explained this to my Kids Helpline counsellors so generally would have a set day to call them. With Libby, it was possible to see her at a consistent time for our appointments, which was really useful. The appointments became part of my 'routine', so were less anxiety provoking.

Provide structure: When working both with Libby face-to-face and with Brooke and Leah on the phone, I found it particularly useful to set an 'agenda' of what we would do in our next appointment, so that I didn't become anxious in between appointments. Particularly with Libby (because seeing someone face-to-face is more intense), I would become really thrown off balance if she took a random tangent in a session that I hadn't expected. This would be really overwhelming for me and sometimes cause me to dissociate. So Libby learned to give me as much warning as possible before starting anything new in sessions, and my anxiety was reduced. For a while, we used a workbook to guide our sessions, which provided me with the structure and warning that I needed. As I became more and more comfortable with Libby, my ability to cope with changes to our plan increased.

Provide warning about your changes: If you are no longer going to see the young person as frequently as you used to, or are going away on a long holiday, this can potentially have a major impact on the young person if they have come to trust and rely on you. You can ease the impact by giving as much warning as possible about any upcoming changes.

Set the young person up to succeed: One thing that I have found particularly useful is when the 'ground rules' with counsellors are agreed upon together. I like to know what you expect of me, and what I can expect from you. When it isn't defined, I am scared that I will 'get it wrong' and embarrass myself. It makes it feel like you have all the power, and makes it harder for me to trust you.

Providing warning about physical movement or touch: As silly as it sounds, if you are with a young person who has experienced abuse, it sometimes helps if you warn them that you're about to move towards them, or even if you're going to get up and open the door, or that it's time to get up and leave. If you just stand up and walk past them without warning it can be very startling because they've become so fine-tuned to peoples' movements and touch. Also, if you're going to touch them at all, again give them warning (and processing time) and make sure it is okay with them. This is particularly important for doctors.

Patience: It is likely that someone who has been abused will yo-yo back and forth with their trust for you, and will sometimes challenge you and lash out at you. You need to understand that this is not personal, but it is just them trying to gauge whether you are a safe person. Sometimes they will want a safe adult by their side, but other times they will feel terrified that you will hurt or abandon them too.

Setting achievable goals: I have found it really useful to set goals that are important to me, and then continually check in with someone about how I am going with my goals. One of my main goals in 2012 was to do more social stuff. I felt really silly when I said to Libby, "maybe I should have a sticker chart or something". The next week when I arrived to my session, Libby had put a packet of cute smiley face stickers on the table for me, to use on my sticker chart. It might seem like a childish idea, but it worked, and I liked it. I found that having the chart and being 'accountable' to Libby really did help to push me towards my goal. I got a sticker for every time I accepted a social invitation from a friend, went along to something outside of work, or organised a social event myself.

Don't get stuck on age: For me, it was helpful that my counsellors could see that despite initially presenting as a competent young person, I was still a scared little child inside, who needed that nurturing that I didn't get earlier on. If you are supporting someone who needs that nurturing, give it to them, regardless of whether it is 'age appropriate' or not. This might be through playing games, or watching a childish movie, or wrapping them up in a blanket. Give them options and help them to tell you what they really need.

Don't shy away from affection: If you have a friend or young person in your life who has experienced abuse, you might think you should never give them any affection. It is good to have an understanding of the difficulties they might have with affection. But once you have a good relationship with them, they might feel safe enough to have a hug from you. They might in fact want that, because it is important for them to learn the difference between safe and unsafe affection. But they might not know how to approach you for affection. The best advice I can give is to just ask them, "Do you want a hug?" They might say yes, they might say no. They might be awkward about it at first, but I think deep down everyone wants to feel safe and secure, and have the occasional hug.

Look for strengths instead of making judgements: Try to avoid making comments about what someone who has experienced trauma does or doesn't need, unless you fully understand all of the difficulties they face. Instead, look for their strengths.

Painting by
Sarah Millicent Elliott

Helping a young person to open up to you

I am also going to include my advice about how you can assist a young person to tell you what they need to tell you. This is particularly relevant to mental health professionals.

Respect: It is very important that you treat anyone who has been abused with respect. I gave some examples of times when I didn't feel respected, for example with my school psychologist, and how this impacted on my ability to accept help from her. It is important to remember that people who have experienced abuse have already had a lot of power taken away from them, so where possible, give them options and a say in what is happening.

Genuine compliments: It helps to give genuine compliments, because young people who have experienced abuse already feel so bad about themselves, and tend to view themselves in a negative light. It is also very empowering for you to tell us what you have learned from us – either personally or professionally. For example, Brooke at Kids Helpline told me that she hadn't realised how sensitive to noise someone who had experienced abuse might be, until she worked with me. I was proud to have taught her something that might help her to better understand what it is like for people in my situation.

Acknowledge the young person's individual story: One thing I noticed was that counsellors always tell you about other people they work with, which I think is meant to make you see that other people have experienced similar things. I sometimes found this quite annoying, because it felt like the counsellor was comparing me to the other people they worked with. It made me feel even more self-conscious, and like they were thinking "Wow, Hannah's really not done very well compared to the other people I see". I suppose in part this comes from my fear of rejection and my bad feelings about myself. My recommendation would be to check with the young person whether they find it helpful to hear about your other clients – some people will say yes, some will say no.

Using humour: One of my biggest barriers with Libby, Brooke and Leah was feeling too embarrassed to give the details of certain things that had happened to me. I ended up asking Libby one day, "Libby, there's something I want to talk to you about, but I am scared you will think it's gross". She said "I wouldn't think it was gross". So to test the waters, I asked "well what do you think is gross then?" She thought about it, laughed and said "I think it's gross when people are driving and pick their noses!" I cracked up at this and felt a bit safer to tell her stuff after that.

Giving the physical space that is needed: Due to their sensitivity to feeling 'trapped', try and give the young person a clear pathway to the door. This ideally should include having them facing towards the door. I can become quite distressed when I feel boxed in as if I won't be able to get to an exit quickly if I need it.

Don't force eye contact: When seeing Libby face-to-face, I found it really difficult to make eye contact with her. This is because the stuff we were talking about was so embarrassing and distressing for me. But Libby didn't force me to look at her, and instead helped me to find things to have in front of me (like colouring in books and pencils), or sometimes we played games together such as Jenga during which we would both be looking at the game, not each other. I was able to tell Libby lots of things when playing games like this. After a while, I was more comfortable and able to make better eye contact with Libby, except when talking about specific details of the abuse.

Find a comfortable place to talk: Another thing I found helpful when I saw Libby was that she let me find a room that I felt comfortable working in. In her actual office, I felt really self-conscious, because there were just the two chairs across from each other, and I felt it was very awkward. But there was another room that Libby had access to, which had a big table in the middle. Libby and I ended up using this room for nearly all our sessions, and at my request we sat with the table in the middle of us. This again gave me a feeling of space and protection, which helped to ease the feelings of self-consciousness a bit. It also helped to have a table to prop myself up on when I was dissociating.

Help the person you are working with to express themselves: They might clam up when they try and talk to you about what happened or what they are thinking. But they might have another way of telling you. With Libby, I would often write things down so that she knew what I wanted to say. I even did that with my GP Dr Camden in my home town. With Brooke and Leah, I would generally send them an email before calling them, so that they knew if there was something in particular that I wanted to talk about. I scanned all of my old diaries (the ones I have now typed) for Brooke when I first started talking to her in 2011, and sent them to her. Brooke felt that she 'got to know me' through my writing, and it meant I didn't have to explain everything to her again. You might have a quiet, grumpy young person in front of you, but they might be an articulate, sad child inside who really wants your help.

Group work

If you are going to put a young person into a therapy group, it is important to be really clear with the young person (and with yourself) about the justification for them going into the group.

When I was 18, the sexual assault centre I attended put me into group therapy as a way of getting me off individual sessions. It was a total disaster though, because I was the youngest in the group. Other than the one 25 year old, other group members were in their 40s and 50s and had experienced great difficulties in their life including imprisonment, prostitution, and drug and alcohol problems. As an impressionable teenager who had only been free from abuse for four months, the group was terrifying! I started to wonder whether my life would end up being as miserable as that of other group members. It made me feel really scared about my future and whether I should even bother to 'keep going'. I found it hard to relate to other group members except for the 25 year old. It had a lasting impact on me and I have since refused to do any group work because my experience was so scarring. My first serious suicide attempt was just two months after the group experience if that is any indication of what a difficult and unstable period it was for me, which again demonstrates just how inappropriate the timing of the group was for me.

I know groups can seem like a great use of resources, but please make sure that you are not doing more harm than good.

Ceasing counselling

Of course, there will always be times when counselling or support has to be ceased for one reason or another. When this is to occur, it is important to have clear planning and warning in place for the young person. If they do not have many adults in their life to rely on for support, you might not realise just how crucial you are in their world.

I was totally shocked when the sexual assault counsellor I had come to rely on suddenly said that it was time to take a break from counselling, a month after I had moved out of home. There was no structure or plan in place and I felt like I had no control over the decision. Counselling should not be ceased at a turbulent time, such as the transition from moving out of home, especially when a young person has very limited supports available.

I think sometimes service providers forget the need to be clear and transparent with young people who have experienced trauma, because sudden, knee-jerk decisions for someone who has already experienced shocking trauma are an unwelcome trigger of a lack of control, chaos and rejection. When ending counselling relationships it is important to allow the young person space to deal with their emotional reaction, as they might feel a sense of loss that you as a professional aren't aware of because to you it is just a normal day at work. It is important to remember that people who have experienced trauma and a loss of family relationships may be triggered emotionally by the severing of relationships, including those with counsellors. I know it sounds obvious but some services really didn't seem to understand that in my case.

It is really important that if you are going to cease counselling sessions with a young person, you ensure they have other supports in place or know who to contact if they need help in the future. This was one of my biggest issues when the sexual assault centre finished counselling with me. I was a teenager and still waiting for the court process to take place. When I asked who else I could talk to, the sexual assault centre recommended a local psychologist that I could see under a Medicare health care plan; however, this was limited to about six sessions. As I have previously explained, this was not a viable long-term option for me due to my financial situation. In hindsight I would have much preferred them to link me in with a local community service or headspace centre.

It is possible for counselling relationships to end in a way that is positive and respectful. I had contact with Kids Helpline for nine years. For the last two years of that relationship, we had a clear plan in place about how I would gradually reduce my contact with them so that I would be supported and not feel too sad at the end of the counselling relationship. We had a 'goodbye' phone call and a closing letter, which helped me a lot as well. I was able to grieve the loss of Leah and Brooke from my life, and my feelings were validated. The clear planning, warning, and room for my input about what would make the process easier for me, made it a positive experience for everyone. Yes, it was still sad, but it was predictable and I felt valued in the process. It has taught me that it is possible to have relationships in life that are positive in their entirety.

My advice for foster carers

I have never been in foster care, but I want to say that I have more than the utmost of respect for people who foster children. I have met some amazing foster parents, including a friend of mine and her husband. One thing that I have sadly seen with this friend is that the foster care system can sometimes be really difficult for foster carers to navigate. Sometimes decisions appear to be made in the best interests of the abusive or unfit biological parents, instead of the best interests of the child. This is extremely unfortunate, as a child's welfare should be the utmost priority.

To people who foster, you really are heroes. You have the ability to completely turn a child's life around. You are a crucial part of society. I hope that what I have written helps you to understand some of the difficulties a child who has experienced trauma may face, including the 'mourning' for the parent they no longer have contact with.

My advice if you suspect a child is being abused or trying to tell you something

If you suspect a child is trying to tell you about something that is happening to them, make it easier for them. Ask if there is something they want to talk to you about. Give them options of where they would feel most comfortable talking to you – for example on the school oval, or in a quiet office? It is important that you show the child that you really do want to listen to them.

If for whatever reason you sense that they do not feel comfortable with you, try not to take it personally. Ask them if there is a particular teacher or adult that they do feel more comfortable talking to. For example, I really did not like my school psychologist, and would never disclose anything to her. If a teacher I liked had been present during my session with the school psychologist, I probably would have felt much more supported.

Be prepared for the details of the abuse to come out slowly, and that the young person will withhold information until they feel safe to share it. For example, I initially wouldn't tell Kids Helpline that I was still being abused. I also withheld my real name, to protect myself. This isn't something you should take personally – it's because there is so much at stake for the young person, and they need to suss you out. Like me, you might have a young person who susses out several people, gradually telling a little bit more information to the people they speak to. This is a way of building up trust and confidence.

If the child really can't get the words out, ask them if they want to write something down or draw a picture instead. No child wants to keep being abused, and if they can see that you are really making an effort and that you care, it is much more likely that they will tell. If they do tell you something, don't get frustrated if they retract their story or start avoiding you. This is, I've been told, extremely normal for children who have been abused and are trying to protect a loved one, and trying to stop a 'report' being made. The child might suddenly be really terrified once they have told you, and feel like their life is falling upside down. As terrible as it is to be abused, home is still home, and family is still family, and most children do not want to lose either of them. If this means retracting their story to keep people happy, well then they will do it. They need you to see through that though, and continue being on their side.

If a child tells you something that you are going to need to report to child protection or another authority – be upfront with them! I was really shocked that in my situation, people were not upfront with me. It is disgraceful that a report was made to child protection without me knowing, and even worse that child protection closed the file without interviewing me.

If you are going to make a report to authorities, it is also important that you reassure the child that you are going to make sure they are safe. If the child feels that you are going to report them and then leave them to deal with all the consequences on their own (angry parents, possible removal from their family, parents getting in trouble), then you can expect them to retract the allegations. They need to know that you will stick with them. They need to know that they are not alone and that people really do care about them. Remember, you are dealing with a child who has already had their trust shattered by the people who they should be able to trust the most. You need to remember that you are in a position of power compared to the child, who might know nothing different to living at home with their family.

I think if a trusted adult had stepped in earlier for me, things would have been much different. But by the time anyone really did try to step in, I was too old to trust them, too cynical, and had already started making plans to move out of home myself.

Another thing I would like to say is that you cannot make assumptions that a child is 'coping well' with a bad situation such as abuse. Children can sometimes be very good at dulling their emotions and not feeling things properly, and that is a way of coping. If you choose not to help as much as possible, or think a child will simply 'be okay', you can expect the child to have ongoing difficulties. You can also expect that they will probably contact you when they are an adult, when they have had a chance to process their anger.

I will include for you now a copy of the letter I sent to my former teacher, Mrs Stanley, in February 2012. I feel it sums up well, how I think adults should respond to and help kids.

Dear Mrs. Stanley,

Just letting you know that I have moved interstate. After everything I endured as a kid, then the court case, and three appeals (the most recent in September last year), I needed to leave.

I have had some time to think things over. I've decided that I still think you really let me down as a kid. I know hindsight always helps, but I still think you had enough information to ask more questions and help much earlier. You chose not to, and that may have been because of stuff going on in your life, or your personality – I don't know. And that's not my fault.

I know you feel like I should have put this behind me – but I do have a right to not respect your actions, and to say how I feel. All I've ever really wanted is for you to say sorry, but also to acknowledge what I had to go through.

When I saw you last year I hoped to get some closure, but it seemed quite awkward and difficult (for both of us).

The one thing I know is that I am going to live a life of not taking chances with kids. If there is ever the slightest chance they're being abused, I will be asking questions (I already have – probably a bit over cautious).

That is the major lesson I have learned from all of this. I am <u>never</u> going to risk a kid being raped or bashed at home because I was too scared to ask if everything was okay, or made the assumption that it wasn't that bad, that they could put up with it. Adults have so much more power and ability to change a situation than kids do.

I feel angry and sad that I was the one who made all the efforts to move out of home. I desperately wanted a trusted adult (you) to take me seriously about needing to leave home. I told you so many times! I felt completely worthless that I had to face so much on my own. Being abused is bad enough, but feeling like nobody cares makes it 100 times worse. I felt like a piece of crap and I just wanted to die.

I'm not mentally unstable, I'm just saying what I've been thinking all these years, and already feel better now that it's out.

I <u>am</u> getting on with my life – I finished uni with honours, went on a trip overseas, and got a great job in a new state. I don't hate you or think you're a bad person, I just don't think you are as strong a person as I thought you were when I was a kid.

You're very welcome to write back or call me, I've included all my contact details. I'd love that, to talk this through with you, but don't expect it to happen.

From Hannah

I did not receive a response to this letter.

The focus on 'mandatory reporting' and 'disclosures'

Since I first published this book online last year, the most common question I have had from professionals is how they should handle informing kids and teenagers about their 'reporting responsibilities' in situations where abuse is suspected. I have given this question a lot of thought and will share my thoughts with you now.

To be honest, I think it is really confronting when the first statement to come out of a professional's mouth is: "While this is confidential, please be aware that in some situations, for example if you or someone else is being harmed, I will need to report it". It is already so intimidating to talk to an adult in the first place – and adults seem to forget that. Then you add a sentence like that and the conversation is pretty much over, well it was in my mind. Once kids learn about the fact that adults 'report' stuff, they will learn to not cross the line by saying too much – that was exactly what I did. I was smart enough to figure out where the 'line' was and never overstep it until I finally trusted a sexual assault and Kids Helpline counsellor. It had to be on my terms.

With the first professionals I spoke to at school, a better way for them to handle things would have been for them to try and build rapport with me first. Clearly I wanted to talk to the school chaplain because I made the appointment myself. I wanted help. She would have seen that, but she scared me right off with her statement about 'reporting'. If she had just given me a chance to get to know her, maybe it would have been different. I did like her and she was gentle, and given time, it could have worked. If I had felt that an adult was genuine and caring and would stick around for the long haul, I would have told them eventually. But as a teenager, if you just think that an adult is going to jump the gun, make a massive big deal and alert the authorities straight away without asking you what you want, then you won't trust them to stick around to help you deal with the aftermath.

I had absolutely no faith in the adults in my school and I think I was very justified to feel that way. None of them showed any signs of truly being there for me past the point of their 'legal responsibilities'. I told them I wanted to move out of home and they offered no assistance whatsoever, instead they just covered themselves by reporting to child protection and doing nothing more. It would have been a great opportunity for them to really link me in with local services and get me out of home... I don't see why it was so hard for them to listen to what I really needed. I don't know why adults often feel it is the responsibility of other agencies to sort out a young person's cry for help and to just say "oh well, nothing we can do, bloody useless child protection!" when child protection services don't intervene. Of course, there are massive inadequacies with child protection systems across Australian states and territories which definitely need to be addressed, there is no denying that. But other community members are still very capable of providing assistance. Don't forget the old proverb:

> *"It takes a village to raise a child".*

How hard is it to link a young person in with local services or Centrelink to help them move out of home when everyone knows they are being abused? a school is central to a young person's life so why they couldn't just make that effort for me, I have no idea.

I also wonder why child protection has to rely on an official 'disclosure' to intervene, which is unrealistic in a lot of situations. I was a teenager who had been abused for years on end. Then I was sent off to the school psychologist, who I didn't know, and was expected to disclose my biggest life secrets. Would you feel comfortable in that situation? If you, as an adult, were forced to speak to a psychologist and asked about the biggest, most shameful part of your life, would you dive right in and tell them all the details in one session — especially if it could mean tearing apart your family? No? So you don't wish to make a disclosure? Well there will be no help for you then!

I felt so disappointed to read the child protection report that was solely focussed on my 'not wishing to make a disclosure'. What kid doesn't want help? Who was this report really protecting? Not me, that's for sure.

In my case, if the school had really wanted to make me feel comfortable with the school psychologist, they could have at least asked me which adult in the school I felt comfortable with, so that they could have accompanied me to the session with the psychologist. It would have also created an opportunity for that trusted adult to follow-up with me after the session, give me a chance to debrief. But I had none of those options presented to me, and nobody to talk to after the appointment. More lost opportunities, and confirmation in my mind of my lack of worth and a complete lack of care or interest in me. And I was supposed to trust these people to care enough about me to keep me safe, when at the end of the day a full disclosure might have meant having no home to go to...

If you were in my shoes, would you have risked it?

Rapport and really listening to the young person need to be at the centre of all work in this area, yet sadly they seem to be missing sometimes!

PART FIVE:
MY PLEA FOR SYSTEM CHANGE

Painting by
Sarah Millicent Elliott

Unless someone like you cares a whole awful lot
Nothing is going to get better, it's not.

(Dr Seuss, in The Lorax)

INTRODUCTION

To conclude the book, I am going to give my ideas about what changes could be made to help prevent situations like mine from occurring in the future.

If you get nothing else from this book, please hear my plea for changes to be made in the way Australia addresses and responds to child abuse.

I am going to give specific recommendations which are relevant to the education, child protection, criminal justice and support systems. I am also including a short section specific to Western Australian readers given that this is the state in which I grew up.

Please note: This section of the book contains my personal opinions about what changes would benefit children and young people, based on my own personal experiences of the service systems.

MY ADVICE ABOUT ABUSE PREVENTION EDUCATION

When it comes to educating kids about abuse, my advice for adults is fairly simple. You need to teach children (and adults) about abuse as much as possible, from an early age. And you need to listen to children and respond to them when they are trying to ask you for help.

What you can do to raise awareness and help prevent abuse and neglect

There are plenty of things you can do in the fight against child abuse. There are several organisations that aim to raise awareness about abuse, and I have listed the ones I know about at the back of this book. You can donate money to any of these organisations, or any other organisations you may know of. Have a look on the internet or in your local phone book and find out what events and organisations there are, and how you can help. You can organise events in your workplace to raise money for an organisation that supports children. In doing so, you will not only be raising money, but awareness amongst staff and other people who frequent your workplace. You might have children who visit your workplace who would also benefit from any awareness raised about abuse, or services available to help kids.

Another recommendation I have is that you advocate for all mobile phone providers to give free access to Kids Helpline. I used to always make sure I was with Optus which used to be the only free provider, but Telstra and a few others have also recently jumped on board, with current details listed on the Kids Helpline website. If kids know that they can access the service for free without it being traced on their phone bill, they are much more likely to seek and access ongoing help. They just need your help to make it possible.

You can also speak to politicians about the importance of keeping children safe. I have done this before – even as a 17 year old I wrote to and then met with a politician, to ask for better education about abuse in our schools. If I could do that as a 17 year old, what's stopping you? Make your voice heard.

I also think it's really important that all adults make time for the children in their lives. Be it your own children, your nieces or nephews, grandkids, neighbours, friends' kids or children you work with, make an effort to listen to them and show them that you care. If they see you as a reliable adult, they're more likely to trust you and want to tell you whatever is going on for them – be it that they are being bullied at school, that they are worried about something, or that they are being abused. If you always appear to be too 'busy' to care, they won't feel able to approach you.

Painting by
Sarah Millicent Elliott

Teaching children about abuse

One factor that worked against me as a kid was that I had insufficient education about abuse at school. This made it impossible for me to go and tell adults what was happening to me because I did not have the words. I also didn't know that abuse was wrong and that it was not my fault. It wasn't until I was 15 years old and stumbled across a Judy Blume book in the school library, that I actually learned for certain what abuse was, that it was not my fault and that I should seek help.

I feel so let down that it was a 1980s Judy Blume book that I found myself that educated me about abuse.

I also feel really disappointed that there were community organisations and protective behaviours organisations in my home state that had been providing abuse prevention education since the early 90s, yet had obviously failed to either reach me or teach me anything that I was able to transfer to my own life. I remember having vague puppet shows about safety, as well as presentations about 'safety houses' and 'stranger danger'. However, nothing I learned made me feel that it would be acceptable for me to talk about what was happening to me, or seek help.

From what I can see, there are now several organisations that are really spearheading the campaign to teach children about abuse including the fact that abusers are generally people known to the child. I don't recall hearing much about these organisations as a child, but as they receive more funding, they are helping more and more children in more parts of Australia. You can support these organisations (and I am sure there are many others) by donating to them, or offering to volunteer. Please refer to the back of the book for more information about these organisations.

I should probably add here that I think it is incredibly important that all abuse education programs are scrutinised to ensure that they contain the information that children and adolescents need. Since publishing the first edition of this book in May 2014, I have been doing my own 'research' into abuse education programs in Australia. Some of them have all the information I feel I would have needed as a child. Others, however, appear much too vague. To me, a good abuse education program is one where, at the end, children can clearly tell you:

- Where it is and isn't appropriate for adults to touch them (including use of correct terminology);

- What to do if someone touches them inappropriately;

- What to do if they are asked to keep an unsafe secret (and they need to be able to define what is an unsafe secret as this is quite a vague term), and

- Who they would seek help from (a network of people), and what they would do if the first person did not listen to them.

Importantly, kids should be able to recall all this information a few months down the track; otherwise the education program was a waste of time! Therefore, schools and parents/carers have a responsibility to continue reinforcing the information throughout the year.

I don't believe that programs about 'safety' alone are enough for children because I had safety education as a child and it was not specific enough for me to generalise to my own life. It is also crucial that we consider the needs of young people with intellectual disabilities who would struggle to generalise any vague information to their life. Therefore, education programs for children really do need specific, clear information about what is and isn't okay for an adult to do to them. There is no need to embed the information into a complex or 'nice' story line – complexity will increase the risk of kids not getting the key messages. You've got to remember that abused kids are already going to be pretty tired a lot of the time, so you really need to be clear with them. I can't say it strongly enough that there is no room for vagueness.

Role of schools in abuse prevention education

Education departments and schools around Australia really need to be taking ownership of abuse prevention education. I have heard the argument around the traps that teachers are 'too busy' or don't have the capacity to add it to an already full curriculum. However, it needs to be a priority, and it needs to be compulsory in all schools. Schools need to be held accountable to this.

I know that not all teachers feel confident to teach content in this area. One of my best friends who has been a primary school teacher for a couple of years, admitted to me that she just 'skimmed over' the abuse prevention education because she felt under-skilled to teach it. This is a friend who knows my history and knows how important abuse prevention is – she just needed a bit more training in this area. It is important that student teachers are trained in child protection and the effective delivery of abuse prevention education; and that all other teachers receive ongoing support and training to carry out this education.

I know some people may say it is an uncomfortable and specialised topic, but in my mind, it is part of the territory of working with kids. If a teacher does not feel comfortable to talk about abuse to their class, how will they feel when a student comes up and tries to disclose that they are being abused? Maybe they will give the same 'shut down' response that I got from my PE teacher. I was the first student she had reported in her 25 years of teaching – now isn't that sad... I wonder how many kids before me could have done with some help.

I think as a kid, having external groups come in and put on plays or education sessions was a bit of a novelty, and as I said, I had a few puppet shows about safety, but what I think really needs to occur is for abuse prevention education to occur in normal, day-to-day school life. That would mean that the kid who is absent will still be able to receive the education they need from their regular teacher. It would mean that the kid who takes a while to grasp the information has a clear 'go to' person for more info – their regular teacher. It would also mean that the kids' regular teacher would have a chance to check in with kids following the education sessions.

When it comes to external organisations providing abuse prevention education to staff or students, there needs to be clear community involvement and planning. There is no point in having an external organisation coming in year after year to deliver all the training. How is that capacity building? That is just teaching schools or communities that it is not really their job and that they don't have the skills to do it. Instead, external education providers really should aim to up-skill key people in each community to eventually run all the training themselves. This could include training a couple of staff in each school so that they could then train all other teachers in the school and therefore become self-sufficient.

Role of other adults in educating kids about abuse

The more people in a child's life who speak with them about keeping themselves safe from abuse, the better. Whether you work with children or have children of your own, you play a vital role in teaching children about what is and isn't appropriate for an adult to do to them, and what they should do if they are ever made to feel uncomfortable. In doing so, you might help a child to disclose abuse far earlier, before they start feeling 'trapped' after having it occur for many years. If you're not sure how to go about teaching kids about abuse, contact one of the abuse prevention organisations that I have listed, and they will be able to provide you with more information. I hope my story has taught you the importance of educating children as much as possible about abuse.

Educating communities to respond to abuse

Of even higher importance than educating children about abuse is the education of adults about how to identify and respond to abuse. As my situation shows, disclosures or signs of abuse achieve nothing if the adults do not know how to identify or respond to them. If adults around me had had increased knowledge and response skills, I am sure I would have received assistance a lot earlier. That is why abuse prevention programs that take a 'whole community' approach are so valuable.

I personally don't believe that educating kids about abuse is a 'first line of defence' in the fight against child abuse. It is really just a 'back up', for when kids do not have adults in their lives who are good at identifying suspected abuse, or actually doing anything about it. However, the responsibility for preventing abuse lies solely with adults.

In many situations, even if kids have been educated about abuse, it is not realistic to expect them to report it to adults. This might be due to fear;

intellectual disability or communication problems which make it difficult for them to report the abuse; a lack of trusted adults in their life; cultural factors; or simply being too young to understand what is happening to them.

For example, it is unrealistic to expect a three year old who is being abused by their immediate family, to go and report the abuse to an adult outside of their family unless they have access to a supportive network of adults (unlikely if they're being abused at home) and those adults know how to identify the signs of abuse. At three years old, kids who have been abused by immediate family members are unlikely to know any different, so won't even know to report the abusive behaviour unless an external adult notices that something is not okay for the child. It is important to remember that some kids, particularly those being abused in their immediate family, do not have a network of trusted adults around them. Examples include a child whose family has moved from interstate/overseas and doesn't have extended family or friendship networks; a child who speaks limited English, or a child who is home schooled or lives in a remote community.

Therefore, I cannot stress enough that it is the responsibility of all adults in the community to play their part in safeguarding all children. This includes understanding abuse, its impacts, and warning signs; monitoring all children in the community; and most importantly, taking action when a child is not safe.

MY INPUT ON PUBLIC DISCUSSION ABOUT SEX OFFENDERS

There has been discussion recently about whether introducing a public register for child sex offenders will better protect children. While I think the intentions behind creating this register are well meaning, personally, I don't think such a register is the most effective way to protect children.

A register would make it possible for users to find out the names and details of sex offenders in their local area. The sorts of parents who would go onto such a register to protect their kids, are the parents who are protective enough to not let their kids hang out with 'strangers' anyway. Which leads me to my biggest concern. Having a register may lull people into a false sense of security when the biggest threat of all is the friends and relatives closest to children. a public register effectively perpetuates the 'stranger danger' myth and further acts to 'demonise' paedophiles. In doing so, we may make it even harder for children and young people to report abuse, due to the increased stigma. Look at how hard I found it to report my dad! If I had known that he was also potentially going to be placed on a publically available sex offender's register, I may have found it even more confronting to make a report as a teenager. Maybe I would not have gone ahead.

It is also important to remember that children pick up on community attitudes and discussions. When I was 15, I was well aware of the double standards in our community when it came to sexual abusers. In my diaries, I reflected on the support offered to a girl at my school who was sexually assaulted by a stranger. The response she received was markedly different from the response I received from those very same staff members:

> *"Do you think I would ever get that much support if I said anything? Absolutely not! Nobody wants to know what's happening to me because there's no easy solution! When someone is attacked by a stranger it's easy to react – everyone just says 'What a monster! Put him behind bars! But when you think about it, there's people doing way worse stuff to their own children, but nobody wants to know because it's too disgusting to understand or believe. People would rather think that people who do these sorts of things are monsters from another planet – outsiders. It's not true though".*

An awareness of community attitudes about sexual abusers as being 'monsters' and 'outsiders' can therefore act as a deterrent for a young person who is being abused by someone they know, due to fear of stigma.

It is also worth remembering that a register will only contain the names of offenders who have been convicted. It is pretty common knowledge that most children take a long time to report abuse, particularly if the abuser is someone they know, and that conviction rates are notoriously low.

A more effective way to combat child abuse is to up-skill communities to recognise and report abuse immediately, which I have already discussed. There also needs to be significant support in place for young people when they have been abused. As my case shows, disclosures and referrals to child protection are useless if there is no follow-up.

It is also crucial that there is a lot of support available to young people who go on to report abuse to police. I would not have gotten through this process without ongoing support from Kids Helpline – without Kids Helpline I would have probably withdrawn my statement, or killed myself. The lack of ongoing support available to me from the local sexual assault centre during the legal process still shocks me. There needs to be better funding for support services if you actually want young people to go through the legal process, and if convictions are to be achieved. And the criminal justice system is in dire need of an overhaul so that it is more user-friendly for young victims of crime. I will give some clear recommendations shortly. I shudder at the memory of being forced to read out every birthday card I had ever given my dad.

Another important area is to work with people who commit (or are at risk of committing) abusive crimes to help them understand the impact of abuse on their victims. I don't have any answers on how to best achieve this, particularly given that my dad refused to do the Sex Offenders Treatment Program and has shown no signs of remorse. But again, there are groups that are attempting to address this need, particularly in working with young offenders to break the cycle of abuse.

THE VALUE OF CHILD PROTECTION

In the media, child protection tends to get slammed a lot, but to me that seems an 'easy way out' instead of addressing the bigger issues. Politicians really need to take child abuse more seriously and put more funding into this important area. I am always very dismayed to hear about terrible cases of child abuse, or even worse, children being murdered by their parents, and then everyone just blames the individual case workers. This is not good enough. Those case workers are loaded up so much that there is no way they can assist all the children who are referred to them. Of course they are going to take short-cuts. If I, as a victim of abuse and the shortfalls of the system can see this, then I think politicians and the general public should be able to as well.

I strongly believe that politicians have a responsibility to advocate for more value to be placed on child protection, including better training and support for people working in this area. This might mean paying social workers more for all I know, or providing better supervision and support. It is also important to value and appreciate the people who are working in the area. They're definitely not in it for the money. They're in it because they care — and there are plenty of children out there needing that care. I urge politicians and policy makers to do everything they can to support those frontline workers in child protection, as their job has a crucial impact on the wellbeing and future of so many young people. While it is easy for members of the general public to slam child protection workers, I don't see many of these 'slammers' putting their hand up to go and work for the department. Since first publishing my e-book in 2014, I have gained a much better insight into what challenges are faced by child protection workers, and I personally can't imagine that I would ever be able to do their job.

It is also important that the foster care system places the best interests of children as its top priority. Though it seems politically correct to try and keep children living with their biological family at all costs, you need to consider the long-term costs of doing so. It is also important to support foster carers in their very important role and this includes lifting unnecessary restrictions on foster carers. We always hear about the lack of foster care placements, and this is used as justification to leave kids in abusive situations. It is time to start improving these systems so that more people feel supported enough to foster.

ADEQUATE SUPPORT IN THE AFTERMATH OF ABUSE

As highlighted in my book, there were definite 'gaps' in the supports available to me following my disclosure of abuse and also through the legal process.

Support to move out of home and the aftermath

Any young person who has been abused and has to move out of home (or has been in foster care and is transitioning to independent living) needs a lot of support through this process. It is incredibly daunting to find yourself at age 18, alone in the world and suddenly having to figure out how to do everything – cooking, managing your finances, juggling work and study, and everything else that comes with the transition to adulthood. Then add on top of that a history of trauma, grief due to the loss of family, and a lack of guidance, and you have a young person who is at risk of feeling extremely isolated, lost and overwhelmed.

All young people will differ in what support and help they require during this transition. I was fortunate enough to be very responsible and good at managing money and domestic responsibilities, but what I hugely lacked was a feeling of 'connection' and adult guidance. Other young people will really struggle to get their head around the financial side of things. It is important that there are services and people in place to provide ongoing support to young people who find themselves trying to navigate this transition alone. I feel heartened to see organisations providing support to this vulnerable population, such as White Lion.

Sexual assault services and support through the criminal justice process

Throughout this book I have discussed the detrimental impact of having a lack of support from local services throughout the criminal justice process. Oh what I would have done for some better support. I was fortunate enough to have Kids Helpline who were always there for me. However, they were not locally based and they were not face to face, so they did not have the same understanding of local systems that a local organisation would have had.

I am heartened by the creation of centres such as George Jones Child Advocacy Centre, which opened in Western Australia the year that I decided to leave the state, so unfortunately I never accessed it. However, I have since visited the centre and felt a pang of sadness that it hadn't been around just a few years earlier. I like this centre in particular because it offers support to the child/young person who has been abused for as long as they need it. I can only imagine how much easier my life would have been through the legal process and aftermath if I had that guaranteed, local face-to-face support which was so sadly lacking in my situation.

The model at child advocacy (or multidisciplinary) centres is that police, counselling and medical services are all located in the one building. The professionals work together to provide information and support as needed. Having one centre as a point of contact would have been much easier than navigating several different departments and buildings and often professionals not being able to clearly tell me where I could go for the information I was seeking. Several of these multidisciplinary centres have started springing up around the country, including in Victoria, and their initiative is to be commended.

I also really like the idea of a case management/advocacy approach where a young person has one local 'go to' person who coordinates the services they receive and also links them in with other services, and finds information to questions, as needed. I think what services sometimes forget is the importance of stable, face-to-face adult support, especially for young people who have experienced trauma and damage in their families. It is important to have a 'human connection' and not just be palmed off between various professionals. If I'd had someone local like that to go to, I can only imagine that the legal process, criminal injuries application and ongoing appeals would have been much easier to deal with.

Criminal injuries compensation

Support needs to be readily available to anyone who is applying for Criminal Injuries Compensation, particularly given that young people or those seriously affected by crime are quite vulnerable, and already 'at the end of their rope' with formal processes. I really regret that I sought informal advice and ended up having to pay a lawyer $7000 of the money that I was entitled to. If I'd had good support and a clear 'go to' person such as an advocate or case manager, this could have been avoided.

When I say 'support', I mean a real person who has rapport with the young person or victim of crime. I don't mean a series of colour coordinated pamphlets. I received plenty of them from victim support services and they were just overwhelming. What I really needed was for a trusted adult, who knew the systems, to walk alongside me on the journey.

THE IMPORTANCE OF TEAMWORK AMONGST ORGANISATIONS AND DEPARTMENTS

Since writing and publishing my book last year, I have become aware that there are many different organisations and departments tasked with the important role of protecting kids.

One thing I have noticed since having contact with the various government departments is that there is a tendency for departments to blame each other for not doing more.

I can read between the lines and hear that child protection workers are saying "Oh, schools aren't making reports to us about kids that we should be seeing, they're just not getting it". And then schools are saying 'Well, why would we bother making a report when most times no action is taken?'Again, this does highlight some definite areas for improvement in terms of staffing and resourcing, but if you find yourself in a situation of being annoyed at other departments, a better way to look at it would be:

"What can I do to help improve my team's relationship with this department so that we can work better to protect kids?"

I have seen examples of this happening e.g. schools and child protection teams meeting together to try and nut this stuff out — which is great! At the end of the day, you've got to remember that you're all in it for the same reasons. You're all there because you want to help kids. So try and be kind to each other, you will achieve so much more that way and feel happier in yourself too! Kids need you to be the adults in the situation and work together, put petty gripes aside and focus on what is important.

Dog-eat-dog is not the answer

I have also become aware that the abuse prevention scene is a bit of a 'dog eat dog' situation amongst organisations in some regions. This to me has been one of the most shocking and disappointing aspects of my journey since first publishing my book in 2014.

For example, I was asked by the Executive Officer of the main 'protective behaviours' organisation in my home state of Western Australia, to write a letter to a Government Minister to say that their program is more deserving of funding than a well known community policing program. If I had expressed interest in providing written support for their organisation and asked where to direct it, this would be different, but to actually ask me, without my initiation, to write such a letter and then tell me exactly what I needed to write ("you need to outline the uselessness of *name of other organisation*") seemed a bit of an unethical request, especially from an executive officer, who also happened to be a police officer, and who was dealing with a young person who had been a victim of extensive child abuse! Talk about a power imbalance! This, from an organisation that supposedly exists to teach young people that it is never okay to be coerced!

It took me six months to process how seriously messed up this request was. It made me worry about other young people who might be subject to similar unethical requests and end up feeling 'used'.

If organisations are so desperate for funding that they will quietly knife each other, something has gone very wrong in our community services sector. This brings me great sadness, especially to see it in my home state where I was abused for so many years as a kid. It made me wonder, if this sort of politics exists behind the scenes, what impact is it having on kids getting the help and support they need?

I was also advised by this protective behaviours organisation that it would be "inappropriate" for me to invite another abuse prevention organisation to a free presentation I was doing for child protection officials because "we don't really work together". This made me feel really uncomfortable and made me wonder why I was going to the effort of using my annual leave to fly back to Western Australia, volunteer my time and give so much of my personal story, only to be thrown into childish politics.

I was stunned to see that this is the world of child protection. Although everyone has surely started out with good intentions, along the way competition has seeped in for some. I don't feel there is any room for competition. The priority here needs to be keeping kids safe. This can only be achieved once everyone works together and pools their resources. There needs to be a government department coordinating abuse prevention and responses so that funding is used in a way that will most directly benefit children. It is a sad indictment of the lack of funding given to this sector that organisations would even feel a need to use such tactics. I don't know what can be done to change this, but I think it is time for open, transparent conversations, goodwill and teamwork.

To counter my negative experiences, I will add that I have come across many collaborative, good-natured and genuine people working in the child abuse prevention sector around Australia. There really is scope for great work to be done in this important area if everyone just works together.

But I'm just one person, I can't change anything...

Since first publishing my book in 2014, I have several times come across a feeling of 'helplessness' from people working in the child protection sector. People know that there are issues that need to be addressed but many feel powerless to change anything. I can definitely hear that there is a lack of staff, lack of resources and huge hurdles to achieve change. I hear that. But please, don't give up! You are important, and one person can achieve a hell of a lot.

To quote my favourite author, from Dr Seuss's book *Horton Hears a Who*:

Don't give up

I believe in you all.

A person's a person,

No matter how small.

You know, one of the biggest life lessons I have learned in this past year is that one motivated, driven person can achieve so much more than 100 unmotivated people who are just turning up to get a pay cheque.

I have come across incredible people in various government departments and organisations who are getting on with it and making things happen. The only extraordinary thing about these people is that they have passion. Passionate people get what they want, because they don't take no for an answer. Of course there are going to be road blocks, but passionate people will keep going and do whatever it takes, while others will say 'oh, it didn't work, wasn't meant to be, ah well I give up... anyone wanna go grab a coffee??'

When you find yourself thinking 'I can't achieve anything, there's no resources' – be resourceful! I have managed to write three books and put presentations together on an old laptop computer which is held together by sticky tape and has frequent and spectacular breakdowns – in addition to my regular full time job in a totally separate area. I initially released the book online instead of hard copy so that there were no publishing costs involved, yet it has still achieved its intended purpose and more. It has achieved a four page feature in The Weekend Australian magazine, it has been used by professionals, educators, young people and carers around the country, and now I have been linked in with fabulous people who have made hard copy publication a reality. All of this has been achieved despite me having no professional resources when I started out, and despite me being a complete 'nobody'.

If you in your professional role think you have no resources — go and take a trip overseas to some less privileged countries and then you will realise just how much potential we have here.

Be brave enough to think outside the box when there is no other option. You are better resourced than you may realise.

THE IMPORTANCE OF SEEKING FEEDBACK FROM YOUNG PEOPLE

Ensuring that services are responsive to the needs of young people

It is incredibly important for service providers in education, child protection, sexual assault response and the criminal justice system to seek the input of young people when evaluating their programs. Young people who have been abused hold crucial information about what changes are needed to make things better in future, because despite the many programs in place, many have still gone on to experience abuse.

Sadly, young people are rarely consulted when decisions about services, policies and programs are made.

The Royal Commission into Institutional Responses to Child Sexual Abuse has definitely opened up discussion on the topic of abuse in Australia, and is to be applauded. However, this commission has focussed predominantly on sexual abuse which occurred within institutions, naming "schools, churches or sports clubs" as examples on their website (Royal Commission, 2014).
This unfortunately is discouraging for young people who have been abused by family and friends, or have experienced other forms of abuse. Sadly, the vast majority of child abuse and neglect is perpetrated by trusted relatives and family friends, with estimates as follows:

In cases of **physical abuse**, 80.5% of perpetrators are a parent or a non-biological parent

In cases of **emotional abuse**, 93% of cases are a biological or non-biological parent

All cases of **neglect** can be attributed to a child's direct caregivers

In cases of **sexual abuse**, 43% of perpetrators are a male relative of the child, and in a further 32.5% of cases are a family friend or acquaintance of the child.

(Australian Institute of Family Studies, 2011).

My experiences illustrate that at present, there are many 'gaps' in the system that are not being adequately discussed in other forums. Unfortunately, my story is one of many. I strongly believe that there are many, many other young

Australians who would be keen to give their ideas on what changes are needed to better protect kids – if only someone asked for their input. It concerns me that despite living in a city, being literate and able to seek help for myself, it was still so difficult for me. It makes me wonder how on earth young people who have fewer opportunities than me would ever manage to break free of their situation. To effectively tackle the issue of modern-day child abuse, we need to hear the feedback of young people across the community – those from cities, remote areas, Aboriginal communities, non-English speaking backgrounds, those who have disabilities, males and females, so that we can best target the needs of children across the country. That is why there is a huge need for a forum, where young people who have been abused can provide feedback to service providers and policy makers.

References for this section:

Australian Institute of Family Studies (2011). Who abuses children? Retrieved from http://www.aifs.gov.au/nch/pubs/sheets/rs7/rs7.html

Royal Commission into Institutional Responses to Child Sexual Abuse (2014). Share your story. Retrieved from http://www.childabuseroyalcommission.gov. au/share-your-story

The need for local feedback

In 2014, one of the child abuse prevention organisations in my home state of Western Australia spent thousands of dollars bringing an American circuit speaker to Australia to discuss implementation of American-based policies. This woman, who has a career in speaking publicly about her experience of childhood abuse, was brought to meet service providers and key government officials, to push for a law to be named after herself in Western Australia. Prior to this visit, she had never been to Australia.

I observed these events with a feeling of confusion. Don't get me wrong. I absolutely have respect for this woman and her work to improve things for other children. But I don't honestly know how an American circuit speaker could know more than young Australians about what changes are needed to better protect children here. That would be like me going to Sweden or Botswana and trying to tell government officials what their young people need – when in reality, I wouldn't have the foggiest idea! I do not understand the use of thousands of dollars of funding in this manner. If organisations in this sector are struggling to find funding to provide front-line prevention and therapeutic services to children, how can this sort of expenditure be justified? Especially considering that there are many, many young Australians who would love to provide their feedback to service providers and would do it free of charge. I do not understand how important discussions are being held without the input of young locals who have been let down by the state and territory-based systems. Ironically, this was the same organisation that had asked me to write a letter to a Government Minister because they so badly 'lacked funding'.

I felt even more confused when an article appeared in the Sunday Times discussing this speaker's proposed law named after herself (remember, this was her first ever trip to Australia), without any young Australians being consulted as part of the piece. I gave my feedback to the organisation responsible for the visit but was told that they as an organisation had to think about "getting our name out there" and that the American speaker would "get more media attention" than young locals.

I was knocked for six.

Do we really find it so impossible to seek feedback from our own young people that we have to spend thousands to fly someone in from overseas? Is this child protection or show business? Where has it all gone so wrong? Is it any wonder that local kids are slipping through the cracks, when we find it so woefully difficult to listen to them and keep them at the centre of discussions?

Any discussions about system changes in Australia must involve many young Australians, so that services are tailored to meet the needs of as many young people as possible. Ideally, discussions should be state and territory-based with local young people providing feedback to service providers and departments. It is the responsibility of government departments and service providers to actively seek out such feedback and implement changes accordingly.

I also feel cynical about the idea of changing policies or legislation based on the experiences of one person. Certainly, the experience of one person can spark great discussion. However, legislation and policies need to be inclusive of all young people. Hey, you could all read my book and think "Hannah has all the answers! Let's have her come and speak at every child protection conference in the country! Let's name a law after her!" That would get me a lot of public recognition and awards and it might make people feel that the problems have been 'fixed'. But is that really the most effective way to achieve the change that is needed? If you listen to me, does that mean you now fully 'understand' the situation – that you can tick that box, pat yourself on the back for having listened to young Australians? No. Not even close.

You must remember that my experience is one of many. I do not have all the answers. In a voluntary capacity, I have provided frank and honest feedback to government departments and service providers in my home state. However, it is not something that I will continually do because it is time for other young people to be approached to give similar feedback. If you only want to hear from me, then you really haven't taken away the key messages from my book at all. Each state and territory needs to give its young people a platform to be heard.

My experience of giving feedback

Since first publishing my e-book in 2014, I have had incredible opportunities to provide feedback to local services and government departments in my home state. Before having these discussions, I didn't fully realise how much anger I was carrying around with me, towards all the people and departments who had let me down. I had huge feelings of worthlessness and betrayal. Having respectful conversations has helped me to realise that the people working in these departments aren't all total morons, they're just human beings working in imperfect systems. There are some people in these systems who are more motivated for change than others, and I have chosen to focus my efforts on the people who will push for change. I feel that because of these people, who genuinely want to hear feedback and do not get their defences up, there is huge potential for improvements to be made.

Some of my feedback-giving experiences have included:

- **Sexual Assault Resource Centre** – In 2014, I contacted the doctor who did my sexual assault examination back in 2007 to tell her about the book I had written. She wrote back immediately to say that of course she remembered me and to congratulate me on writing the book. She asked if it was okay for her to pass on some of my feedback to management of the centre. She even organised a meeting for myself with the head of counselling and therapy, as well as the new centre manager because I asked if I could provide the feedback in person. To be treated with such respect over so many years by this doctor has had a lasting impression on me. And to be able to provide feedback to the counselling component of the service and to be met with respect from those listening, was also a very positive experience.

- **Department for Child Protection** – I sent the link of my book to an advocate who worked for the child protection department in my home state. I expected to hear nothing back, so was quite surprised to get a lovely email back from the advocate thanking me for sharing the book, which she had read in its entirety. I was then invited to provide any feedback that I wished to, in whatever format I felt comfortable with. I said that I would be happy to do a presentation for a group of clinical staff, so it was arranged for me to speak to a group of 30 staff. I was very well supported with this and we had great, open discussion. It made me realise that there are some incredible workers in that system who really do want the best for kids and young people. I am still in touch with several of them and it has been very healing for me. I also had the opportunity to meet with the case worker who had closed my file in 2005. You see, she was still working for the department and had actually gone on to become a team leader, so I called her up to speak with her... I was shocked that she not only answered the phone, but talked with me at length, and then had the guts to come to my presentation. Again, another healing experience for me, and potentially for the case worker too. We have not stayed in touch but I do respect her for 'facing' what I had to say, instead of running away.

- **Education Department** – I have also had the opportunity to meet with staff from the education department who are responsible for implementing better student education and teacher training about abuse. They have also respectfully received my feedback and been very supportive of my efforts with these books. Again, this was a pleasant surprise to me because I expected that they would not want to hear from me. But instead, some of them couldn't have been more accommodating of me and my viewpoints. Once you meet the right people, it is amazing what can be achieved.

- **Criminal justice system** – I have had the opportunity to meet with the new Victims of Crime Commissioner in Western Australia. That was emotionally intense for me because I had such negative experiences in the criminal justice system. However, to feel so listened to and respected by the Commissioner was again a healing experience for me, and she is helping to set up further opportunities for feedback with key authorities such as the parole board and criminal injuries compensation board.

These opportunities to give feedback do not take away the damage the abuse has done to my life. They also do not eradicate my bad memories of system failure. They do, however, help me feel in some small way that something good has come of my experience, if it can help another young person to not have as difficult time as I did. However, change will only be achieved if people in these systems have not only listened to my feedback but actively led further discussion, consulted more young people and made changes accordingly. Time will tell whether this happens or not. Life has taught me to not hold my breath when it comes to big systems.

SOME QUESTIONS FOR FURTHER DISCUSSION

I know this book has raised lots of issues which might be overwhelming. So I thought I would narrow it down for you by concluding the book with a list of key topics for professional and public discussion. I don't want you to read this book, put it on your shelf and think no further about the issues I have raised. I intensely hope that instead, my book provokes discussion around Australia about the huge room for improvement in the current systems and the need to seek further feedback from other young people who have endured these systems.

Judging by the many emails I have received since first publishing my book, these questions hold relevance across the country. I have concluded with some questions specifically for Western Australian readers given that I grew up and experienced inadequate system responses in that state.

Abuse prevention and education

- What can be done to ensure that abuse prevention education is mandated in all schools and that all teachers feel confident to carry out this important training? It is crucial that even in universities, teachers are given adequate training in this area.

- Who is monitoring schools to measure how frequently abuse prevention education is being carried out and also the effectiveness of this training? What outcome measures are being used to ensure that children are taking away the crucial information from any abuse prevention education, and retaining it months down the track? (It is not enough for kids to have one education session a year – it needs to be ongoing).

- Who is coordinating the abuse prevention approach in each state and territory? In states like Western Australia where there is so much competition in the abuse prevention 'industry' it really should be a government department such as the Education or Child Protection department, to ensure that all abuse prevention programs/organisations are working together to ensure that kids are the priority. There really is no room for competition.

- What can be done to make abuse prevention information more mainstream? I had never even heard of the term 'protective behaviours' until I published my book in 2014. It sounded like martial arts or something, and I actually had to Google it to figure out what it meant (and I am someone who has a university degree). This seems a shame to me because if young people don't know what information to look for, they are less likely to stumble across it. It also means that parents/members of the general public will feel less comfortable teaching such a 'specialised' topic. What can be done to ensure that crucial abuse prevention information is easily accessible and understood by members of the public?

- How are we ensuring that any abuse prevention education and resources are what kids and young people who have been abused really feel is needed? I have reviewed the resource *a Teenager's Guide to Personal Safety* which has been used in some schools in Western Australia. When I was younger, if I had stumbled across this resource but not been forced to read the inside content, I would have disregarded it and not realised it was aimed at teens like me. The front cover (a picture of a teenager on a skateboard) and the title would have made me think it was a book about remembering to wear a helmet when skateboarding or similar. When resources are created we need to make sure that they meet the needs of their intended target audience.

Child protection

- What changes are needed so that child protection workers have the capacity to respond to referrals for suspected abuse in a consistent and timely manner?

- What level of peer and senior supervision is in place to ensure that workers are coping and that they are performing at the expected level, including their ability to provide clear and accurate records and documentation (which in my case was extremely unsatisfactory)?

- What can we do to make the foster care system easier for potential foster carers to navigate, so that children requiring foster care can access it more readily?

Support services

- What improvements can be made so that young people have the long-term support they need following abuse?

- How easily accessible are support services for young people?

- What changes are needed so that young people can feel better supported through the legal process? How can we avoid having young people 'cut off' from services right after making a police report?

- What supports are being made available to young people to pursue criminal injuries compensation so that they are not left with hefty lawyer bills at the end of the process?

Criminal justice system

I think the average member of the public would be shocked to realise just how difficult the criminal justice system is for young people to navigate. Sadly, you don't hear much feedback from these young people because on top of the abuse they have suffered, they have gone on to be further victimised by the criminal justice system. With their spirits crushed, it is no wonder that this population does not have the energy to go on and advocate for changes to the system. That is why it is important for you to step in and help to advocate for change.

I would love you to discuss the questions below.

Trial/appeals process

- What can be done to reduce the waiting time between making a police statement and going to court? As a young person, having to wait over a year for your case to go to trial is excruciating. It puts you further and further behind your friends because instead of wanting to socialise and get on with life, the upcoming court proceedings are always lingering in the back of your mind. It also impacts on your studies/employment.

- Is it really fair that relevant evidence is being excluded from sexual abuse trials, therefore jeopardising the likelihood of a conviction? I am at a loss to understand why all counselling evidence was excluded in my trial. Dad's lawyer found a loophole in the laws, stating that all counselling evidence is confidential for the protection of victims of crime. However, I was consenting to the information being used as it strengthened the case a great deal. If my dad had been found 'not guilty' due to a lack of evidence, I would have been extremely angry that this important evidence was excluded. The jury were not getting a true picture of what had happened and my attempts to get help.

- What can be done to get rid of demeaning courtroom practices which compound the trauma and abuse already experienced by young people?

In my experience, the court process shows little understanding of the dynamics of abuse, especially when it occurs in families. I cannot fathom why I was forced to read out a pile of birthday cards and Father's Day cards that I had given my dad, as though this was proof that he had not abused me. I also don't know why I was questioned several times about the fact that Dad had helped me with my maths homework. Why are such ill-informed questions allowed?

- What can be done to address poor or lack of communication between government legal departments? It is crucial that departments work together to support young people instead of leaving young people to chase all the information themselves. As I learned in the trial and appeals process, communication between departments is often non-existent.

- What changes can be made to criminal injuries compensation appeals so that no victim is again 'sued' by an offender? I cannot understand how my dad got away with launching civil legal action against me. Is this happening in other parts of Australia?

The parole process

- What level of consideration is given to remorse in the parole process? I cannot understand why my dad, who continually harassed me, appealed against his convictions and refused to do the Sex Offender's Treatment Program, was awarded parole. How much consideration is being given to these factors when considering an offender's true level of remorse?

- How appropriate are some of the current sex offenders treatment programs, and what are victims' views on these? My dad completed a program called the Sex Offender Denier's Program, which is run in both Western Australia and New South Wales. This program is essentially based on denial of the crime! Doesn't that scream 'red flag' to you? Does it really demonstrate remorse? How is this deemed 'good enough' for the community and the victims of sex crimes? To me, it is an insult.

Post-parole

- Why do we not have nationalised restraining orders as a matter of due course for crimes of sexual assault or domestic violence? Now that Dad's parole has ended, there is zero protection in place for me. Why is the onus on me, the victim, to sort this out myself, and risk giving the offender my new location by getting the order put through by police in my new home state? Do you have any idea how much stress this has brought to my life and that of many others in similar situations? We need to change this.

- Is it fair that victims of sexual and violent crimes are unable to access basic information about offenders that can have a significant impact on their life? Imagine if your child was sexually abused, and the perpetrator was allowed to move right back into your neighbourhood without you being told? Or imagine if you were raped, and the rapist was allowed to work in the same building as you without you being told. These are the sort of scenarios that are surely faced by families around Australia who like me, do not have a right to any information. There is a huge difference between making information about sex offenders available to the general public (I don't agree with this) vs. making information available to victims of crime who specifically request it. I lost all rights to privacy when I was raped, so I think it is fair for me to be entitled to basic information about the person who has so badly violated me.

Some Western Australia specific questions about the criminal justice process

Please note that all of the above questions are extremely relevant to Western Australian readers because those were the systems I directly experienced. A few additional questions that I have are as follows:

- Why did I have to deal with the State Solicitor's Office when Dad appealed my criminal injuries compensation? Why was I forced to become the defendant in a civil action? If the defendant has a problem, it should be kept between them and the Criminal Injuries Assessor, not the victim. And what right does the offender have to say how deserving a victim is of receiving compensation?

- How was Dad allowed to get away with attaching correspondence to me with his criminal injuries compensation appeal? How did he suddenly get to cross the line from criminal to civil court, without any intervention from the courts that supposedly should be protecting victims?

- Why was the parole board so unfriendly to contact, to the point that the Victim Offender Mediation Unit quietly advised me to not contact the board directly? And when I became distressed about hearing dates changing, the guy at the parole board was unable to understand or empathise that it might actually have an impact on my life. What can be done so that these services are more understanding of victims' needs and the huge impact of crime on a victim's life?

DISCUSSION IS THE KEY

I know I have asked some confronting and direct questions throughout this section of the book. Please remember that there is nothing wrong with healthy discussion, in fact, that is what is needed in all regions of Australia.
If you find yourself having a particularly strong or defensive reaction to any of the questions I have asked, then that shows to me that it is something which is worth further discussion.

It is important that other kids and young people around Australia are given the opportunity to add their insights and questions into the public discussion. I see my questions as merely a starting point, but there is much more feedback needed to get a true understanding of what changes are needed in Australia.

There is no room for 'preciousness' from organisations or individuals.
The wellbeing of kids and young people needs to be kept at the centre of all discussions. They deserve a better experience than what I and many others have had to go through. I hope you are passionate enough to push for this.

Painting by
Sarah Millicent Elliott

EPILOGUE

Writing this book has been both challenging and rewarding. It has helped me to reflect on the journey I have had, the difficulties I have overcome, and the people who have helped me to get my life on track. It has particularly made me grateful for the amount of support I received from Kids Helpline. If it wasn't for them, I can't imagine that I would still be alive, or I at least would not be the person I am today. I ended my contact with Kids Helpline in 2014 when I reached the age limit for their service. With their help, I have dealt with a lot of my issues, and am no longer needing so much support. I am ready for the next chapter in my life, and I hope it will be a good one.

Through writing this book, I have now had my voice heard by people who do and don't know me. This is very empowering and scary at the same time. It is very humbling for me to know that my words are helping people to understand what it is like for a young person who has been abused. It has also given me a great opportunity to speak directly with government departments and service providers, to provide feedback about what could be done differently in future.

I will never forget the honest and open discussions I have had with people across Australia since first publishing my book. It gives me some hope for other kids now that I have met some incredible people working in the fields of child protection, victim advocacy, education and reform, who really do want to make things better. However, it is hard for me to know whether these discussions merely provided a bit of short-lived inspiration or whether they will lead to any further discussion and action. What you choose to do with my information and ideas is out of my control. Life has taught me to be cynical about people's willingness to step in, advocate for the vulnerable and make changes.

I hope you prove me wrong.

It is time for me to step away now from speaking about my own story and to get on with my life, knowing that I have done my best to improve the situation for other kids and young people here in Australia. It is hard for me to say what the future holds for me. I will continue to face difficulties as a direct result of the abuse. It would be impossible not to, when you consider that I was abused for many years, followed by all those years dealing with the criminal justice system and its issues. Sometimes I am scared that I won't get to fulfil my dreams. Sometimes I wonder why I bother to keep going – getting out of bed can feel so hard, especially with the nightmares I still have to deal with. But I have done everything possible to give myself the best chance at succeeding at the things that are important to me in life. Even when things don't turn out exactly the way I plan, hopefully I can be happy with whatever life throws my way. There are no guarantees, but I will just continue to do my very best, and surround myself with people who have my best interests at heart.

USEFUL CONTACTS

Please note: This is by no means an exhaustive list. For services specific to your local area, see your phone book or community directory. I cannot endorse any of these organisations other than Kids Helpline, which is the only organisation on this list that I had direct contact with as a teenager/young person.

Crisis phone lines

Kids Helpline (1800 55 1800) — Australia's only free, private and confidential telephone and online counselling service specifically for young people aged 5–25. You can speak to the same counsellor each time, and can request to speak to a male or female. http://www.kidshelp.com.au

Lifeline Australia (13 11 14) — Crisis support and suicide prevention helpline for adults. Also offers online chat services. http://www.lifeline.org.au/

1800 Respect (1800 737 732) — Family Violence and Sexual Assault helpline. Offers telephone and online counselling, and can also assist you to link in with local services. https://www.1800respect.org.au/

Youth support organisations

headspace — Australia's national youth mental health foundation. They provide services for people aged 12–25, including medical services, counselling, alcohol and drug services, and education/employment services. See the website to find the phone number for the headspace centre closest to you. http://www.headspace.org.au/

White Lion — a non-profit community organisation that provides support, mentoring and role-modelling to young people who have been disadvantaged. Many of their young clients have experienced abuse and have little support. http://www.whitelion.asn.au/

Apps (both free to download)

Hear Me — An app developed by Parkerville Children and Youth Care Inc. which gives info about child abuse and how to get help.

iMatter — An app developed by Doncare which gives information about relationships and domestic violence.

Websites with information about child abuse
(appropriate for young people)

Bursting the Bubble – Helps young people work out what's OK in a family and what isn't. Also provides information on what to do if a family member is hurting or abusing you or another member of your family. http://www.burstingthebubble.com/default.htm

Carly Ryan Foundation – a charity created by the family of Carly Ryan, a 15 year old Australian teen who was the victim of a man she met online. The foundation provides information for teens and young people about how to stay safe online. http://www.carlyryanfoundation.com/

CyberSmart Website – Provides kids and teens with info about staying safe online. http://www.cybersmart.gov.au

Child Abuse Prevention Service Helpline – The National Child Abuse Prevention Service provides counselling, advice and referral service to victims and families of child abuse.
Phone: 1800 688 009 (freecall) http://www.childabuseprevention.com.au/

Domestic Violence and Incest Resource Centre Victoria – a state-wide resource centre providing information about domestic violence and sexual assault – for those affected by family violence as well as for workers and researchers. http://www.dvrcv.org.au/

Join The Dots (run by Bravehearts) – a website where young people can anonymously report inappropriate contact from adults on the internet. Bravehearts will pass the information on to police to help keep other kids and young people safe. http://www.bravehearts.org.au/join-the-dots/

Kids Helpline website – Information page with links to websites about child abuse. http://www.kidshelp.com.au/teens/get-help/who-else-can-help/helpful-links/child-abuse.php

Lawstuff – Provides good information about the laws in each of the states and territories, including sexual relationships and sexting.

Love: The Good, the Bad and the Ugly – This website gives you information and advice from the personal experiences of other young people who have been there. http://lovegoodbadugly.com/

Reachout: What is Child Abuse? – Website that provides good information about the different types of abuse, possible impacts and where to get help. http://au.reachout.com/

State-based sexual assault organisations

Australian Capital Territory – Canberra Rape Crisis Centre. Provides support to men, women and children who have experienced sexual assault. http://crcc.org.au/

New South Wales Rape Crisis – Provides telephone and online crisis counselling for anyone in New South Wales who has experienced or is at risk of sexual assault, and their non-offending supporters. The website also contains links to local sexual assault centres throughout the state. http://www.nswrapecrisis.com.au/

Northern Territory – Sexual Assault Referral Centre (SARC) – services located in Darwin, Tennant Creek, Katherine and Alice Springs to provide support to adults and children who have been sexually assaulted, recently or many years ago. http://www.health.nt.gov.au/Sexual_Assault_Services/

Queensland – Please see the list on Queensland government website to find your local service http://www.health.qld.gov.au/sexualassault/html/contact.asp

South Australia – Respond SA. An information hub that provides information and resources for people who have been affected by childhood sexual abuse. http://www.respondsa.org.au/

Tasmania (north and north-west) – Laurel House. Provides therapeutic services and support for people who have experienced recent or past sexual abuse/ assault. http://laurelhouse.org.au/

Tasmania (south) – Sexual Assault Support Service (SASS). Includes counselling and crisis support. http://www.sass.org.au/

Victorian Centres Against Sexual Assault – The peak body of 15 Centres Against Sexual Assault, and the Victorian Sexual Assault Crisis Line (after hours). Provides information about support services available, as well as education programs being held within the state. http://www.casa.org.au/

Western Australia – Sexual Assault Resource Centre (SARC). Provides services to males and females aged 13 and over who have experienced sexual abuse/ assault recently or in the past. http://www.health.wa.gov.au/services/detail.cfm?Unit_ID=319

Western Australia (child-specific) – George Jones Child Advocacy Centre in Perth. Doctors, police, child protection workers, psychologists and child and family advocates form a multi-disciplinary team to provide services to care for all the needs of a child or young person who has been abused, and their family. http://www.parkerville.org.au/Child-Advocacy-Centre

Abuse prevention/education organisations
(in alphabetical order)

Australian Childhood Foundation (1800 176 453 – free call) – An organisation that assists children to recover from experiences of abuse, neglect and domestic violence, through specialist counselling and providing education to their supporters. http://www.childhood.org.au/

Bestlife for Children – Organisation based in South Australia that provides advice for parents on abuse prevention actions and strategies, as well as webinars and coaching. http://www.bestlife-coaching.net/bestlife-for-children-main-page

Bravehearts (1800 272 831) – An organisation that runs education programs for children to prevent childhood sexual assault, and also provides counselling services for victims of sexual abuse. http://www.bravehearts.org.au

Daniel Morcombe Foundation – An organisation created by the parents of Daniel Morcombe, which aims to educate children about their personal safety, and also provides support to child victims of crime. http://www.danielmorcombe.com.au

National Association for Prevention of Child Abuse and Neglect (NAPCAN) (02 8073 3300) – Organisation that raises awareness about child abuse and neglect, as well as prevention programs. NAPCAN founded national child protection week which occurs in September every year. http://napcan.org.au/

Protective Behaviours Australia – An organisation that aims to reduce the incidence of abuse and violence in the community through empowerment and education. There are branches in most of the states and territories of Australia. http://www.pbaustralia.com/index.html

Safe4Kids – An organisation in Western Australia which specialises in child protection education. The organisation also runs education programs which target Indigenous children in regional/remote communities of Western Australia and the Northern Territory. http://www.safe4kids.com.au/

Some Secrets Should Never Be Kept – Website contains details about the picture book of the same name that has been created to educate young people about abuse. http://somesecrets.info/

White Ribbon Australia – An organisation that aims to stop violence against women, including domestic violence and sexual assault. The organisation works hard to engage both men and women in the solution. http://www.whiteribbon.org.au/about

ABOUT GEORGE JONES CHILD ADVOCACY CENTRE

In Western Australia, *Parkerville Children and Youth Care (Inc)* have been providing services for children who have been harmed or neglected since 1903. In 2007, the Board of Parkerville confirmed their intention to raise capital funds to build the *Child Advocacy Centre* (CAC) in Armadale and to work with government and other stakeholders to develop this model of service delivery for children, young people and families. It was agreed by all stakeholders that the purpose of the CAC would be to prevent and respond to child abuse by:

- Providing a multidisciplinary team response to meet the needs of each child and family with compassion, understanding and skill, and

- Uniting stakeholders and agencies to strengthen the response to the safety, treatment and well-being of abused children.

Internationally, CACs are a well-established mode of service provision with over 900 centres in operation across the U.S.A., Iceland, Denmark, Sweden, Poland, Canada, Turkey, Israel and South Africa. CACs cater for all children who have been harmed and support a child to disclose what has happened to him/her and provide appropriate follow-up. This includes planning multi-layered interventions to protect the child, investigate harm, gather evidence, and provide medical treatment and psychosocial support services. a CAC also provides support to non offending carers/parents so they in turn can support their child well.

The Premier of Western Australia opened the George Jones Child Advocacy Centre (GJCAC) in Armadale, Western Australia in March 2011. Within the GJCAC, a Child and Family Advocate are assigned to a child and their family. The Advocate's role is to undertake a holistic assessment with families who may be hampered by many issues (such as unemployment, single parenthood, housing or health issues) and link them to other community services with the aim of reducing stress and strengthening the family. Other services may also include therapeutic interventions for parent(s) to address their own abuse issues or receive additional support. Services at a CAC are seamless and comprehensive and the child and family have a clear ongoing contact point for subsequent services and follow-up.

In May 2015, interviewers and investigators from Western Australian Police and the Department of Child Protection and Family Support will co-locate with Parkerville Children and Youth Care staff at the GJCAC to implement the CAC model more fully. The Australian Centre for Child Protection will conduct an evaluation of the pilot to review the impact on the wellbeing, mental health and justice outcomes for children and young people attending the centre.

For more information visit:

http://parkervillechildadvocacycentre.com.au

and

http://www.parkerville.org.au

ABOUT KIDS HELPLINE

Kids Helpline is Australia's only free, private and confidential, telephone and online counselling service specifically for young people aged between 5 and 25. It is a service of BoysTown.

Kids Helpline officially opened in March 1991. More than 3,200 young people called the first day, and despite a number of hitches 122,000 calls were logged in the first 17 days. Within a year of opening, Kids Helpline had answered 75,000 calls – this is the GABBA sporting ground filled twice! By Child Protection Week in October 1993, it had registered one million calls. Kids Helpline expanded state by state across Australia, and became a national service in 1993. Email counselling started in 1999 and the web counselling service was launched in May 2000.

Since 1991, Kids Helpline has answered more than 6 million telephone calls and online contacts. As at 2015, Kids Helpline counsellors respond to almost 4,500 calls each week about issues ranging from relationship breakdowns and bullying, to sexual abuse, homelessness, suicidal thoughts, and drug and alcohol use.

The service aims to empower young people by assisting them to:

- Develop options;

- Identify and understand the consequences of a particular course of action;

- Facilitate more productive relationships with family and friends, and

- Provide information on local support services.

Kids Helpline counsellors are fully qualified professionals who undergo additional accredited training at Kids Helpline. This ensures that each young person who contacts Kids Helpline receives the very best of care. Counsellors are based in Brisbane, where calls from all around Australia are answered 24/7.

Information for this section was gathered from the Kids Helpline website. Please visit www.kidshelp.com.au for more information. Their phone number for young people aged 5-25 is **1800 55 1800**.

ACKNOWLEDGEMENTS

There are several people and organisations I would sincerely like to thank for their assistance and support with my books.

Kids Helpline for your encouragement when I first wrote a draft of this book and your ideas on how to 'get it out there'. Thanks in particular to **Sarah, Sam, Leo** and **Maya**.

Carol Ronken (Bravehearts) for your encouragement with the original manuscript. Thanks also to **Jo Compagne** for being a friendly first contact.

Cameron Stewart (The Weekend Australian) for covering my story with such compassion, patience and sensitivity, and your ongoing encouragement.

Sarah Millicent Elliott for so kindly donating your paintings for me to use in this book. You are a beautiful person and extremely talented too!

Mark and **Jayneen Sanders** for generously donating your time to assist with the formatting and production of these books. I would have been lost without your assistance!

Cherie Zamazing for the logo art for Wallace Publishing. Wallace is very pleased!

Adam Guerin (Oz Web Shop) for kindly donating your time and resources to build and host my website for free!

George Jones Child Advocacy Centre and **Parkerville Children and Youth Care**: Thank you to all of the staff who have been supportive of my books. Huge thanks to **Natalie Hall**, you're such an inspiration to me and it has been a pleasure working with you! Thank you to **Basil Hanna** for your encouragement and assistance. Thanks also to **Jennifer Hall, Emma King, Yvette McGuinness, Amanda Paton, Vicci Smith, Kris Gorbert, James Herbert** and **Lisa McAneny**.

Education Department of Western Australia: Thank you **Teresa Delany** (and **Grant**) for going well beyond 'the extra mile' and making sure I felt respected, comfortable and heard. Thank you **Julie Gower** for your encouragement and time.

Department for Child Protection and Family Support (WA): Thank you **Judy Garsed** for being so keen for my voice to be heard. Thank you to all of the clinicians who attended my presentation in September 2014. Thanks to those who have stayed in touch and provided further ideas/feedback, including **Simone Rist, Karen Walker** and **Angela Hislop**.

Kelly Hinton (White Lion New South Wales) for believing in the value of my story and for helping it to be heard.

Others who have supported me with my books: **Dr Maureen Phillips, Jennifer Hoffman, Maggie Woodhead, Julie Graham, Nikki Mitchell, Petalynne Hay, Joanna Guerin, Greer, Hayley, Wallace, Penny, headspace.**

Finally, I would like to say a major thanks to you, the reader, for taking the time to read my book. It means the world to me to have my voice heard, and I hope I have helped someone, in some small way.